DATE DUE

APR 1 0 2014			
APR 1 6 2014			
MAR 2 5 2015			
			PRINTED IN U.S.A.

Z

N

Zoo Station
The Story of Christiane F.
by Christiane F.

© 2013 by Zest Books LLC
First published in 2013 by Zest Books
35 Stillman Street, Suite 121, San Francisco, CA 94107
www.zestbooks.net
Created and produced by Zest Books, San Francisco, CA

Teen Nonfiction / Biography & Autobiography / Social Issues / Drugs, Alcohol, Substance Abuse

Library of Congress Control Number: 2012936083

ISBN: 978-1-936976-22-5

Cover Design: Tanya Napier
Book Design: Keith Snyder
Translation: Christina Cartwright
All photos courtesy of Deutscher Taschenbuch Verlag
Typeset in Sabon

Manufactured in the U.S.A.
DOC 10 9 8 7 6 5 4 3 2 1
4500390748

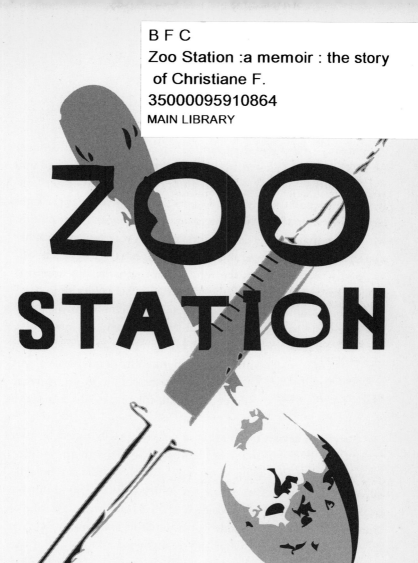

ZOO STATION

[a memoir]

the story of christiane f.

FOREWORD

This is the haunting, real-life story of Christiane Vera F.—a daughter, a sister, a student, and a typically rebellious teenager in 1970s Berlin. Like so many young people in every age and time, Christiane is eager to fit in and prove herself after her family first moves to the city. She desperately wants to wear the right clothes, listen to the right music, and hang out with the cool kids. More than that, though, she wants to find a way to deal with her abusive, alcoholic father, and learn the ropes at her new school.

Sadly, Berlin was in the midst of a major heroin epidemic when Christiane's family arrived. Nothing was cooler than "H," and in Christiane's search for acceptance and community she was always bound to encounter heroin at some point. Unfortunately for her, it all happened very fast. By the time she was 14 years old her daily concerns had already degenerated from questions about who she should date and which party she should go to, to what kind of a client she should be willing to tolerate in order to score her next fix.

In telling her story Christiane was originally aided by two journalists (Kai Hermann and Horst Rieck), and they did a wonderful job of letting Christiane simply speak for herself. Whether she's talking about drugs, johns, clothes, David Bowie, or boyfriend troubles, her voice is always loud and clear. She is completely unguarded, and her profound self-consciousness gives us a very clear sense of what she sees when she looks out at the world; meanwhile, a fuller picture of Christiane's life is provided by the simultaneous accounts from Christiane's mother and a number of other adults involved in Christiane's life.

Christiane's story has had a major impact on German culture to this day. Locations such as the Bahnhof Zoo subway station, the housing projects in Gropiusstadt, and even certain public bathrooms have all gained a share of notoriety and fame. Christiane's book is required reading in much of Germany, and has been translated into many other languages as well. When it was first released in the United States, in 1980 (under the title Christiane F.: Autobiography of a Girl of the Streets and Heroin Addict), it became an instant hit, resonating with teens, parents, and even David Bowie—who provided music for the film adaptation.

Although Christiane's experiences on the streets of Berlin will be quite foreign to most readers, Christiane, as a character, does not wind up feeling distant on that account. In fact, even at the book's conclusion, after so much hardship and misery, Christiane remains in many ways a very typical teenager. We can all find something to relate to in the way that Christiane struggles for acceptance, resists all attempts to rein her in, and fights against herself, uncertainly. The urgency in her voice is timeless. For all these reasons and more, we are proud to be able to bring Christiane's story back to America with Christina Cartwright's excellent new translation.

Even at the darkest times, Christiane manages to maintain a surprising kind of integrity. She always sees with the same eyes and speaks with the same voice. As a result, she has provided us with a stunningly honest and vital account not only of her own teenage years, but also of the powerful forces—both internal and external—that determine the course of our lives. Sometimes they lead us away from ourselves, and sometimes they bring us back home.

Hallie Warshaw

Hallie Warshaw
Publisher, Zest Books

TRANSLATOR'S NOTE

In translating this story I've made every effort to preserve Christiane's unique perspective and tone. Christiane has a biting, cynical wit that is still typical of many young Berliners (and which becomes especially prominent in the face of various authority figures), and it is my hope that the updated slang will help to hone the edge that is present in a lot of her commentary. In an effort to give a better sense of Christiane's surroundings, we've added footnotes about many of the locations, and also provided additional information about some especially German expressions and institutions. In all of my translation choices I have worked to maintain not only the tone of Christiane's voice, but also its vitality.

This book has a very strong hold on me personally. As a teenager in the 1970's I spent a lot of time in Berlin, and I remember well what life was like in Berlin as a divided city. I know most of the locations mentioned in the book, and visited them at roughly the same time that Christiane did (although under very different circumstances). As a single parent, I can also sympathize with Christiane's mother's frustration, anxiety, and fear. I have a teenage son myself, and this book made me think more deeply about his daily life, and pay closer attention to his own set of trials. I think I've become a more compassionate listener as a result of the time I've spent with Christiane.

Despite the measures that have been taken against teenage drug use and child prostitution in Germany and in the United States, these are still very real problems. And it goes without saying that, when it comes to peer pressure, alcoholism, depression, and familial strife, today's teenagers have it no easier than the teens of 1970s Berlin. I hope that this book will help teens gain some perspective on their own problems, and encourage them to take a fresh look at the choices that remain open to them—whatever their situation. I strongly believe that both teens and their parents both stand to gain a lot from reading Christiane's story.

I am honored to have worked on translating this book into current, American English (with the help of my very talented editor, Daniel Harmon). I hope that it does justice to Christiane's voice and personality.

Christina Cartwright

THE CHARGE

Excerpts from the state's attorney's charge against Christiane Vera F. at the state courthouse of Berlin, dated July 27, 1977.

The student Christiane Vera F. is charged as a legally responsible juvenile with having used regulated narcotic substances continuously after May 20, 1976, without authorization by the Federal Department of Health.[1] Moreover, the accused has been using heroin since February 1976, injecting herself with approximately one quarter of a gram each time—at first only intermittently, but then later on a daily basis. She has been criminally responsible and accountable since May 20, 1976.

On March 1 and March 13, 1976, the accused was found in the halls of the Zoo and Kurfürstendamm subway stations, and searched for drugs. She had two substances containing heroin on her person, one weighing 18 mg and the other 140.7 mg.

On May 12, 1977, the mother of the accused, Mrs. F., found a heroin-containing substance among her daughter's personal belongings, which she sent to the criminal division of the police. As a result, on that same day, a tinfoil packet containing 62.4 mg of a heroin-containing substance was confirmed to be among

---

1 In the 1970s and 1980s, the German government's policy on drug use was extremely strict. In the years that followed, a number of experimental new policies were put into place, including "harm reduction," a policy in which drug addicts are given low doses of drugs in a controlled environment. But at this time in Germany all drug users were considered criminals and expected to become drug-free.

the personal effects of the accused. Heroin-related paraphernalia was also found among her personal effects. Laboratory tests revealed that there were heroin-containing substances adhering to the paraphernalia. Also, analysis of her urine revealed the presence of morphine.

In her defense, the accused stated that she had been using heroin since February 1976. In addition, she had worked as a prostitute since the winter of 1976 to acquire the money she needed in order to purchase the drugs.

It must be assumed that the accused continues to consume heroin today.

THE VERDICT

*Excerpts from the verdict of the Neumünster County
Court, dated June 14, 1978. Verdict in the name of
the people.*

In the criminal case against the student Christiane Vera F., for
offenses against narcotics laws: The accused is guilty of continuous purchase of narcotics in concurrence with continuous
tax evasion. Sentence of youth detention is suspended and the
accused is placed on probation.

Grounds: The accused experienced normal development up
to her thirteenth year. She possesses above-average intelligence
and fully understood that the purchase of heroin represented a
punishable offense. Although there is sufficient evidence that the
accused was already addicted to drugs by May 20, 1976 (before
becoming criminally liable), this fact precludes neither her criminal responsibility nor her criminal liability. The accused was
able to recognize the seriousness of her situation, and made an
effort to stop using these drugs. She was therefore fully capable of
recognizing the illegality of her conduct, and to act on that
realization.

The prognosis for her future is, at the moment, positive—
even though her sobriety is far from guaranteed. In the near
future, the continued progress of the accused must be monitored
with care and attention.

ZOO STATION

It was all incredibly exciting. My mom had been packing suitcases and boxes for days. We were going to start a new life together.

I had just turned six, and I was going to start attending school right after we finished with the move. While my mom was packing and getting more and more anxious, I hung out almost every day on the Völkl farm. I waited for the cows to be herded into the barn for milking. I fed the pigs and the chickens, and ran around and played crazy games in the hayloft with the other kids. I was able to carry the farm's kittens around with me. It was a wonderful summer, the first one that I remember consciously enjoying.

I knew that we were going to leave soon and move to a large faraway city named Berlin. My mom flew ahead because she wanted to set up the apartment first. My little sister and my dad and I followed a couple of weeks later. It was the first time that my sister and I had ever flown anywhere. Everything was unbelievably exciting.

My parents had told us wonderful things about the huge apartment with the six big rooms that we'd soon be living in. My parents were going to make a lot of money in Berlin. My mom said that we would each have our own big room. They were going to buy really nice furniture. She would describe what our rooms would look like in vivid detail. I know, because as a kid I never stopped fantasizing about that room. In my imagination, it became more and more beautiful with every passing day.

I'll never forget what the apartment looked like when we actually arrived. I felt this deep-seated fear when I was in it. It was so big and empty that I was afraid I would get lost. If you spoke loudly enough, there was a spooky echo, too.

Only three rooms had any furniture in them. In the kids' room there were two beds and an old kitchen cabinet for our toys; in the second room was my parents' bed; and in the biggest room we only had an old couch and a couple of chairs. That's how we lived in Berlin-Kreuzberg,[2] on the north bank of the Spree River.

After a few days, I finally took a chance and rode my bike down the street all by myself because I saw a few of the older kids playing outside. In the town where I grew up, the big kids always looked out for the little kids, and played with them. But right away the kids out front said, "What's she want here?" and took away my bike. When I got it back it had a flat tire and a bent rim.

My dad spanked me because the bike was broken. From then on, I only rode my bike around our six rooms.

Three of the rooms were actually supposed to function as an office because my parents wanted to run a dating service out of the apartment. But the desks and armchairs that my parents

---

2 Berlin-Kreuzberg was a neighborhood in West Berlin. Today it is an urban district within Berlin that was combined with Berlin-Friedrichshain to form Friedrichshain-Kreuzberg.

talked about never arrived. The kitchen cabinet stayed in the bed-room that I shared with my sister.

One day a moving truck arrived, and the couch, beds, and kitchen cabinet were all transported to one of the tall apartment buildings in Gropiusstadt.[3] So now, instead of living in the big place in Berlin-Kreuzberg, we were confined to two and a half small rooms in an eleventh-floor apartment. The big, expensive furniture that my mom always talked about would've never fit into the room now meant for us kids.

Gropiusstadt: the projects. Home to 45,000 people, but mainly just a forest of high-rises, with some patches of green and shopping centers in between. From far away, it looked new and well taken care of. But when you got up close, you realized that the whole place reeked of piss and shit—because of all the dogs and kids that lived there. The stairwells smelled the worst.

My parents hated the trashy kids who treated the staircases like their own personal bathrooms, but most of the time it wasn't their fault. I figured that out the first time I played outside and needed to pee. By the time the elevator arrived and I'd made it up to the eleventh floor, I'd already wet myself. My dad gave me a spanking. After the same thing happened a few more times, and after a few more spankings, I learned to just find a place where nobody could see me. And since people in high-rises could see almost everywhere, the safest place to pee out of sight was in a staircase.

On the streets of Gropiusstadt, I was known as the stupid country kid. I didn't have the same toys as everyone else—I didn't even have a water gun. I wore different clothes. I talked differently.

---

3 Gropiusstadt is a subsection of Berlin devoted almost entirely to public hous-ing. It was named after Walter Gropius, the architect who first envisioned the complex.

And I wasn't used to the games they played (but I also didn't like them). In the town where I grew up, we would ride our bikes into the woods, to a bridge over a little stream. When we got there, we'd build dams and forts—sometimes together and sometimes apart, but always side by side. And when we destroyed everything afterward, it was only after everyone had agreed to it, and we'd have fun tearing it all down. We didn't have a leader. Anyone could make suggestions for what kind of game we should play. Then we'd all argue back and forth until someone's suggestion won out. It wasn't even unusual for the older kids to let the younger ones have their way once in a while. We'd created a real democracy amongst us kids.

In our section of the Gropiusstadt projects, there was one boy who was definitely in charge. He was the strongest and he also had the best water gun. We liked to play this game where we would pretend to be a gang of robbers, and he would always be the leader (of course). The most important rule for all of the other robbers was that they had to do whatever he said.

But it didn't matter what kind of game we were playing—we were always competing with each other. The goal was to always try to annoy somebody else. So we'd do things like try and steal or break someone else's toys. The name of the game was superiority: beating people up to show you were bigger and stronger than they were, and finding other little advantages that made you look better than everybody else. It was a dog-eat-dog world.

If you were the weakest, you'd obviously get the most abuse. My little sister wasn't very strong, and she always looked scared, so people picked on her, but I couldn't really help.

Then I started school. I'd been looking forward to it. My parents had told me to behave and to always do what the teachers said, but I thought that was a given. In the town where I came from, the kids respected the adults as a matter of course. And that's probably one of the reasons I was looking forward to school, because I thought that it would keep all of the other kids in line.

But school was totally different than I expected. After just a few days, the kids would get up during class and run around playing tag. Our teacher was completely helpless. She kept yelling, "Sit down!" but then the kids would laugh at her, and everything would get even more chaotic.

●

I'VE ALWAYS LOVED ANIMALS, ever since I was really little. Everyone in my family was crazy about animals. It made me proud. I didn't know any other family that loved animals like we did. I felt sorry for the kids whose parents didn't like animals and who weren't allowed to keep pets.

It didn't take long for our already cramped living space to be transformed into a small zoo. I had four mice, two cats, two bunnies, one parakeet, and Ajax, our brown Great Dane, whom we'd brought with us when we moved to Berlin. Ajax always slept next to my bed. At night, I'd let one arm dangle out of my bed so that my hand was on his fur while I fell asleep.

I found other kids who also had dogs, and I got along with them pretty well. It turned out that in Rudow—which was a neighborhood just outside of Gropiusstadt—there were still pockets of nature left. So that's where we headed with our dogs. We played on the old, earth-covered hills of the garbage dump, and our dogs were always a part of whatever it was we were doing. Our favorite game to play was a version of hide-and-seek that included our dogs. One of us would hide, and somebody else would hold onto that person's dog. Then the animal had to track down and find that person. My Ajax had the best nose of all.

Sometimes I would bring my other pets into the sandbox or even into school with me. My teacher used them as show-and-tell opportunities in biology class. Some teachers even allowed me to bring Ajax into the classroom. He never disrupted anything. Until the bell rang, he'd lie peacefully next to my chair or under my desk.

I would've been really happy there with all my animals if things hadn't gotten progressively worse at home. While my mom was out at work my dad just sat at home, doing nothing. The dating service didn't pan out, of course, so now he was waiting for a different job. He wanted something that he'd enjoy, but he just sat on the worn-out couch and waited for something to fall into his lap. Meanwhile, his rage-filled outbursts happened more and more often.

My mom always helped me with my homework when she got home from work. At one point, I was having a hard time telling the difference between the letters H and K. So one night, my mom was explaining the difference to me (with the patience of a saint), but I wasn't really paying attention, since I could see how worked up my dad was getting. I could always tell when it was going to happen: He got the hand broom out of the kitchen and started beating me with it. During a break in the thrashing, I was supposed to explain the difference between H and K to him. At that point, I was obviously incapable of understanding or explaining anything to anyone, so my rear end received another dose of the same, and then I was sent to bed.

That was his idea of helping me with my homework. He wanted me to be a good student and work toward a better future.

After all, his grandfather had made a lot of money: He owned a printing company, a newspaper in East Germany, and some other businesses as well. After the war, everything that was privately owned in the DDR[4] was expropriated by the state. So now my dad totally freaked out whenever he thought that I wasn't getting something in school because I was supposed to continue the financial success of his family instead of succumbing to the apathy generated by the socialist policies in East Germany.

There were evenings that I can still remember down to the last detail. Like one time when I was supposed to draw houses in my math notebook. They were supposed to be six squares wide and four squares high. I had already finished one house and knew exactly how to do it, when my dad suddenly sat down next to me. He asked me how the next house should be drawn—where the squares should go. Frozen with fear, I didn't count anymore but started to guess. Every time I pointed to a wrong square, he slapped me across the face. When I couldn't give any more answers because I was crying so hard, he stood up and went over to the rubber plant. I knew what that meant. He pulled out the bamboo stick that was acting as a support for the plant, and then he beat me on the rear with that bamboo stick until my skin was so raw it was peeling off all by itself.

By the time I sat down at the dinner table every night, I was already afraid. When I dropped a crumb on the tablecloth, I got slapped. When I spilled something, I got a spanking. I could hardly bear to touch my glass of milk anymore. I was so nervous that I caused some small disaster at almost every meal.

---

4 DDR stands for Deutsche Demokratische Republik—although most English speakers know this country more familiarly as East Germany. East Germany was dissolved and joined with West Germany in the German reunification on October 3, 1990—not long after the fall of the Berlin Wall.

In the evenings, I always asked my dad (as sweetly as I could) if he had any plans for the night. He went out a lot, and the first thing we did after he left was breathe a very deep sigh of relief. Those evenings were wonderfully peaceful. But when he got back later on, there was always the threat of another disaster. Usually he was drunk by then, so just one small thing could cause him to go totally apeshit. It could be toys or even just a piece of clothing that was lying around because no one had put it away. My dad always said that nothing was more important than tidiness. And if he saw something that hadn't been cleaned up when he came home, he'd drag me out of bed and beat me. After he was done with me, my little sister would also get a beating. Then my dad would throw all our stuff onto the floor and demand that we pick it up and put everything away in just five minutes. Of course we could almost never get it done, so we'd get another spanking.

My mom would usually just stand in the doorway and cry while all this was going on. She didn't dare defend us because then he would beat her, too. Only Ajax, my Great Dane, would intervene. While my dad was beating us, he would whimper in a really high voice and stare at us with his big, sad eyes. Ajax was the only one who could bring my dad to his senses because he loved dogs as much as we all did. He once yelled at Ajax, but never beat him.

Despite all that, I still loved and respected my dad. I thought he was way better than other kids' dads, but I was still terri-fied of him—despite the fact that I thought it was completely normal when he would smash things or hit whoever happened to be around him. It wasn't any different at the other kids' homes in the projects. Sometimes they even got black eyes, and so would their moms. There were some dads who even passed out drunk in the street or woke up in the playground. Sometimes furniture came flying out of the windows from the apartments above us, and women would yell for help so that the police would have to come. It wasn't anywhere near that bad with our family. My dad never got that drunk.

My dad constantly nagged my mom about spending too much money—even though she worked and he didn't. Sometimes she would tell him that most of it financed his drinking escapades, his women, and his car. Then their fights would get physical.

His car, the Porsche, was the one thing in this world that my dad loved most. He buffed and polished it every day (or at least every day it wasn't in the repair shop). There couldn't have been another Porsche in all of Gropiusstadt—and certainly not owned by somebody who didn't have a job.

Back then, I didn't have a clue about what was really bugging my dad—why he was constantly going berserk on us. It didn't dawn on me until later, once I started talking with my mom a little bit more often. Little by little, I began to see things for what they really were. He just couldn't make it, didn't have it in him to hold down a job and support a whole family. He always wanted to make it big, aimed high, and fell back down again. His dad despised him for that. Grandpa had warned my mom before the wedding that his son was a "good-for-nothing son of a bitch." My grandpa used to have big plans for my dad: The family was supposed to regain the wealth and status that it had in the old days, before the DDR seized all of its possessions.

If he hadn't met my mom, he might have become a farm manager or certified dog breeder, in which case he would have probably bred Great Danes. He was studying farm management when he met my mom. She got pregnant, so he quit his studies and married her. At some point, the idea got lodged in his mind that my mom and I were to blame for his misery. All that he had left of his grandiose dreams was his Porsche—that, and a few snobby, cocky friends.

He didn't just hate his family, he completely rejected us. He didn't want anything to do with us. He even went so far as to deny our existence to his friends. They weren't supposed to know that he was married and had kids. When we met his friends, or when someone picked him up from home, I always had to call him "Uncle Richard." Because of the regular beatings, I'd learned to keep things straight, and I never made a mistake. As soon as other people were around, he was my "uncle."

It wasn't any different with my mom. She was never allowed to tell his friends that she was his wife, and she wasn't allowed to act like his wife either. I think he always said that she was his sister.

My dad's friends were younger than him. They still had their lives ahead of them, or so they said. My dad wanted to be one of them—he wanted to be young again and not have to worry about providing for a family (or failing to do so). That just about sums up my dad. As far as he was concerned, we were just deadweight, holding him back and dragging him down.

But back then—when I was six, seven, eight years old—I didn't have a clue, of course. My dad simply reinforced the code of conduct that I'd learned at school and in the street: It was a dog-eat-dog world—eat or be eaten. My mom, who'd received enough beatings in her life, had arrived at the same conclusion. "Never start anything," she drilled into me. "But if someone hurts you, then you hurt them back. Punch, and keep punching—as long and as hard as you can."

It took me a while to completely absorb that lesson. At school I started with the weakest teachers. I kept interrupting class with my own running commentary. It made the others laugh, at least, but I didn't start to win any respect from my classmates until I started doing the same thing with the stricter teachers.

I'd learned how you got your way in Berlin: You had to show no fear, and always be ready with something quick and cutting. No one got anywhere without a big mouth. The bigger the better. After I learned how to intimidate people with my insults, I started to back it up with muscle. I wasn't really that strong, but when I got angry, I got angry. I learned that a big mouth combined with a bit of well-timed fury could win out over someone much stronger than me. It got to the point where I would even look forward to pissing people off because then I'd get a chance to prove myself again after school. Often, I didn't even have to get physical. The kids just respected me.

In the meantime, I turned eight. All I wanted was to just grow up already, to be an adult, like my dad, and to have real power over others. Whatever power I already had, I experimented with and used as much as possible.

At one point, my dad actually found a job. It didn't make him happy, but it at least paid for his Porsche and for his alcohol. And so now that he had a job, my younger sister and I got to stay home alone in the afternoons. I'd also become friends with a girl who was a couple years older than me. Being friends with her made me proud and gave me even more credibility at school.

Almost every day after school, we played this game with my little sister: We collected cigarette butts out of garbage cans and ashtrays; then we straightened them out, held them between pinched lips, and puffed away. When my sister tried to get a piece of the action, though, she got a slap on the fingers. We ordered her to do the housework—to wash the dishes, dust, and do whatever else our parents had asked us to do. Then we grabbed our doll carriages, locked the apartment, and headed out for a walk. We kept my sister locked up until she'd finished all of the chores.

AT AROUND THIS SAME TIME, when I was about eight or nine, a riding stable opened up in Rudow. At first, we were really pissed off, because it meant that we were going to lose the last bit of wilderness and nature in the area—the one place where we could escape with our dogs. It was going to be fenced in and cleared of trees. But then I started talking with the owners, and we got along really well. I helped them with cleaning stables and taking care of the horses, and in exchange I was allowed to ride for fifteen minutes or so in down times during the week. I thought that was the best thing that had ever happened to me.

I loved the horses and also the donkey they had there. But there was something else that I thought was incredible about riding: the feeling of power that it gave me. The horse I was riding was much stronger than me, but I could force it to bend to my will. When I fell off, I had to get back on. I had to get back up again and again, until the horse finally obeyed me.

They didn't always need help at the stables, and when they didn't, I'd need to find another way of getting money for my fifteen-minute ride. We hardly ever got an allowance at home, so I began to pull little scams. I cashed in discount coupons and collected redemption money by returning my dad's beer bottles.

When I was about ten, I started shoplifting, too. I'd try to grab stuff that we couldn't get from our parents—usually from local supermarkets. Stuff like candy. Almost all the other kids were allowed to eat candy. But my dad said that it caused your teeth to rot.

In the projects, we all eventually learned the same lesson: You couldn't have fun without breaking some rule. All of our best games were forbidden in one way or another. Actually, pretty much everything was forbidden—whether it was fun or not. There was a sign at every corner in Gropiusstadt. The "recreational parks" between the high-rises were really just sign parks.

And most of the signs were directed at kids, prohibiting one thing or another.

I liked to copy the strangely contradictory language from the signs into my diary. The first sign that I noticed was right next to our front door. Kids were basically only allowed to tiptoe around the apartment and the staircase: playing, running, roller-skating, or bicycling—everything else was prohibited. Then when you walked outside to the lawn, you'd see more signs, at every corner with even a bit of green: KEEP OFF THE GRASS. We weren't even allowed to sit on the grass with our dolls. Next, there was an anemic rose garden and again a big sign in front of it: PROTECTED PUBLIC GARDENS. Right below this bit of advice there was a paragraph that pointed out that punishment would follow should anyone get too close to the pathetic little roses.

So we were only allowed onto the playground. Every few high-rise apartment buildings were allotted one playground, usually consisting of some sand (which was also used as a urinal), a few broken climbing structures, and of course a huge sign. The sign was installed inside an iron box, under glass, and the glass was protected by an iron grate, in case we got the crazy idea to smash that piece of nonsense. The sign was titled "Playground Rules," and it instructed kids to use the playground exclusively for "fun and relaxation." That simple goal was actually made pretty difficult, though, since we weren't allowed to "relax" at our convenience. In bold, underlined letters, we were also told that the park was only open "from 8 a.m. until 1 p.m., and from 3 p.m. until 7 p.m." So by the time we got home from school, we could forget about any fun and relaxation.

Technically speaking, my sister and I weren't even allowed on the playground, since the sign declared that kids could play there "only with permission from and under supervision of their legal guardians." And even if our parents had been with us, we would still have broken the rules, since "the community's need for quiet should be especially respected." According to these rules, we could only really just play catch—silently, of course, and under supervision. But the fun stopped there, because even then, "Any ballgames of athletic nature are not allowed." So no dodge-ball, no soccer. This was especially hard on the boys, who had to release their extra energy (and pent-up frustration) on the climbing structures, benches, and, of course, all those signs. It must have cost a lot of money to keep replacing the signs over and over again.

The property manager kept watch and made sure that everyone followed the rules, so I wound up on his shit list pretty quickly. Pretty soon after our move to the housing projects, the playground (which was basically concrete, sand, and a slide) bored me to the point of insanity. But then I found something interesting: the storm drains. They were supposed to divert all the rainwater from the concrete area, but back then you could still lift off the grate that covered the drain. (Later on, of course, they corrected that mistake.) So my sister and I lifted off the grate and tossed all sorts of junk down into the drain hole. The property manager came, grabbed us by the collar, and dragged us into his office. We were only five or six years old, but once he had us in there, he treated us like criminals and made us give him all our personal information (or as much as we could provide at the time). Our parents were notified, and my dad had another good reason to beat us.

I didn't understand what was so bad about plugging up the drain. In the town where I came from, we did all sorts of things like that near the stream, without any adults ever complaining. But I did understand that in the projects, the kids were supposed to obey the grown-ups' rules, above all else. You were supposed to slide down that one slide they'd given us and play around in the urine-soaked sandbox. It was dangerous to make your own rules or be at all creative.

The next run-in with the property manager was about something more serious. It happened like this: I was walking Ajax, my Great Dane, and got the idea to pick some flowers for my mom. Back in our hometown, I would pick flowers all the time and make beautiful bouquets. But here in between the high-rises, there were only these pathetic roses. My fingers were getting all bloody trying to pick just a couple of blossoms off of the rosebushes. Either I couldn't read the sign, PROTECTED PUBLIC GARDENS., or I didn't understand what it meant.

But I knew I'd done something wrong when I saw the property manager running toward me (he broke the rule about not stepping on the grass), screaming something and flailing his arms like a crazy person. Overcome with fear and panic, I said, "Ajax, attention!" My big dog's ears went up, his body went rigid, his hackles went up, and he stared down the property manager. The guy stopped dead in his tracks and started retreating back over the lawn. He didn't dare start yelling again until he was within range of the building's entrance. I was relieved but hid the roses behind me, as by that time, I definitely knew that I'd broken the rules again.

When I got home, the property management office had already called to say that I'd threatened the manager with my dog. Instead of a kiss from my mom, I got a spanking from my dad. No one cared that I'd brought flowers.

The heat was unbearable in the summer. The concrete, asphalt, and stones all seemed to soak it up and pour it out again. If there were any trees at all, they were so small that they gave no shade. And the wind was blocked by all the apartment buildings. There was no swimming pool, not even a small plastic kiddie pool. Only a measly fountain in the middle of the concrete square in front of our building's entrance. You weren't allowed to play in it, but we sometimes splashed around in its basin and squirted water at each other for a minute before we were chased away again.

At one point, we all got really into marbles—which presented a problem because where were we supposed to play? You couldn't build marble runs on concrete, asphalt, or the small patches of lawn that said, KEEP OFF. And you couldn't play in the sandbox either because you need pretty firm earth to make good holes and effective hollowed-out runs in the dirt.

But we eventually found an ideal spot under the puny maple trees that they'd planted among the apartment buildings. In order to keep the little trees from suffocating, they'd left space around each tree for earth instead of concrete. The round openings they'd left consisted of firm soil that was raked clean and level. Simply ideal for making marble runs.

But now it wasn't just the building managers who were after us, but also the gardener. They all kept chasing us away, hoping to scare us off with their wild threats. Of course, we ignored them. Then, unfortunately for us, one day our tormentors came up with a good idea: They didn't rake the soil (which made it flat) but turned it over. That was the end of our marble runs.

But we had other entertainments: When it rained, the entrance halls and corridors on the ground floors were slippery and ideal for roller-skating. The noise didn't even bother anybody at first, since there weren't any apartments on the ground floors. We tried it out a few times, and nobody bothered us—much to our surprise—except for the wife of the property manager. After a while, she said that the roller skates left marks on the floor. So, another failed undertaking. And another spanking from my dad.

During bad weather, it sucked to be a kid in Gropiusstadt. Nobody was allowed to have any friends over because the rooms were too small. Most of the kids we knew lived in a half-size room, just like we did. When it rained, I sometimes sat by the window and thought about what we used to do back in our town in similar weather. Wood carving, for example. We were always ready for rainy weather. When the weather was nice, we'd go into the woods and collect thick pieces of oak bark for making little boats. And then, if it rained for so long that we actually finished with our carving before the rain stopped, we'd just put on our rain gear and head down to the stream to try out the boats. We'd even build harbors and organize races.

So, we couldn't have each other over, but there was also nothing entertaining about hanging out between the high-rises when it was raining. We had to think of something. Something fun. Something that was totally against the rules. And then it hit us: We had the elevators.

At first, the objective was just to annoy the other kids. We'd grab a kid, lock him in an elevator, and then push all the buttons. The other elevator we'd hold at the ground floor. Then the kid had to rattle all the way to the top, stopping on every floor. They did that to me a lot, too. Especially when I came back from a walk with my dog and had to be back on time for dinner. It would take forever to get to the eleventh floor, plus it made Ajax really nervous.

It was even worse for the kids who had to pee. If they got pranked, then they'd usually end up having to pee in the elevator. But the worst thing of all was when it happened to a kid who had no wooden spoon (or whose wooden spoon had just been grabbed). All the little kids made sure to never go outside without our wooden spoons because we could only reach all the elevator buttons with something that had a long handle. The easiest thing to grab and take along was a long-handled wooden cooking spoon out of your mom's kitchen. Without such a wooden spoon, you were screwed. If you lost it or the other kids took it away, you had to trudge up flights of stairs. The other kids wouldn't dare help you, and the grown-ups wouldn't either because they thought that you just wanted to play with the elevator and break it.

The elevators broke down a lot, and we weren't entirely blameless there. We also liked to hold elevator races, because even though they went at the same speed, there were a few tricks you could use to shave a few seconds off your time. For one, the outer door had to be closed quickly but with a delicate touch—because if you slammed it too hard, it would bounce open again just a little. Also, the safety door closed automatically, but if you manually helped it along, it closed faster. Sometimes it also just broke. I was pretty good at racing the elevators.

Soon, our thirteen floors weren't enough for us anymore. Besides, the caretaker was always right on our heels, which added an unpleasant element of stress. We needed new terrain, but going into other apartment buildings was absolutely forbidden for us. And we couldn't get in anyway because we didn't have a master key. But then we found a way: There was a second entrance for furniture and other large delivery items. It was blocked by a gate, but I figured out how to get through: You needed to go headfirst, and it was a real puzzle to figure out how to turn your head to squeeze past, but somehow we did it. (The skinny kids, at least.)

Once we'd made our way through, we found ourselves in the midst of a veritable elevator paradise: a high-rise building with thirty-two floors and unbelievably sophisticated elevators. Suddenly we had a whole new set of games and activities, which would never have been possible in our old building. One of our favorite new activities was "jumping." When we all jumped up at the same time during the ride, the thing came to a stop. The safety door opened. Or, if you jumped right when you got in the elevator, the safety door wouldn't close at all. No matter what happened, it was pretty exciting.

Another crazy thing you could do was push the handle for the emergency brake to the side, instead of down, so that the safety door would stay open during the entire ride. It made you realize how fast the elevators actually went. It was crazy how fast the concrete dividers and elevator doors flashed past us.

Those games were all pretty good for some quick excitement, but the true test of courage was to push the alarm button. It set off a bell, and then the caretaker's voice would come through the loudspeaker. That was the signal to hightail it out of there. A building with thirty-two floors presented good odds for escaping the caretaker. He was always trying to ambush us but didn't have much luck.

The most exciting game during bad weather was the one we invented for the basement. It was probably also the most dangerous—or at least the most forbidden. We somehow found a way into the area of the basement where every tenant had a storage space screened in with wire fencing. The fencing didn't go all the way to the ceiling, so you could climb over the top. So that's where we played hide-and-seek. We called it "no-holds-barred hide-and-seek"—meaning, you could hide anywhere. It was really creepy. It was already pretty scary to hide among the unfamiliar stuff of strangers in that dusty, dim light. Add to that the fear that someone could show up at any moment. We suspected that we were pretty much doing the most illegal thing we could possibly be doing.

We also played this game where we tried to outdo each other in finding the most outrageous things in those storage spaces— toys, or junk, or clothing (which we'd then play with, or mess with, or try on). Afterward, of course, we usually couldn't remember which storage spaces the stuff had come from, and so we just tossed it anywhere. Sometimes, if there was something really cool, we'd take it with us. Of course, then it was discovered that someone had "broken in" down there. But we were never caught. That's how we came to learn the following rule: If it's allowed, it's probably boring, and if it's forbidden, it's probably fun.

There was a shopping center across from our apartment house, which was also more or less off-limits for us. It was guarded by a fanatical caretaker, who chased us off whenever he saw us. He went really nuts whenever I came remotely close by with Ajax. He said that we were the ones who trashed the place and brought all the dirt into the shopping center. The place looked okay from a distance, but if you got up close, you saw how dingy and dirty everything was. Each shop tried to be more swanky, more exclusive, and classier and hipper than the last. But the dumpsters in the back were always overflowing and stank, and you always risked stepping in melted ice cream or dog shit, or knocking over soda cans and beer bottles.

The caretaker of the shopping center was supposed to clean it up at night. No wonder that he'd lurk around all day, hoping to catch someone making a mess. But he was powerless to do anything about the store owners, who threw their trash next to the dumpsters. And he didn't dare approach the drunk teenagers who freely tossed empty beer cans anywhere they wanted to. And the old ladies with their little dogs just snapped sassy replies back at him. So he let out his primitive rage against us kids.

They didn't like us in the shops, either. When one of us got some money—whether by allowance or some other means—we'd go straight into the coffee shop, where they also sold penny candy. And all the other kids would follow behind, because that was a big event. It drove the salesladies nuts when a half-dozen kids came into the store and started arguing over what they should buy for a few pfennigs.[5] Eventually we started hating the store owners and didn't think twice about stealing from them.

There was also a travel agency in the shopping center, where we liked to stand and press our noses against the window until we were shooed away. They had these fantastic pictures in the shop windows showing palm trees, beaches, native people, and wild animals. In the middle of it all hung a model airliner from the ceiling. We all liked to pretend that we were sitting in that plane on our way to that beach, climbing palm trees to watch rhinos and lions.

Next to the travel agency was the Bank for Commerce and Industry. Back then, we didn't think it was weird for there to be a bank for commerce and industry in Gropiusstadt, of all places (where everyone earned their paltry wages by working for industrial and commercial establishments). We liked the bank. The refined gentlemen in their fancy suits were always friendly to us. They also weren't as busy as the ladies in the coffee shop. They would let me change my pfennigs (which I'd swiped from my mom's penny jar) for larger coins. And it was necessary, too, since in the coffee shop, they'd get furious if you paid for anything with pennies. And at the bank, if we said please, like sweet, well-behaved kids, they'd give us little piggy banks. Or little banks shaped like elephants sometimes, too. Maybe those nice gentlemen thought that we needed so many piggy banks because we were such diligent savers. But I, for one, never put a penny into any of them. Instead, we used the animals to play "zoo" in the sandbox.

As our pranks got worse and worse, they built something they called an "adventure playground" for us. I don't know what they really meant by "adventure." But it had nothing to do with actual adventure. I guess it was there for the parents, so that

---

5 One German pfennig was worth a little less than one US penny.

they would think their kids were having fun. Anyway, it must have cost a ton of money. It certainly took them long enough to build. And when we were finally allowed on it, we were greeted by friendly social workers: "So, what would you kids like to play today?" and shit like that. The so-called adventure consisted of us being constantly supervised.

They gave us real tools and smooth-planed boards and nails. So one was allowed to build something, it would seem. A social worker would make sure that we wouldn't smash our fingers with the hammer. Once a nail was in the wood, it was in. No taking it out or changing anything. Of course, we always changed our minds before it was finished and wanted to make it look different.

I was explaining to one of those social workers once that where I used to live, in the country, we built caves and real tree houses. Without hammers or one single nail. With whatever boards and branches we could find. And every day, when we came back, we kept tinkering with it and changing everything. And that was fun. I'm sure the social worker was trying to understand what I meant about changing a project before it was finished, but he had his responsibilities and instructions.

In the beginning, we still had our own ideas about what we could do on this adventure playground. For example, once we wanted to be a pretend Stone Age family and cook real pea soup over a fire. The social worker thought that was a great idea. Unfortunately, he said, cooking pea soup wasn't allowed. How about building a cabin, he asked, with hammer and nails. A hammer and nails—in the Stone Age?

But soon the playground was closed off again. They said they wanted to rebuild it, so that we could also use it in bad weather. Then iron beams were unloaded, and cement mixers and a team of construction workers arrived. They built a concrete bunker with windows. Seriously, a real concrete bunker. No log cabin or anything like that, but a block of concrete. Its windows were smashed in after a few days. I don't know if the boys smashed the windows because the sight of the concrete thing made them aggressive, or whether the playhouse was built out of concrete because in Gropiusstadt everything not made out of iron or concrete ended up being broken. The concrete bunker now took up most of the space of the adventure playground. Then they built a school directly adjacent to it, which got its own playground, one with a slide, monkey bars, and a few short, assorted-sized round logs driven into the ground vertically, which provided good cover if you had to pee. The school playground was built partly on the adventure playground and surrounded with mesh wire fencing. That didn't leave much adventure playground.

The little adventure playground that was left was gradually taken over by the older boys, whom we called rockers. They arrived in the afternoons, already wasted, terrorized the younger kids, and just smashed everything. Breaking stuff was their hobby and just about their only amusement. The social workers couldn't deal with them. So then the adventure playground was closed down most of the time.

Instead of the adventure playground, we kids were given a real attraction. They built a sledding hill. It was awesome the first winter. We could choose our own runs down the hill. We had a "death run" and an easy run. The boys whom we called rockers liked to make sledding dangerous. They formed chains with the sleds with the goal to run us over. But we could dodge them and go down other runs. Those days when there was snow were among my happiest days in Gropiusstadt.

In the spring, we had almost as much fun on the sledding hill. We'd run and play with our dogs and roll down the hill. The most fun was fooling around on our bikes. The downhill rides were insane. It looked more dangerous than it really was. Because if you actually did crash, you landed in the soft grass.

But guess what? Soon they didn't allow us to play on the sledding hill anymore. They said, "This is a sledding hill, not a playground, and certainly not a racetrack for bikes." The scars we had made in the lawn had to grow over and recover, etcetera. By now we were no longer little kids, so the word *forbidden* had lost its effect on us, and we kept on going to the sledding hill. Then one day, the men from the landscaping department arrived and put up barbed wire fencing all around the sledding hill. But we only conceded defeat for a few days. Until someone found some wire cutters. We cut a hole into the barbed wire that was big enough to get through with our dogs and bikes. When they patched the hole, we cut it open again.

A few weeks later, the little army of construction workers was back. They started walling off and paving over our sledding hill. Our "death run" got turned into steps. Paved walkways cut through all of our runs. Onto the top of the hill, they put a cement platform. One strip of grass remained for sledding.

During the summer months, there wasn't a thing left for us to do on the hill. In the winter, the one remaining sledding run was way too dangerous. But the worst was having to walk to the top. You now had to negotiate stone slabs and steps that were always iced over. We bloodied our knees, bumped our heads, and, if it was really bad, got a concussion.

You see, everything was made more and more perfect in Gropiusstadt.

When we moved there, this grand example of a model suburb was not finished yet. Especially right outside the high-rise quarter, there was much that had not yet been perfected. What we considered to be our paradise playgrounds were just a short walk away, so even we younger kids could get to by ourselves.

The most beautiful spot was near the Wall,[6] which wasn't far from Gropiusstadt. There was an undeveloped strip alongside it that we called the "little woods," or no-man's-land. It was almost twenty-two yards wide and nearly a mile long. There were trees, bushes, tall grass you could disappear in, old boards, and water holes.

There we climbed around, played hide-and-seek, and felt like explorers who every day discovered a new part of our little wild wood. We could even make campfires and roast potatoes and make smoke signals.

But inevitably, one day, it was discovered that kids from the projects were playing over there. Then the troops arrived again to create order and clean up. And they put up the all-too-familiar signs. Nothing was allowed anymore; everything was forbidden: biking, climbing trees, letting dogs run off-leash. The policemen, who were lurking around the area anyway because of the Wall, made sure that the new rules and regulations were obeyed. Apparently our no-man's-land was now a bird conservation area. A little later, they turned it into a garbage dump.

But there was still the old landfill, which had been covered over with earth and sand. We often played on it with our dogs. This was also secured against us, first with barbed wire, then with tall fencing, before a scenic restaurant was built on top of the dump.

Another beautiful spot to hang out was in a few fields, that the farmers no longer cultivated. There, the corn and cornflowers and poppies and wild grasses and nettles grew so high that you would soon sink into them up over your head. The government had bought these fields with the intention of turning them into real recreation areas. Piece by piece they were fenced off. A riding stable swallowed up one portion of the old fields,

---

6 The Berlin Wall, which divided East Berlin from West Berlin from 1961 to 1989.

and tennis courts were built on another part. So now there was nothing left for us. That took care of all the places we could go to get away from Gropiusstadt.

At least my sister and I worked and rode horses at the riding stable. In the beginning, we could ride wherever we wanted to go. Later, it was forbidden to ride on all streets and even country roads. They had built a dedicated riding path for that purpose. Exactly the way a proper riding path was supposed to look, with nice sand and everything. Probably cost a lot of money. This riding path ran right alongside the railroad tracks. Between the fence and the railroad tracks, you could just barely fit two horses side by side. That's where we were supposed to ride now, as the freight trains came thundering past. I'd like to see a horse that doesn't bolt when a loaded freight train thunders by a couple of yards away. In any case, our horses always freaked out. And the only thing you could think about at that moment was, I hope my horse doesn't run into the train. But I was a lot better off than the other kids because I had my pets. Sometimes I took my three mice with me to the sandbox at the playground. At least the playground regulations didn't say, "No mice allowed." We built tunnels and caves for them and let them run around.

One afternoon, one of the mice ran into the grass that we weren't allowed to step on. We couldn't find it again. I was a bit sad but consoled myself with the thought that the mouse was probably much happier outside than in the cage.

Of all evenings, my dad picked that one to come into our kids' room and look into the mouse cage. He asked in a funny tone of voice, "Why are there only two? Where is the third mouse?" I didn't sense any danger yet, didn't pick up on the weird tone of voice. My dad never liked those mice and always told me to get rid of them. I told him how the mouse got away on the playground.

My dad looked at me like a lunatic. I knew that now he'd go totally psycho. He screamed and immediately started beating me. He was hitting me, and I was wedged into my bed and couldn't get out. He had never before hit me like that, and I thought he was going to kill me. When he also started in on my sister, I got a couple of seconds of air and instinctively tried to get to the window. I believe I would have jumped, right out of that eleventh-floor window.

But my dad grabbed me and threw me back on the bed. My mom probably stood crying in the doorway again, but I didn't see her. I only became aware of her when she threw herself between my dad and me. She pounded on him with her fists.

He'd completely lost it. He was punching and beating my mom in the hallway. Suddenly I was more afraid for my mom than I was for myself. So I ran after them into the hallway. My mom tried to escape into the bathroom and close the door before my dad could get there. But my dad had a good grip on her hair. The tub was full of laundry soaking in soapy water like every evening because we didn't have the money for a washing machine. My dad thrust my mom's head into the full tub. At some point she emerged from the water. I don't know if my dad let go of her, or if she managed to free herself.

My dad had turned deathly pale and disappeared into the living room. My mom went to the closet and put on her coat. Without a word, she left the apartment.

That was without doubt one of the most terrible moments of my life, when my mom simply left without a word. Left us alone in the apartment. At first, all I could think was that he'd come back and continue beating us. But in the living room, all was quiet, except for the TV, which was on.

I brought my sister into my bed with me. We hung on to each other. My sister had to go pee. She didn't dare go into the bathroom, and she was trembling. But she also didn't want to pee in the bed because that would result in more beatings. At some point, I don't know when, I took her by the hand and walked with her to the bathroom. From the living room, my dad said good night to us.

Nobody woke us up the next morning. We didn't go to school. Some time before noon, my mom returned. She hardly spoke a word. She packed a few of our things, stuffed Peter, the cat, into a bag, and told me to put Ajax on the leash. Then we were off to the subway. The next few days we stayed with one of mom's work colleagues in her small apartment.

My mom explained to us that she wanted to get a divorce.

My mom's colleague's apartment was too small for my mom, my sister, Ajax, Peter, and me. After a few days, her colleague showed signs that we were getting on her nerves. So my mom packed up our stuff again; we grabbed the animals and headed back to Gropiusstadt.

My dad came into the apartment just as my sister and I were taking a bath in the tub. He came into the bathroom and said real normal-like, as if nothing had happened, "Why did you go away? You really don't need to sleep at strangers' houses. The three of us would've had a nice time together." My sister and I just looked at each other awkwardly. My dad pretended that my mom was invisible for the rest of the evening. He looked right past all of us, as if we weren't there. And he never said another word to us about it. That was somehow worse than beating us.

My dad never beat me again. But the fact that he now pretended that he was no longer part of our family was horrible. He was there but not there, and that made me miss having a dad even more acutely. I never hated him; I'd only been scared of him. I'd also always been proud of him. Because he loved animals, and because he had such a cool car, his '62 Porsche. In a weird way, he no longer was our dad, although he still lived with us in

our small apartment. And then something else really terrible happened: Ajax, my Great Dane, suffered a fatal abdominal infection
and died. Nobody consoled me. My mom was totally preoccupied with herself and the divorce. She cried a lot and didn't laugh
at all anymore. I felt very alone.

One evening the doorbell rang. I opened the door, and it was
Klaus, one of my dad's friends. He wanted my dad to go bar-
hopping with him. But my dad had already gone out.

So my mom asked him in. He was much younger than my
dad—in his early twenties. And this Klaus guy suddenly asked
my mom if she wanted to go out and get something to eat. My
mom didn't hesitate: "Sure, why not." She got changed, walked
off with him, and left us alone.

Other kids might have been pissed or afraid for their mom.
I had those feelings for a moment, too. But then I was honestly
happy for her. She looked positively perky when she left, even
if she tried not to show it. My sister noticed it too: "Mom was
really happy."

Klaus came by more often now, when my dad wasn't there.
It was on a Sunday, I still remember it very well, when my mom
sent me out to take the trash downstairs. I was very quiet when I
returned upstairs. Maybe I was quiet on purpose. When I peeked
into the living room, I saw Klaus kissing my mom.

I felt really weird and tiptoed into my room. Neither of them
had seen me. And I didn't tell anyone about what I had seen. Not
even my sister, from whom I usually didn't keep anything.

I began to feel pretty weird and uncomfortable about this
new guy who was always over at our apartment. But at least
he was always nice to us—and (even more importantly) always
really nice to my mom. She was laughing again, and she'd almost
completely stopped crying. She even started thinking about the
future again. She talked about moving into a new apartment
with Klaus and about this new room that my sister and I were

supposed to get if we all moved in with him. But of course we didn't have that new apartment yet. And my dad wasn't moving out anytime soon. In fact, he stuck around even after my mom and he were finally divorced. My parents continued to sleep in the same bed even though they hated each other. There wasn't really another choice: We still had no money.

And when we finally did get another apartment, one subway stop away, in Rudow, things weren't ideal either. Klaus was a permanent fixture now, and even though I still thought he was kind of nice, he was always getting in the way. He soaked up a lot of my mom's attention and also got in the middle of fights between my mom and me. I just didn't accept him as one of us. I didn't think that this guy, who was just in his early twenties, had any right to tell me what to do. And so, as a result, I had less and less patience with him.

We started getting into fights—just over little things at first. Sometimes they were my fault. Most of the time, we fought about music. My mom had bought me a record player for my eleventh birthday, just a little cheap one, and I had a few records: some disco and teenybopper music. And, in the evenings, I'd put on a record and turn the volume all the way up, loud enough to burst your eardrums. One evening, Klaus came into our room and asked me to turn down the record player. I didn't. He came back and yanked the arm off the record. I put the arm back on and positioned myself in front of the turntable so that he couldn't get at it. At that point, he pushed me away, and as soon as that man touched me, I freaked out.

When we had these fights, my mom would cautiously take my side. That was also awkward because then it would escalate to a fight between Klaus and my mom, which made me feel kind of guilty. There was definitely one person too many in the apartment (and I had a strong suspicion about who that one person was).

That being said, for the most part our fights weren't that bad, and they weren't that frequent either. What was worse than the fights was the quiet, when we'd all sit together in the living room. Klaus would be leafing through some magazine or flipping through channels on the TV and my mom would try to start a conversation, first with Klaus, and then with us, and then with Klaus again, and nobody would respond. It was so uncomfortable. When my sister and I couldn't take it anymore, we'd ask if we could go outside to play, and nobody ever objected. Klaus, for his part, usually seemed happy when we left. So we'd stay away for as long as possible.

Looking back, I can't really blame Klaus. After all, he was only in his early twenties. He didn't know what it meant to have a family. He didn't get how much our mom loved us and how much we loved her, and he probably couldn't understand that we needed some time alone with her during the short periods that we got to spend together in the evenings and on weekends. He was probably jealous of us, and we were just as jealous of him. My mom wanted to be there for us, but she was also worried about losing her boyfriend, so it wound up really stressing her out.

I responded pretty badly to the situation—with a lot of anger (and a lot of yelling). My sister, however, got more and more quiet and was clearly hurting inside. She probably didn't know why she felt so bad herself. But she started to talk more and more often about moving back in with my dad. I thought that idea was totally crazy after all that we'd been through with him. But he actually offered to let us stay with him. It was as if he'd become a different person after we left. He had a young girlfriend. And he always seemed to be in a good mood when we saw him. He was really nice to us, and, for the first time, I hoped he might actually live up to the image I'd always had of him as a nice person. He gave me another Great Dane—a female this time.

I turned twelve, and my breasts started growing. I started to get weirdly interested in boys and men. They were like these strange creatures, and they were hard for me to figure out. They were also all so brutal: the older boys on the street, and my dad, and, Klaus, too, in his own way—they all were. I was afraid of them, but they also fascinated me. They were strong and they had power. They were just like I would've liked to be. Their power, their strength, drew me in like a magnet.

I began to use a blow-dryer on my hair. I used the nail scissors to cut my bangs a little shorter and then combed them to the side. I spent a lot of time on my hair because people had started to tell me how beautiful and long it was. I also didn't want to wear kids' pants anymore; instead, I wanted jeans. Then, when I got jeans, I absolutely had to have high-heeled shoes. My mom gave me one of her old pairs.

With my new jeans and high-heeled shoes I'd go parading through the streets until 10 p.m. almost every night. I felt like the new me was being rejected back at home. But even though that hurt, their rejection gave me a kind of freedom, too, which I loved. I also kind of enjoyed my fights with Klaus. It made me feel powerful to fight with an adult.

My sister couldn't stand it though, and as a result, she did what was for me the unthinkable: She moved back in with my dad. In so doing, she deserted my mom and left me behind as well. So I became even lonelier, and our mom was totally distraught. She started crying again. She was torn between her kids and her boyfriend and she didn't have any idea what to do or who to choose.

I thought that it wouldn't take long for my sister to come back. But she liked it at my dad's. She got an allowance. He paid for her riding lessons and bought her a pair of real riding pants. That was pretty tough for me to see. I had to keep on earning my riding lessons by mucking out the stalls. But that didn't always pan out, and before long, my sister, with her fancy riding pants, was a way better rider than I was.

But my dad made it up to me by inviting me on a trip to Spain. I'd done really well in sixth grade, and as a result, I'd been recommended for the Gymnasium—the college preparatory track.[7] I was registered for the comprehensive school[8] in Gropiusstadt.

So before the start of this new chapter of my life, which would culminate in the college entrance exams,[9] I flew to Torremolinos, Spain, with my dad and his girlfriend. It was an amazing vacation. My dad was great, and I was able to see that, in a way, he did love me. He treated me now almost like an adult. He even let me go out with him and his girlfriend at night.

He finally seemed to have his head screwed on right. He had friends that were his own age, and now he managed to actually tell them that he'd been married once before. I didn't have to call him Uncle Richard anymore. I was his daughter. And he seemed to be really proud of the fact that I was his daughter. However, as was typical for him, he'd planned his vacation according to what was most convenient for him and his friends. At the end of my school break. Which meant I started my new school two weeks late. So I began my college prep years as a truant.

---

7 After sixth grade, students in Germany are divided into different schools, or tracks, depending on their performance up through sixth grade. The least difficult of these is known as Hauptschule; the intermediate track is called Realschule; and the most advanced college preparatory track is Gymnasium.

8 In the 1970s, the comprehensive school (called Gesamtschule in German) system was created as an alternative to the traditional three-way division of schools into Hauptschule, Realschule, and Gymnasium. In this single system, students could study different subjects at different levels of difficulty.

9 College entrance exams (called Abitur in German) are taken at the end of twelfth grade and are required for attending university. Completing twelfth grade in Germany is roughly the academic equivalent of having completed approximately two years of college in the United States.

Coming in late made me feel like an outsider in the new school. New friendships and new cliques had already been established. I sat by myself. But the biggest issue was that, during the first two weeks, while I was in Spain, they'd explained to the newcomers how the comprehensive school system worked—how you can pick classes, how difficulty levels vary, etcetera—and it's actually really complicated, especially when you've just arrived from elementary school. Everyone else had gotten help with selecting their courses and setting their schedules. Meanwhile, I was lost and alone. I had absolutely no idea how the school functioned. And I never figured it out either. It wasn't like elementary school, where each grade would have a designated teacher who would look out for his or her own group of students. Here, every teacher taught a couple hundred students, all in different grades and courses. If you wanted to successfully complete your college entrance exams in comprehensive school, you really had to know what you were doing: You had to be self-motivated and make the conscious decision to study and work your way up into the advanced courses. And to do that, you had to have parents who would tell you exactly what you needed to do and who got on your case if you started to fall behind. I just had no idea what was going on; I was totally lost.

I didn't feel accepted there either. Everyone else had had a two-week head start—and that's a huge advantage at a new school. I reverted to my old elementary school tactics and started annoying the teachers with interruptions and contradictions. Sometimes I'd do it because I actually knew something, and other times, just because I felt like it. I was fighting again, against the teachers and against the school as a whole. But I just wanted to be accepted.

The coolest kid in our class was a girl named Kessi. She already had boobs. She looked at least two years older than the rest of us, and she acted more mature, too. Everyone liked having her around. I admired her, and more than anything else, I just wanted her to be my friend.

Kessi also had an awesome boyfriend. He was in the same grade as us (in a different class) but was also a year older already. His name was Milan. He was at least 5'7" tall and had long, black, curly hair down to his shoulders. He wore jeans and these badass boots. All the girls at school liked Milan. Kessi wasn't just popular because she had boobs and acted so mature, but also because Milan was her boyfriend.

Back in those days, we had very specific ideas about what a "hot" boyfriend should be like. He couldn't ever be seen in baggy pants. Skintight jeans were a requirement. Guys with sneakers also looked stupid. Instead, they had to wear really dramatic, decked-out boots. We thought that the guys who still played immature pranks—like shooting spitballs or chucking apple cores around—were ridiculous. They were usually the same kids who still drank milk and played soccer during recess. The cool guys, the ones we all had crushes on, disappeared into the smoking corner every recess. And if a guy wanted to be really cool, he also had to be comfortable with drinking beer. I still remember how impressed I was when Kessi told me a story about how drunk Milan had been at some point.

I kept wondering about how I could transform myself into the kind of girl that would matter to someone like Milan—into someone that he would want to talk to or ask out. Or—and this was actually one and the same thing—how I could become accepted and respected by someone like Kessi. I already thought her nickname, Kessi,[10] was super cool. I wanted to be the kind of person who had a cool nickname.

---

10 "Kessi" stems from the German word *kess*, which means someone who is brash and has a tendency to talk back.

After a while, I started to ask myself why I was so worried about my teachers, when I only saw each of them for an hour or so each day. Why was I so worried about getting their approval? It's way more important to be accepted by the people who you actually spend your time with. So from that point on, all bets were off: I was the teachers' worst nightmare. I didn't have personal relationships with any of them. And most of them didn't seem to really care anyway. They didn't have any real authority over us, and as a result, they tried to intimidate us with their insults and threats. But whatever they dished out to us, I gave back to them with both barrels. Before long, I'd become an expert in wreaking havoc in the classroom; without hardly even trying, I could mess up the teacher's entire lesson plan, and the more destructive I was, the more recognition and respect I got from the other students.

I used every extra cent to buy cigarettes so that I'd have something to smoke in the smokers' corner. And once I started smoking regularly over there, Kessi warmed up to me. We started talking and hanging out after school as well. Eventually she even invited me to her house, where we shared a couple of beers (until I felt kind of giddy and woozy). We talked about our home lives. We were both stuck in pretty similar situations, but Kessi's home life was even more fucked up than mine.

Kessi's father wasn't part of her life, and her mom went through a lot of different boyfriends (who obviously didn't accept Kessi as part of the deal). She'd just gone through a rough time with one of these boyfriends who went ballistic on her. He beat up on Kessi and her mom and one day wrecked all the furniture in the apartment. Then, when he was done, he threw the TV set out of the window, as a kind of exclamation point to the episode. Kessi's mom was different from mine in one crucial respect though: She was strict, or tried to be. Kessi had to be home by 8 p.m. almost every night.

So I'd finally made it in school: I'd earned the respect of my classmates. But keeping it up was tough—it was a constant struggle, and it left hardly any time for studying. My triumphant new social status was written in stone the day Kessi finally invited me to sit next to her.

Kessi was the one who taught me how to cut class. If she didn't feel like being at school, she just left for an hour or two and met up with Milan or did whatever she felt like. At first I was scared. But then I caught on quickly that it was hardly ever discovered if you missed single classes in the middle of the day. Attendance was only taken at the beginning of the first class of the day. During the following classes, the teachers had way too many students to keep track of who was there and who wasn't. And most of them didn't care anyway.

At that point, Kessi had already made out with a few different boys. And she was already going to the Center House, which was a meeting place for young people, affiliated with the Protestant church. It had a kind of disco club in the basement known simply as "the club." You had to be at least fourteen to get into the club. But Kessi already looked a lot older than thirteen.

I begged and begged my mom until she bought me a bra, even though I didn't really need one yet. I just wanted one because it would make my boobs look bigger. I started to use makeup, too. And then Kessi took me along to the basement club, which opened at 5 p.m.

The first thing that I noticed once I was inside the club was a boy from our school. He was in ninth grade, and he was, I thought, the coolest guy in school. Even cooler than Milan (and better-looking, too). And more than anything else, he was just so overwhelmingly self-confident. He acted like a rock star. It was obvious that he thought he was superior to everybody else. His name was Piet. Piet belonged to a group that always sat or stood at the edge of things. They gave the impression that they were different from the other teenagers who hung out at the club. The whole group was super cool. All the guys looked hot. They wore skin-tight jeans, big, crazy boots, and their jackets were all either denim or else these crazy things that were scrapped together from a lot of discarded old materials—but they looked amazing. Kessi knew these guys and brought me over. I couldn't believe that she was introducing me to these guys, considering that everyone else was in awe of this group. They seemed to be cool with Kessi though, and let us sit with them. When I came to the club the next night, that same group had brought a huge hookah with them. At first I had no clue what it was. Kessi explained that they were smoking hashish and told me that it was okay for me to go join them. I didn't know exactly what hashish was supposed to be. I only knew that it was a drug and totally illegal.

They lit the stuff in the pipe and passed it around. Everybody took a drag. Kessi did, too, but I passed on it. I didn't really want to say no, since I wanted so badly to fit in. But I couldn't get myself to do it yet—to smoke hash. The idea of doing drugs still scared the shit out of me.

I felt really insecure. I wanted to just sink into a hole in the ground and disappear. But I couldn't leave the table because then it would've looked like I didn't want anything to do with these guys, just because they smoked hashish. So I told them that what I really wanted was a beer and not hash. I got up and collected the empty bottles that were lying around. For four empties I could get eighty pfennigs, or one beer. That night I got drunk for the first time in my life while everyone else sucked on the hookah. They talked about music, too—music that I didn't know about yet. I was into all the teenybopper bands. I liked to listen to Sweet.[11] I couldn't hold up my end in their conversation anyway, so it

---

11 A British glam rock band.

was just as well that I was drunk and relaxed and didn't get too worried about it.

It quickly became clear what kind of music they thought was cool, and I decided right away that I agreed with them. They loved David Bowie and that sort of stuff.

These guys in the club seemed like rock stars to me all by themselves. From behind, they all looked like David Bowie, even though they were all only sixteen or so.

The people in this clique were cool in a way that was completely new to me. They weren't loud, they didn't get into fights, and they didn't show off. They were pretty quiet. They just kind of exuded superiority. And it was the same whether they were out at the club or just hanging out amongst themselves: They were always just effortlessly cool. They never argued with each other. And when they greeted each other, they did it with little kisses on the mouth. And although the guys always set the tone, the girls were treated as equals. Unlike other groups, they never had those stupid immature fights between guys and girls.

Not long after I got drunk at the club, I cut class again with Kessi. Just the last two classes. Kessi had a date with Milan in the Wutzkyallee subway station. As we were hanging out at the subway station waiting for Milan, we also kept an eye out for teachers because sometimes they'd show up around this time, too.

Kessi was just lighting a cigarette when I saw Piet and his friend Kathi, another guy from their group. It was the moment I'd been hoping for and fantasizing about. I'd always wanted to run into these guys during school hours. And then, in my daydreams, I'd ask Piet if he'd come home with me. Honestly, I didn't have any lecherous thoughts at the time. I wasn't interested in fooling around with guys yet. After all, I was only twelve years old, and my period hadn't even started yet. All I wanted was to be able to say that Piet had been to my house. Then the others would've thought that he and I were an item, or at least that I was definitely a solid member of their group.

So here were Piet and Kathi. I knew for a fact that nobody would be at my apartment right then, since both my mom and her boyfriend had daytime jobs. So I said to Kessi, "Let's go say hi to these guys." My heart was pounding. But after only a few minutes, I got my bearings (sort of), and confidently asked Piet, "Hey, you guys wanna come over to my place? Nobody else is there. And my mom's boyfriend has some awesome records —Led Zeppelin, David Bowie, Ten Years After, Deep Purple, and the Woodstock Festival album."

I'd already come a long way. Not only did I know the music that they were into, I'd also learned to talk like them. Their language was different; everything with them was different. I'd paid close attention to the new slang that I'd heard them use. This was much more important to me than memorizing English vocabulary at school, or math formulas.

Piet and Kathi were both really into my idea. And I was ecstatic. Their enthusiasm made me that much more self-assured. So once we'd made it back to my place I said: "Shit, guys, I don't have anything to drink." So we pooled all our change and Kathi and I went off on a mission to the supermarket. Beer was too expensive. You needed more than a few marks[12] to get enough beer for a buzz. So instead we bought a liter of red wine for 1.98 marks. "Hobo wine" they called it. We sucked down the whole bottle of wine, and then we just talked—mostly about the police. Piet said that he had to be really careful and keep an eye out for the cops because of the pot. They called hashish *pot*, because that's what they'd heard the Americans call it. They were convinced that we lived in a police state and kept piling insults on all the local cops.

---

12 At the time, one German mark was equal to about $1.50–$2.00 US

This was all totally new to me. Up to that point, the only authority figures I'd really hated were our buildings' caretakers, who were always hounding you just when you started to have fun and just because you were having fun. But the police still represented an unassailable authority to me. My new friends told me that the housing project caretakers were actually just a part of the police state, but that cops were much more dangerous than caretakers. For me, whatever Piet and Kathi said was the be-all and end-all, and I accepted it as the truth.

When we'd finished the wine, Piet said that he could go back to his place to grab some hash if people wanted to smoke. Everyone was really into that idea.

Piet left via the balcony. Since we'd moved to our new apartment on the ground floor, I had also started to go out that way. I loved it after living on the eleventh floor for all those years. Piet came back in a bit with a disc of pressed hashish about the size of his hand, which was divided into gram pieces of ten marks each. He took out a chillum, which is a wooden tube, like a pipe, about eight inches long. He stuffed tobacco into the top so that you didn't have to smoke down to the wood. Then he mixed some tobacco in with the hash and put the mixture on top. To smoke it, you had to tilt your head back and keep the tube in a vertical position so that none of the hot ashes fell out.

I watched the others very carefully to see how they did it. There was obviously no way I could say no, now that Piet and Kathi were here in my house. So I played it cool and talked about how much I wanted to smoke some hash that day. And I pretended that I was already an expert when it came to chillums.

We'd let down the blinds. Thick clouds of smoke were visible in the dim light that still filtered through. I'd put on a David Bowie record and took a drag on the chillum and held the smoke in my lungs until it made me cough. Everybody had grown quiet.

They were all dozing off, drifting away into their own worlds, listening to the music.

I waited for something to happen to me. I thought, Now that you've taken drugs, something really crazy, something totally outrageous should be happening. But I didn't actually feel anything. I just felt a little tipsy—but that was from the wine.

I didn't realize that most people don't feel a thing the first time they smoke pot. You actually need to "practice" smoking pot before you start getting a high. Alcohol has a much stronger, more immediate punch.

I saw Piet and Kessi move closer together on the sofa. Piet was stroking Kessi's arms. After a while, they got up, went into my room, and shut the door.

Now Kathi and I were alone. He sat down next to me on the side of the armchair and put his arm around my shoulders. Right away, I liked Kathi much better than Piet. And I was so happy that Kathi came over to me and showed me that he was interested in me. I'd always been afraid that it would be obvious to guys that I was only twelve and that they'd dismiss me as just a little child.

Kathi started stroking me. I didn't know anymore whether I was okay with this or not. I started feeling incredibly hot. I think because of fear. I sat there frozen like a stone and tried to make small talk about the record that was playing. When Kathi put his hand on my breast (or at least on the little bump that was growing there), I stood up, walked over to the record player, and started fiddling around with it.

Then Piet and Kessi came back into the living room. They had weird looks on their faces. They were upset and somehow sad. Kessi was really red in the face, and the two of them were completely ignoring one another. Neither one of them said a word. It seemed to me that Kessi had had a bad experience—one that she didn't get anything out of, one that wasn't satisfying for either of them.

Piet finally asked me if I'd come with them to the Center House that night. That cheered me up again. I'd accomplished a lot that day. Things had turned out exactly as I'd hoped they would. Piet and Kathi had come to my house—in real life!—and I'd become a part of their group.

Piet and Kessi left over the balcony. Kathi was still wandering around the living room. I felt something like fear rise up again. I told him pretty bluntly that I needed to pick up around the apartment and then do some homework. Suddenly I didn't care what he thought. He left after that. I lay down in my room, stared at the ceiling, and tried to make sense of it all.

Kathi was good-looking, definitely, but I'd somehow lost interest in him. After an hour-and-a-half the doorbell rang. Through the peephole in the door, I could tell it was Kathi. I didn't open up, and instead I tiptoed back to my room. I was really afraid to be alone with him. He was freaking me out, and yet somehow I also felt guilty. I didn't know why. It could have been the pot. But nothing ever happened with him anyway.

As I thought about this, I started feeling kind of depressed. Even though I was part of the clique now, I didn't really fit in. I was still way too young to fool around with the guys. I knew for sure that I just couldn't do that yet. And whatever they said about the police and the government was way over my head—not that it mattered to me, anyway.

Even so, at 5 p.m. I was back at the Center House. This time, however, we didn't go to the club; instead we went to the movies. I wanted to sit next to Kessi and a stranger, but Kathi squeezed himself in between us. Then, during the movie, he started touching me again. At some point, his hand slipped between my legs.

I didn't resist. It was like I was paralyzed. I was scared to death of something, but I wasn't sure what. Once, I thought about running out of there. But then I reminded myself, Christiane, this is the price you have to pay for being part of this clique. So I let him do whatever he wanted, and I didn't say a word. After all, I had incredible respect for this guy. But when he said that I should touch him too, and when he tried to pull my hand toward him, I clamped my hands together tightly in my lap and ended things.

I let out a huge sigh of relief when the movie was finally over. I broke immediately away from Kathi and went over to Kessi. I told her everything, and I also said that I didn't want any part of Kathi anymore. I'm sure Kessi told him what I thought later on because a little later I found out that she'd had a huge crush on Kathi herself. She started crying right there in the club because Kathi didn't pay any special attention to her. Eventually she did finally confess to me how crazy she was about Kathi; she said that she always felt like crying whenever he was around.

Despite the thing with Kathi, I was now a solid member of the group—despite the fact that they all referred to me as "the baby." But that didn't matter; I belonged to them. None of the guys tried to touch me. Word had gotten around, and everyone was fine with the fact that I was still too young for fooling around with. That was totally different with the drunks—the teenagers who spent all their time drinking beer and schnapps. If any of their girlfriends didn't want to fool around or drink with them, they treated them horribly, almost brutally. They made fun of them, insulted them, and ostracized them. In our group, there was none of that emotional brutality. We accepted each other just the way we were. After all, we were all on the same journey—or at least all on the same drug trip. We understood one another without a lot of talking. Nobody was ever loud or obscene. We didn't pay much attention to what the others were gossiping about—we felt like we were above all that.

With the exceptions of Piet, Kessi, and me, everyone else already had jobs. And they all had a similar outlook on things: They hated life at home and they hated their jobs. Unlike the drunks, who were always worked up about something, carried their stress into the club with them, and let their aggression out on others, the people in our group could kick back and chill out. After work, they'd put on different clothes, smoke pot, put on some hot new music, and make a perfect little world for themselves. When we were together, it was love and peace all around us, and we forgot about all the shit that happened in the real world that existed outside of our little clique.

But I didn't quite feel everything the others felt; I didn't "get it" completely. For that, I think, I was still too young. Still, they were my idols. I wanted to be exactly like them. I wanted to learn from them because they knew how to make their own rules; they knew how to live a life that was actually cool. They didn't let all the assholes out there get them down. Reality hardly mattered anymore. Parents and teachers couldn't tell me what to do; I was through with them. The only thing that mattered to me now was my group of friends—well, that and my pets.

The reason I was so obsessed with my friends at the time was partly due to what was happening at home. I couldn't take it anymore. The worst part was that Klaus, my mom's boyfriend, hated our animals. At least that's what it seemed like to me at the time. It started with him constantly complaining about how our apartment was too small for so many animals. And then he wouldn't let my new dog—the one my dad had given me—lie down in the living room.

That's when I lost it. The dogs had always been a part of our family. They were treated like any other family member. And now this jerk comes along and says my dog isn't even allowed in the living room? But worse was still to come. He tried to prevent my dog from sleeping beside my bed. What was I supposed to do? Klaus seriously wanted me to build a dog crate for my big dog, in my tiny room. Of course I didn't do it.

Then Klaus had his final meltdown: He exclaimed that the animals absolutely had to get out of the house. My mom took his side and said that I didn't take care of the animals anymore anyway. I thought that was the last straw. Sure, I wasn't home much at night, and so one of them had to always take the dog out one more time. But otherwise, I thought, I took care of the dog and the other animals with every free minute that I had.

I could threaten, yell, and howl all I wanted—there was nothing I could do. They gave my dog away. At first to a woman whom I thought was okay because she really liked the dog. But the woman got cancer soon afterward and had to give the dog away again. I heard that it ended up in a bar somewhere. My dog was an extremely sensitive animal, and she was terrified by loud noises. I knew that in a bar she would be completely traumatized, and I blamed Klaus and my mom for this. That's when I decided that I was done with people who hated animals.

●

THIS WAS ALL GOING on around the time when I started going to the Center House a lot, and started smoking pot. The only pets I had left now were two cats, and they didn't need me during the day. At night, they slept with me on my bed. With the dog gone, there was no reason, no purpose for me to be at home. Without the dog, I didn't even enjoy going for walks anymore. So now I just waited for 5 p.m. to roll around, when I could go back to the club at Center House. And even then, I'd often have already spent the early afternoon with Kessi and some of the others from our group.

I smoked pot every night. The people who had enough money for drugs would share it with the others. I didn't think twice about smoking pot anymore. After all, we were able to do it right out in the open at the club. The social workers from the church, the ones who supervised the club, would occasionally try to say something when they saw us smoking. They didn't all feel the same about pot, but most of them would admit that they used to smoke, too. Most of them were recent college and university graduates and had been part of the student movement,[13] where smoking pot and hashish had become normal. So they generally just told us not to overdo it and not to use it as an escape, etcetera. More than anything else, they were worried that it would be a gateway drug and lead straight to harder stuff.

All that talk went in one ear and out the other. What right did they have to moralize like that, when they themselves admitted to having done the same things? Someone from our group confronted one of those young guys once: "So you think that when college students smoke pot, it's okay, because they're smart. But when workers or interns smoke pot, then it's dangerous. That seems like kind of a double standard to me." The guy didn't have a response for that. You could tell he felt uneasy.

I didn't just smoke, either; I also drank wine and beer—especially when I didn't have any marijuana. I usually started drinking right after school, and sometimes had something in the mornings, too, if I was skipping classes. I always had to have something.

---

13 The German student movement was a protest movement in the late 1960s in West Germany. German students had been largely conservative until the '60s, but protest movements across the world encouraged them to rise up against the perceived authoritarianism and hypocrisy of the German government, and the poor living conditions of students.

I was constantly spaced out. I needed it to keep from dwelling on all the shit that was happening at school and back at home. I couldn't care less about school anyway. My grades started plummeting around then, going from B's to D's and F's.

I started to look different, too. I got super skinny because I hardly ate anything anymore. All my pants were suddenly way too big for me. My face looked gaunt. I stood in front of the mirror a lot, and I liked what I saw, the changes I was seeing. I looked more and more like the others in my group of friends. The innocent look on my face had finally fallen away.

I was totally obsessed with my appearance. I made my mom buy me high heels and skinny jeans. I parted my hair in the middle, grew long bangs, and combed them so they hung long across my face. I wanted to look mysterious so that nobody would see the real me. So that nobody would notice that I actually really wasn't as cool as I wanted to be.

One evening at the club, Piet asked me if I'd ever dropped acid. I said, "Of course." I'd heard a lot about LSD by that time. There was always a lot of talk about somebody's latest crazy trip. Piet grinned at me, and I could tell that he didn't believe me so I started making stuff up. I pieced together a story from what I'd heard other people say and concocted my own fantasy trip. But I could see that Piet still didn't buy any of it. He was pretty cynical. By the time I'd finished stumbling through my story, I was pretty embarrassed. Piet just said, "If you want to try, I'll have some really good stuff on Saturday. You can have some if you want."

I was looking forward to it. I thought that once I dropped acid, no one could doubt my belonging anymore. When I arrived at the Center House that Saturday, Kessi was already tripping. Piet said, "If you really want to, I'll give you half of one. That's enough for the first time." He gave me a bit of crumpled cigarette paper with a crumb of acid wrapped in it. But I couldn't just toss it down like that in front of everyone! I was unbelievably excited.

I was also kind of scared of being caught. Besides, I thought this occasion called for a more private, ceremonious place. So I went into a bathroom stall, locked myself inside, and swallowed the crumb.

When I came back, Piet clearly thought that I'd just flushed the pill down the toilet. I waited impatiently for something to happen to me, to prove to the others that I'd swallowed the pill.

When the club at the Center House closed at 10 p.m., I still didn't feel any different. I went to the subway station with Piet. At the station, we met up with two friends of his, named Frank and Pauli. They were dressed exactly alike, like twins. They were incredibly calm and serene. I liked them. Piet said, "They're on H." That's what they called heroin. It didn't make an impression on me just then. I was at that very moment even more self-absorbed than usual because I was busy dealing with the effects of the acid, which had just started to kick in.

After we got into the subway and started moving, I freaked out. It was totally insane. For some reason, I was convinced that I was inside a tin can, and that someone was stirring us around with a gigantic spoon. The banging and clanking of the subway going through the tunnel was terrifying. I didn't think I could take the noise for even one more second. The people in the subway all had horribly distorted faces, too, like masks, like pig faces. By which I mean, they looked exactly like they always did: like a bunch of losers. But now I could see so much more clearly how disgusting and ignorant these working stiffs really were. I could imagine them all having just left some fucking bar or some shitty job. All of these grotesque, porky faces finish their day and then it's back to bed, and then it's back to work again, and then they turn the TV on, and then that's it. I thought, Wow, you're lucky that you're not one of them. You're lucky that you have friends. That you're on acid and know what's important and can recognize how ridiculous and stupid these common people are. That's kind of what I was thinking. And I had the same sequence of thoughts on later acid trips, too. Then I started feeling terrified by those faces again. I looked at Piet. He was also somehow uglier than usual. His face was really small compared to the pig faces. But despite that, he still looked kind of normal.

I was so glad when we got out in Rudow, because by that time I was really tripping. All the lights were insanely bright. One of the streetlights above us seemed to be even brighter than the sun. In the subway, I was freezing, but now I was boiling hot. I thought I was somewhere in Spain, instead of in Berlin. It was like in one of those beautiful posters in the travel agency office in Gropiusstadt. The trees were all palm trees, and the street was a beautiful beach. Everything was unbelievably bright. I didn't tell Piet that I was tripping. I kind of wanted to be alone on my crazy but awesome trip.

Piet, who was also tripping, said that we could still go to his girlfriend's because her parents weren't there. He loved this girlfriend of his. We walked into the underground garage of his girlfriend's house. He wanted to see if her parents' car was there. But the garage was something out of a horror movie—at least in my eyes. The low-hanging ceiling seemed to crush us, bulging further and further downward. The concrete pillars swayed back and forth. The parents' car was there.

Piet said, "Man, what a crazy fucking garage." And then he must have suddenly felt self-conscious, thinking that he was the only one tripping and asked me, "So where did you throw that pill back there in the club?" He looked at me and said after a few seconds, "Whoa, baby girl, I shouldn't have said anything: Your pupils look like they've been sucked into your eyeballs!"

Once outside, everything was beautiful again. I sat down on the grass. The wall of one house was so orange that it seemed to offer a reflection of the rising sun. The shadows all seemed to move away to make room for the light. The wall bulged out and suddenly seemed to be devoured by flames.

We went to Piet's house. Piet was an incredible painter. In his room, he'd hung up one of his paintings. It was a picture of a skeleton riding a really fat horse, and wielding a scythe. I was obsessed with that picture. I'd seen it a couple of times before and thought it was just about death. But now the painting didn't scare me at all. My thoughts were all much simpler now, almost naïve. I thought, There's no way that that skeleton would be able to control such a big horse. It seemed like the horse was already in command. We talked a long time about that picture. Then Piet gave me a few records to listen to. He said, "This stuff is amazing when you're tripping." I went home.

My mom was still awake, of course. She started in with the usual questions: Where had I been, what had I been doing, and things could definitely not go on like this, etcetera, etcetera. My mom seemed completely ridiculous to me—all fat and dumpy in her white nightgown, her face distorted with rage. Just like all of the other losers in the subway.

I didn't say a word. I wasn't talking to her anymore. Even when I did say something, it was only about the most necessary and trivial things. I didn't need any love or affection from her. Sometimes I even believed that I didn't need a mom or a family at all.

My mom with her boyfriend lived in a completely different world from me. She didn't have the slightest clue as to what I was up to. She thought that I was a completely normal kid, just going through puberty. What could I have said to them anyway? There was no way they'd get it. They would've only told me to stop. That's what I thought at the time. The only thing I felt for my mom was pity. Pity for how stressed out she always was when she'd come home from her job and then immediately throw herself into her housework. But it was her own fault for buying into that mundane, tedious lifestyle.

Christiane's Mom

I often ask myself why it took me so long to realize what was going on with Christiane. The answer's simple, but I couldn't really bring myself to admit it until I'd heard some other parents say the exact same thing. I was in denial. I couldn't bring myself to face up to reality. I just didn't want to believe that my daughter was a drug addict.

My boyfriend, who'd been living with me since the divorce, started to suspect something was up way before I did. "What are you talking about?" I'd ask him. "She's only a child." That was probably my biggest mistake, to believe that the kids were somehow "too young." When Christiane began to isolate herself, when she avoided contact with family and would rather hang out with her friends on the weekends, that's when I should have paid closer attention and investigated what she was up to. I shrugged a lot of things off.

When you have a full-time job, it's hard to pay close enough attention to your kids. You're glad when you get some quiet time to relax, and you don't really mind when they go off to do their own thing. Sure, sometimes Christiane came home too late. But she always had some excuse that I was eager to believe. I thought that her recklessness and defiant behavior were just part of a developmental phase that would eventually end.

I didn't want to force her to do anything. I'd had enough of that kind of parenting myself already. My dad was extremely strict.

In the Hessian[14] village, where I grew up, he was the owner of a quarry, and everyone respected him. But his theory on child rearing consisted only of saying no. If I even talked about boys, he'd hit me.

I still remember one particular Sunday afternoon like it was yesterday. I was out for a walk with a girlfriend of mine, and trailing more than a hundred yards behind us were two young men. My dad happened to pass by us, so he immediately pulled over and slapped me across the face, right there on the street. Then he threw me into his car and took me home. And all this just because there happened to be two high school guys walking behind us. That made me furious. I was sixteen at the time, and already I was wondering how I could eventually get away.

My mom, who was kindness personified, didn't really have a say in any of this.

I wasn't allowed to pursue my dream of becoming a midwife. Instead, my dad insisted that I get trained in business and office work so that I could do his bookkeeping. Around this time I met Richard, my future husband. He was a year older than me and was an apprentice farmer. He was supposed to become the manager of a farm or an estate (at his dad's insistence). At first we were just friends. But the more my dad tried to destroy our friendship, the more obstinate I became. I only saw one way out: I had to get pregnant. That way I'd have to get married, and then I'd have my freedom.

It happened when I was eighteen. Richard interrupted his apprenticeship immediately, and we moved to northern Germany, to the town where his parents lived. The marriage was a fiasco right from the start. Even during the pregnancy, I couldn't depend on him. He wound up leaving me alone over and over again, night after night. All he could think about was his Porsche

---

14 Hesse is a state in Germany.

and his stupid, grandiose plans for the future. No job was good enough for him. He always wanted to be someone more powerful and more impressive than he actually was, so that people would finally respect him and look up to him. He loved to talk about how important his family was in the old days, before World War II, when his grandparents owned a daily paper, a jewelry store, and a butcher shop in East Germany. And they also owned land.

That was the vision he had for himself. He desperately wanted to be an independent businessman like his dad and grandfather. Sometimes he dreamed about starting a mail-order company; other times he wanted to open up a car dealership, and then there was the time he wanted to open a landscaping business with his friend. He never got beyond the initial planning stages with any of these plans. And then he'd let out his anger and frustrations on the kids, and when I got in the middle, the fights got worse, and he'd turn on me.

I was the breadwinner of the family. When Christiane was four years old, I landed a great job working for a dating service. When contracts needed to be closed on weekends, Richard would help me out. That worked pretty well for a couple of years. Then Richard started arguing with my boss, and I wound up losing my job. At that point Richard wanted to start his own dating service—but this time bigger, better, and more prestigious, of course. And he decided that Berlin would be the ideal location for his new business.

So in 1968, we moved. I had hoped that the move to Berlin would mean a fresh start for our marriage, but instead of the elegant housing and offices we'd talked about, we ended up with two-and-a-half rooms in Gropiusstadt, on the outskirts of Berlin. Richard had failed to raise the necessary capital to start up the business. Everything was exactly the way it had been before. As a result, Richard vented his rage on the people around him: on me and the kids. The best job he could find was a temporary position as a salesman, and he hated himself for that. He just couldn't stand being another one of the lower-middle-class people that the housing projects were made for.

I often thought about divorce but didn't have the courage. Whatever self-confidence I'd managed to salvage after my dad was done with me was crushed by my husband.

Luckily I got a job in Berlin pretty quickly and netted one thousand marks weekly as a stenographer. Being appreciated again and having a real job gave me new sense of strength. I wasn't as willing to put up with the usual amount of grief from my husband. He and his grand plans started looking ridiculous to me. The arguments between us became less and less tolerable. We tried separating several times, but that never really worked, since I still felt attached to him. Maybe it was because he was my first love, or maybe it was because of the kids. I'm not sure. I couldn't manage to find spots in either preschool or kindergarten for the girls—but at the time, I couldn't have afforded it anyway. So I didn't mind that at least Richard was home every now and then. The divorce got postponed again and again, until in 1973 I was strong enough to correct my mistake and finally went to see a divorce attorney.

I wanted to give Christiane a better life than I'd had up to that point. Right after Christiane was born, I swore that she'd never find herself in the kind of miserable marriage that I'd wound up in. Christiane would be allowed to develop her talents freely, and she wouldn't be forced to be a secretary or a bookkeeper like me; she would have the freedoms I never had and be raised like a modern child, according to modern practices. Based on that thinking, I probably let her get away with way too much later on.

After the divorce, my top priority was finding a new apartment. (I couldn't just stay in our old place because Richard refused to leave.) Luckily I found one in a new tax-incentivized housing development. The rent was fairly reasonable, and I also got a spot in the garage, even though I didn't have a car. It was still way too expensive for me, when it really came down to it, but I didn't have a choice: I had to get out of that marriage, once and for all. I wanted a new beginning for myself and for the kids, whatever the cost.

Richard wasn't even able to pay child support. So I told myself, There's only one thing you can do: You have to pull yourself together, work the occasional overtime shift, and find some way to provide for the family. The girls were now ten and eleven, and up to that point they'd only experienced the absolute minimum in terms of furnishings and comfort. We didn't even have a real couch—just a hulking thing to sit on, cobbled together from a lot of other discarded bits and pieces. I was deeply hurt by the realization that I couldn't even provide a decent home for my kids.

I wanted to make it up to them after the divorce. I finally wanted to have a pretty apartment, where we could all feel at home. That was my dream. That's what I worked for. But I also wanted to be able to indulge them a little bit. I wanted to be able to buy them pretty clothes and go on weekend trips where we didn't have to watch every penny.

With that new goal in mind, I worked myself to the bone. I was able to finally provide a nice room with pretty furniture for my daughters, and I let them choose the wallpaper, too. In 1975, I was able to give Christiane a record player as a present. Those things made me happy. I was so glad to finally be able to afford something special for my girls.

And when I got home from work in the evening, I'd often bring some treats back with me. Little things. But I had fun going to Wertheim or Karstadt[15] to pick something up. Usually I'd just get whatever was on sale. Sometimes a new candy; sometimes a funny pencil sharpener or some other trinket. When I came back with things like that, they'd be so happy and give me these giant, heartfelt hugs. Those days felt like Christmas to me.

Today I understand of course that I was hoping to compensate for my absence with money and gifts. I shouldn't have worried so much about money. I should've spent more time with the kids, instead of working so much. To this day I don't understand why I left the girls alone so often. As if money could make up for a mom's time. I should've taken advantage of the welfare money I could have received instead. But welfare was out of the question for me back then. My parents had always pounded it into me that one should never be a burden to society.

Maybe I should've taken my ex-husband to court for his refusal to pay child support. I don't know. In any case, in my effort to create a pretty house, I totally lost sight of what was really important. I can spin it any way I want, but in the end, I always wind up with only myself to blame. I left the kids alone, and they had to take care of themselves. Christiane certainly needed much more support and guidance than I was able to provide. She's more sensitive, less stable, and more susceptible to peer pressure than her younger sister is. Back then, I never even considered the possibility that Christiane could end up going down the wrong track—despite the fact that I was able to see the daily struggles of so many other families in the suburb where we lived. There were constant domestic fights and beatings. Drunkenness was out of control, and it wasn't uncommon to see a man, woman, or teenager lying drunk in the gutter. But I lived with the delusional belief that if I set an example for my girls, and

15 Wertheim and Karstadt were the names of two large department stores in Germany.

didn't mess around with a lot of guys, and didn't let myself go, then they would follow my example.

I really believed that we were on our way up. In the morning, the kids would go to school. They made their own lunches back then. And in the afternoons, they'd often go to the riding rink and head over to the stables in Rudow. They were always crazy about animals.

Apart from some jealousy issues between the kids and Klaus (my boyfriend, who had moved in with us), things were going really well. When I wasn't working, or tending to the house, or managing the kids, I still wanted to have some time to take care of him, too. He was a source of real calm for me. But because I wanted to have more time with Klaus, I made a serious mistake: I let Christiane's sister move in with her dad—who was lonely at the time and had managed to win her allegiance with all sorts of promises.

So now Christiane was alone when she got home from school. And at this point, she got mixed up with some much more dangerous kids. But I wasn't able to notice. Kessi, her girlfriend who lived nearby, and who hung out with her in the afternoons, seemed to be really sensible and mature. And Kessi's mom kept an eye on them off and on. Sometimes Christiane was at Kessi's, and sometimes Kessi was at our house.

They were both about twelve or thirteen years old, the age where you get curious and want to try everything once. And it didn't bother me when they went to the youth club at the Center House, which was set up and run by the church community in Gropiusstadt. I was sure that Christiane was in good hands with those church people. I never could have imagined that the teens in Center House would be allowed to do things like smoke pot.

I was envisioning something totally different. I was comforted that Christiane was growing into a happy teenager and not

68

*just missing her sister all the time. Since she'd made friends
Kessi, she'd started laughing again. Sometimes those two were s
ridiculously silly that they made me laugh, too. How was I supposed to know that they were giggling so much because they'd
been smoking pot—or even something worse? It never would've
occurred to me.*

✳

THE CLIQUE WE HAD THEN was like my family. We had
friendship, affection, and love, too, I think. Even the way we said
hello to one another had something magical to it. We kissed each
other on the cheek, and it was tender and affectionate. My father
had never kissed me like that.

In our clique, problems didn't exist; we didn't talk about
them. No one wanted to weigh anyone else down with whatever shit was going on in their life. When we were together, the
nightmare of the "real world" completely disappeared, and we
were like our own little island of peacefulness and friendliness
surrounded by a world of people living unhappy, miserable lives.

We talked about music and pot. Sometimes about clothes, and
sometimes about people who rebelled against what we viewed as
a police state. We liked people who took instead of being taken—
people who stole cars and robbed banks. And after I dropped
acid that first time, I felt like I was finally one of them—especially
since it had been such an awesome trip, and I felt as though I'd
handled it like a cool pro. I felt like I had proved myself.

Suddenly I had a new outlook on things. I went out into the
country again. When I was younger, I'd go there with my dog,
and somehow I experienced the countryside through him. Now, I
would never go out there without either getting high or tripping. I
started experiencing nature in a totally different way. It dissolved

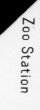

...ounds that were reflective of my moods. ...tten a handle on things. And for a few ...happy with myself.

...s started to get old. Pot and acid didn't ...ore. We'd gotten used to them. We were used to getting high like that. There wasn't anything new or exciting about it.

Then one day somebody came into the club and said, "I've got something really new: ephedrine. This stuff is awesome." I took two ephedrine pills without knowing exactly what I was swallowing, but obviously (or as I know now) they're a kind of upper. I washed them down with a beer because that's what everyone else was doing. But even that wasn't easy for me at the time because I hated beer, and I hated all the drunks I saw every day around the city, always drinking, and always totally shitfaced.

All of a sudden, it seemed like there were tons of pills floating around in the club. That same night I took a Mandrax, which is a kind of a high-octane sleeping pill. Once I'd done that, I was convinced again that everything was perfect, and I loved everyone in our little group.

In the weeks that followed, we took a prolonged cruise through the entire pharmaceutical industry.

Things were starting to deteriorate at school. I didn't do any homework anymore and always woke up tired. Despite that, I did manage to advance to eighth grade. I sometimes still got decent grades in language arts or social studies because the topics interested me—sometimes, at least—and because I was just naturally good at them.

But especially in those classes in which I didn't totally space out, I got into trouble more and more often. Sometimes I'd get into arguments with the teachers, and sometimes with the other students. I just thought it was horrible the way people treated each other there. I hated the way the teachers were so hypocritical, since the high morals and ideals they were teaching were in such stark contrast to the way they treated the students, and also the way they turned a blind eye to the students who were treating each other so horribly.

I still remember a big fight I had with a teacher who wanted to talk to us about environmental conservation. The whole class was totally apathetic. They weren't interested in anything. Still, that wasn't really their fault, since there was nothing to take notes on and nothing to learn. The teacher's self-righteous ramblings and the way he paid no attention to any of his students really got on my nerves. So at one point I lost it. "What sort of shit are you talking about?" I yelled at him. "What the hell do you even mean by 'environmental conservation' and 'respect for the environment'? I mean, that has to start with us, with human beings learning how to treat one another. That's what this shit-for-school should teach us first—that as a human being you should show interest in and care for others. The goal shouldn't just be to be louder and stronger than everyone else, or to lie and cheat and rip people off just to wind up on top, with the best grades! It's about time the teachers finally got a clue, and addressed the real problems in this school, and started treating the students fairly!" And so on. I actually kind of liked that teacher—at least compared to the others. That's why I got so furious at him for ignoring us and thought it would make a difference to let him know how I felt—loudly and clearly.

So in a word, the school sucked, and I hated it. We didn't have any contact with the teachers outside of the classroom. And because everyone's class schedule was always changing, it was hard to make and maintain friends. Here again it was dog-eat-dog. Nobody helped anybody, and everybody wanted to be better than everybody else. In this meat grinder, the teachers took it out on the students because they had the power to hand out grades. The students knew that if they pissed off a teacher, that teacher could retaliate by slapping them with a bad grade. And the students, in turn, took advantage of any of the teachers who were too good-natured to assert themselves.

I realized how profoundly unfair everything was, but I kept trying to fight back—sometimes because what I had to say really mattered to me, and sometimes just to disrupt class. By now, most of my classmates only paid attention to me when I was screaming about something or other; they didn't have any interest in hearing my thoughts about how shitty everything was.

That didn't really bother me though—not like it used to—because the only people I wanted to accept me were the people in my clique. When I was with them, there wasn't any of that stress or fighting. But even then, when I was hanging out with my group, I often sat by myself. I participated less and less in the conversations. But it didn't really matter, since our conversations were always about the same things: pot, music, the events of the previous night, and, more often now, the street prices for things like acid and pills. I was usually so stoned that I wanted to be just alone and not have to talk about anything

I did, however, have a new goal: I wanted to get into The Sound. The Sound was a club on Genthiner Street in the Tiergarten[16] neighborhood. All over the city there were posters about how The Sound was Europe's hottest club. A lot of the people in our group were regulars there, but it was only for people sixteen or older—and I'd just barely turned thirteen. So I was always afraid that they wouldn't let me in, even though I'd already changed the birth date on my student ID.

---

16 Tiergarten means "animal garden" or "Zoo" in German. It is a neighborhood in central Berlin.

The Sound was the place to be. You could buy anything there—from pot to quaaludes to Valium and even heroin. Also, I'd heard about a bunch of really cool people who hung out there and seemed almost magical to me. It sounded like heaven to a young girl like me, who divided most of her time between dreary places like Rudow and Gropiusstadt. I imagined The Sound to be a kind of palace—with lights and glitter and crazy effects and music that was so incredible I couldn't even imagine it yet. And of course, I also thought about the guys that I'd meet there.

I'd planned to go along with the others on a few previous occasions, but it had never quite worked out before. So Kessi and I drew up a detailed plan of action that was guaranteed to work. One Saturday, I told my mom that I was sleeping over at Kessi's, and Kessi told her mom she was staying at my house. Both of our moms fell for it (luckily). A girlfriend of Kessi's was also supposed to come along, named Peggy. She was a bit older than us. We also had to wait for Peggy's boyfriend, Micha. Kessi told me some important news: Micha was shooting heroin. I was excited to meet him because up to that point I'd never personally met a junkie.

When Micha arrived, I was very impressed. Somehow he was even cooler than the guys from our group of friends. Immediately my old inferiority complex surfaced again. Micha treated us very condescendingly, as if he was a step above us. I was reminded again of the fact that I was only thirteen, and that this heroin fiend was much too worldly, much too grown up for me. I felt like a loser again. Incidentally, Micha died just a few months later.

We got into the subway and went to Kurfürstenstrasse station.[17] That was a pretty long ride for me back then. I felt like I was

---

17 Kurfürstenstrasse (Strasse means "street" in German) is not to be confused with Kurfürstendamm, which is a broad, long boulevard full of shops, houses, hotels, and restaurants. Kurfürstenstrasse is neither as famous nor as glamorous.

very far away from home. The street corner nearest the station, the corner of Kurfürstenstrasse and Potsdamer Street, looked pretty grungy. There were some girls milling around. At the time, I didn't realize that they were hookers looking to get picked up by passing cars. There were some guys there, too. Peggy said that they were the dealers.

If someone had told me then that one day I'd be like them, hanging around a dismal place like this every day, I'd have said they were totally crazy.

The next thing I knew, we were finally doing it: We were going into The Sound. As soon as I walked inside, I stopped dead in my tracks. This was nothing like I had imagined. "Europe's hottest club" was a basement with a low ceiling. It was loud and filthy. On the dance floor, everyone was dancing by themselves, just doing their own thing. Strangely enough, nobody was touching anyone else. There was no physical contact. The air was unbelievably stale and gross. An oscillating fan pushed the nauseating odor lazily around the room.

I sat down on a bench, afraid to even move. I had the feeling that people were staring at me because they'd somehow noticed that I didn't belong. I was a complete outsider. But Kessi was into it right away. Right away she started hustling around the room, looking for hot guys. She told me that she'd never seen so many hot guys all in one bunch. Meanwhile, I was glued to the bench. The others had brought some kind of pills and were drinking beer. I didn't want anything. All through the night I hung onto two glasses of juice. What I really wanted to do was go home. But that was out of the question because my mom thought I was at Kessi's. I was just waiting for 5 a.m. to come around, when the club would finally close. For a moment, I even wished that my mom would figure out what I'd been up to and suddenly show up and take me home. Then I fell asleep.

The others woke me up at five. Kessi said that she was going home with Peggy. I had a really bad stomachache, but nobody cared about what was going on with me. I walked alone to the Kurfürstenstrasse subway station at five in the morning. There were drunks everywhere in the subway. I felt like puking.

It'd been a long time since I'd been this glad to unlock our front door and see my mom come out of her bedroom. I told her that Kessi had woken up so early, and I'd decided to come home and sleep in where it was quiet. I grabbed my two cats and carried them into my bed with me and snuggled down under the blankets. Right before I drifted off to sleep I thought to myself, Christiane, that is not your world. It's wrong, so just let it go.

When I woke up around noon, I still felt awful. I needed to talk to someone about what I had experienced, but I knew that no one from my group of friends would understand. So I could only talk about it with my mom.

I didn't know how to begin. "Hey, mom," I began, awkwardly. "So last night Kessi and I went to The Sound." My mom looked shocked. "Actually," I said, "it was kind of fun. It's such a big place. They even have a movie theater in there."

My mom immediately started in with her usual reprimands. In the meantime, I kept waiting for some questions. But my mom didn't really ask any. Between cleaning and dinner and Klaus, she was completely stressed out that afternoon. She probably didn't want to suffer anymore stress by having a long mother-daughter talk with me. Maybe she didn't even want to know all the details, anyway.

I didn't have the courage to speak up on my own. I wasn't even really aware that I wanted and needed to talk. I wasn't really that conscious about anything at that time in my life. I lived according to my subconscious thoughts and moods. I never thought about consequences. I had no plans. What did I know about planning? No one in my house ever talked about the future.

The next weekend, Kessi had to stay with me because that's the way we'd sold our story of alternating sleepovers to my mom. I actually had to drag her to our house because she was already tripping so hard. She'd dropped acid earlier. I'd also taken half a pill of something, but I could still think pretty clearly. Kessi stood on the street in front of our house, hypnotized like a deer by the two headlights that were coming toward her. I had to yank her off the road so that she wouldn't get hit by a car.

I pushed her into my room right away. But my mom followed us in, of course. As she stood in the doorframe, Kessi and I somehow shared the same crazy, distorted vision: For some reason, we were convinced that my mom was too fat to fit through the door. We started to giggle and pretty soon were convulsing with laughter. I thought my mom looked like a fat, kindhearted dragon with a bone in her hair. We laughed, and my mom naïvely laughed with us. She must have thought we were just a couple of silly teenage girls.

●

FROM THAT POINT ON, Kessi took me with her to The Sound almost every Saturday. I went along because I didn't know what else to do on a Saturday night. I gradually got used to everything there. I was honest with my mom and told her where we were going on the weekends. She told me I could stay out until the last subway train.

Everything went well for a few weeks, until one Saturday in the summer of 1975. We wanted to stay out all night and once again told our mothers that we were staying with friends. That still worked because back then my mom still didn't have a phone. So the moms couldn't check on us or spy on us. First we went to the Center House and guzzled two bottles of wine. Then we loaded a killer bong. Kessi tossed down a couple of ephedrine pills, and at some point after that she started to bawl. I saw that one coming. After ephedrine you sometimes get hyper-emotional, and fall apart.

When Kessi suddenly disappeared, I started to worry. I had an idea about where she'd gone, so I headed over to the subway station. There she was, hanging off the side of a bench, totally passed out, with a pile of French fries in front of her. Before I could wake her up, a subway train pulled in and Kessi's mom got out. She worked at a sauna and was just now at 10 p.m. getting out of work. She recognized her daughter (whom she thought was safe in bed at my place) right away. She grabbed Kessi, still asleep, and slapped her, hard, across the face several times. You could hear the sound of her hand smacking her daughter's face echoing off the walls of the station. Then Kessi puked. Her mom grabbed her, just like a police officer would, and hauled her off.

That little beating that Kessi received from her mom at the Wutzkyallee subway station probably saved her a lot of grief. Without that bit of corporal punishment, she might have ended up in the drug scene, on the streets, selling herself, even before me—which means she wouldn't be finishing her college entrance exams now either.

After that, Kessi wasn't allowed to hang out with me anymore; she wasn't allowed out in the evenings at all. That made me feel pretty lonely at first. I didn't really like hanging out at Center House anymore. I saw everyone from that scene during the school week. But I couldn't imagine weekends without The Sound anymore. Everyone there, and everything that was happening there, seemed to incredibly cool to me. They were real rock stars in my mind. The guys from Gropiusstadt just couldn't compare—and besides, they never really made it out of Gropiusstadt anyway. But it meant that I was constantly short on cash now. Before she was grounded, Kessi had always received an allowance of one hundred marks a month, which we spent on pot and pills. Now I had to find my cash somewhere else, borrowing from friends, or stealing.

I had to go to The Sound by myself now. The next Friday afternoon, I went to a drugstore and bought a packet of ephedrine for 2.95 marks. You could get that without a prescription. I'd gotten to the point where I was no longer taking two, but four or five ephedrine pills. Then I made one more stop at Center House and bummed a joint from someone. I walked to the subway station feeling like I was on top of the world. I didn't think about Kessi; I didn't think about what was going on. I was simply there. I was just floating along in a beautiful, intoxicating, carefree world.

When I was in the subway, I could tell right away, at every stop, if the people who'd gotten on were going to The Sound. There was a kind of uniform we all shared: bold, fashion-forward clothes, long hair, and outrageous shoes with four-inch platform soles. These people were my idols; they were the stars of The Sound. I wasn't nervous at all anymore when I went out there, even when I was alone. I was really high, and I felt amazing. The weed I'd smoked earlier was obviously good stuff.

On the steps of The Sound, I bumped into a new boy, whom I hadn't met before, and he said something to me. He seemed really cool: tall; slim; long, blond hair; and incredibly calm. I managed to initiate a conversation with him while we were still on the stairs. Since, after all, I was feeling so awesome and super confident. From the very first sentence, we seemed to understand each other completely. We liked the same music, and we even tripped the same way. His name was Atze. He was the first boy who really made me stop in my tracks. I was crazy for him, right from the start. For the first time in my life, I was in love.

Once we were in The Sound, Atze introduced me to all of his friends, and they were all really cool. I had no problem jumping right into their conversation. The most popular topic was always drugs and the best ways to get high. And at that point in time, I'd had as much experience as anyone else I was likely to run into. Atze's friends also talked a lot about heroin, or "H," as they called it. Everyone agreed that it was the end of the line, the ultimate low point. Once you started with H, they thought, you might as well put a bullet through your head and save yourself some money. I remember saying something around that time about people shooting up being "total loser assholes." Then we talked about how to alter jeans so that they'd have a tighter fit.

Since I'd been losing so much weight recently, I'd become a kind of expert in the subject of tailoring. I had to alter my jeans almost weekly. Skintight pants were a kind of uniform for people who spent their nights at The Sound. I was able to give people sewing tips. But making jeans fit tighter was the only kind of sewing that I'd ever done.

I was accepted into Atze's clique almost immediately. I didn't even have to fight for it. I was on a lot of drugs, of course, and I had this new sense of serenity and self-confidence that was surprising even to me. There was another guy in this new clique who I felt an instant connection with. His name was Detlef. He was totally different from Atze. He was cute, kind of childlike, and soft. They called him "babyface." He was sixteen. He was the one that I felt most at ease with. We could talk about anything. Then there was also this awesome girl, Astrid. She really had her shit together. She was always making these witty comments that would have everyone laughing hysterically. She always knew what to say, no matter what. I admired that. The only one you really had to watch out for was Ralph. He'd really tear into you whenever he saw any sign of weakness or insecurity. When I told this story about the time I was tripping on the subway and started playing with a little kid—who seemed like an angel to me at the time—Ralph cut right in with something about how naïve I was and made my story seem ridiculous. So you had to really watch what you said. I also didn't think this other guy, named Stinger,[18] was that cool. He thought he was God's gift to girls, but my experience earlier on with Kathi had made me really suspicious of that kind of character. But Stinger only sort of belonged to the clique; he wasn't a regular.

So we all talked and talked, and then we finally took a break to go outside to smoke some weed. When The Sound closed down at 5 a.m., I followed the others to the Kurfürstendamm.[19]

In the subway back to Rudow, I couldn't help it: I felt so incredibly happy. When I came down from all the pills and the pot, it was like landing on a cloud. I was tired but I was happy; for the first time in my life, I was in love.

From that day on, I was always impatient for the weekends. Atze was so gentle and affectionate. When we met for the third time in The Sound, he kissed me and I kissed him back. It was pretty innocent. I didn't want any more than that, and Atze seemed to sense as much without us having to talk about it. But that was the difference between the druggies and the drunks: Most of the druggies were really empathetic—at least when it came to their own group of friends. Meanwhile, the drunks would all become really aggressive when they were drunk. All they cared about was sex. For us, other things were more important.

Atze and I were like brother and sister. He was my big brother. We always walked arm in arm, and he made me feel secure. Atze

18 Stinger's German name was Bienenstich, which means "bee's sting."

19 This is one of the most famous avenues in Berlin—a very broad, long boulevard full of shops, houses, hotels, and restaurants. Before the Wall was dismantled, especially, this avenue was comparable to the Champs-Élysées in Paris.

was sixteen, and even though he hated the work, he had a job as an apprentice to a glass cutter. He had very specific ideas about what a girl should look like. I did my hair the way he wanted me to. And because he was crazy about long overcoats, I went to a secondhand store and found one for myself that had a long slit up the back, which was super stylish.

I couldn't imagine life without Atze anymore.

When The Sound closed at five, I didn't bother going straight home anymore; instead, I stayed with the clique. Since we'd all gotten high together, we'd all come down together, too. Then we just bummed around the city until the afternoon. We'd go to see exhibits or head over to the zoo, or we'd just hang out on Kurfürstendamm (or Ku'damm, for short). A lot of the time, these hangout sessions lasted all day long. I kept telling the same old Kessi story to my mom, and I also made up some new girlfriends, at whose houses I was supposed to be staying overnight. I developed an unlimited capacity for creativity and imagination when it came to convincing my mom where and how I spent my weekends.

During the week I still saw my old friends at Center House. I always sat kind of by myself, looking mysterious. Sometimes I talked about the things I'd seen and done at The Sound. The others couldn't help but admire me. I was just one step ahead of them. But at that time, I didn't know that it was one step further into hell. Neither did I know that many of my old friends would follow me into hell a little later on.

On the drug scene at The Sound, you could get just about anything. For my part, I did everything, except for heroin. I experimented with Valium, quaaludes, ephedrine, an amphetamine called Captagon (which we called "Cappis"), and of course we always smoked a lot of pot and also managed to drop acid once or twice a week. Uppers and downers—it didn't matter—we swallowed them by the handful. The pills we'd taken conflicted with one another or supplemented each other; often-times we didn't know which was which—and we didn't really care. We were totally out of control.

With the drugs on hand, you could make yourself feel however you wanted. You could eat more uppers or take more downers. When I was up for dancing, I'd swallow some Cappis and ephedrine, but if I wanted to just sit quietly in a corner or watch a movie at the theater, I'd toss back some Valium and quaaludes. I was really happy and contented at the beginning. At least for a couple of weeks.

And then something awful happened. I arrived at The Sound on Saturday, as usual, and ran into one of the guys in our clique, on the steps. He said, "Did you know that Atze quit his job?" He was quiet for a while and then said, "Atze's here every night now, you know." He said it in a kind of funny way, and I realized something was probably seriously wrong. If Atze was here every night, then he would've met other girls, too.

I asked, "Is something up with Atze?"

He looked at me and said, "He's got a girlfriend. Moni."

I felt like I'd been kicked in the stomach. But still I had some room for doubt; I had to believe it wasn't true. I ran down into the club. Atze was standing there by himself. It was just like always. He gave me a kiss and then locked my things into his locker. (At The Sound you always put your things in a locker because of all the theft.)

A little later, this girl Moni arrived. I'd never really noticed her before, but she sat down with our clique as if it was the most natural thing in the world. I stayed to the side, watching her.

She was completely different from me. Short and plump and always happy—or at least pretending to be. She seemed to be almost mothering Atze. I kept thinking, This can't be happening. How could he dump me for this ridiculous, overweight slut? But

I had to admit that she had a really pretty face and beautiful, long, blond hair. Maybe he needs a girl like that, I thought. One who's cheerful and takes care of him. And then what started out as a creeping suspicion grew into a conviction: I was absolutely sure that Atze was dating this girl because he needed someone who would sleep with him. She was clearly the kind of girl who would do that.

I was totally sober. I didn't want to do anything that night. And when I couldn't stand to watch the two of them anymore, I went to the dance floor just to release some of that energy. When I came back, the two of them were gone. I ran like mad all over the place. When I finally found Atze and Moni, they were in the movie theater that was an extension of The Sound, with their arms wrapped around each other.

Eventually, I somehow made my way back to the group. Of course, the one person who knew right away that something was wrong was Detlef. He put his arm around my shoulder. I didn't want to cry. I always thought it was tacky to cry in front of everyone, but I'm not sure exactly where I first got that idea. When I couldn't hold the tears back anymore, I ran outside, across the street, and into the park across from The Sound. The tears were just streaming down my face.

Suddenly, Detlef was standing next to me. He handed me a tissue, and when I had used up that one, he handed me some more. I was too preoccupied with myself at the time to really notice Detlef. Only later did it occur to me how sweet it had been of him to come looking for me.

I never wanted to see Atze again. I didn't think I would even be able to look him in the eyes again. Especially now, after everyone had seen me sobbing so hysterically. Now everyone knew how dependent I'd been on him. But at least Detlef managed to pull me back into The Sound.

But when it came down to it, I had to go back anyway because Atze still had the key to the locker. I worked hard to pull myself together, walked into the movie theater (scaring Atze so much that he jumped out of his seat), and got the key. After I got my stuff, though, I wasn't quite up to going back and returning the key. Detlef (who'd never left my side) did it for me instead.

It was almost 2 a.m. The last subway was gone. I stood in front of The Sound with no idea where to go. I felt like getting high. It didn't matter on what. I just wanted something, and I wanted it right away, in the worst way. But at the same time, I was totally broke. Just then, someone from our Center House clique came by. His name—or his nickname—was Panther, and he was dealing some LSD and always had really good stuff. I hit him up for some and asked if he could give it to me as a present. It worked out, and he gave me one of those really awesome crystal pills. He didn't even ask me why I was so desperate to get high so late at night.

I immediately swallowed the pill and went back downstairs onto the dance floor. It was a crazy time. I danced like a maniac for an hour or so—probably more. When I stopped, it didn't feel like I was actually tripping yet. I thought that maybe Panther had scammed me. Luckily, a few people from the Center House were there. I went to Piet. He was also on acid. I told him the story with Atze. But of course Piet was already pretty far gone and wasn't really listening. He kept saying things like "Forget it, girl" or "Don't let it get to you."

I needed to eat something, so I got myself a vanilla pudding. The whole world just sucks, I thought to myself, and it's depressing as shit. I wanted leave—to return the bowl for the pudding and get my deposit back (there was a theft problem at The Sound so they made you pay a deposit on every glass and bowl to discourage stealing) and go. But then the acid hit me, all at once. It happened like a flash. The bench and I tipped over, and after that, all I remember is just dancing. I danced until the place shut down.

After closing, I went outside and met up with everyone again—including Atze and Moni. I didn't care at all. I was completely absorbed with some poster outside of the club. Atze and Moni went up to Atze's room.

The rest of us walked off in the direction of the zoo. Somebody got the idea, on the way, to go to the Europacenter[20] instead, and we ended up at the ice-skating rink over there. It was a pretty warm night—it had rained, and there was water on top of the ice. I was sliding through the water, and it seemed to me like I was walking over the ocean.

Then, out of nowhere, I heard the sound of breaking glass. The boys were over at the ticket booth, and one of them reached through the window he had broken, then broke open a cash register drawer, and was tossing out rolls of cash. Before I caught on to what was happening, everybody was already running away. I was still on the ice, so the first thing I did in my high-heeled boots was fall flat on my face. I was soaking wet. But Detlef waited for me and took me by the hand.

On the Kurfürstendamm in front of the Café Kranzler, we split up the loot. Everybody got something. I thought that was awesome. I got two rolls of coins totaling ten marks. Everyone was overjoyed—not only because of the money, but also because we'd fooled the two private security guards who watched the Europacenter at night. They'd been after us for a long time. We were totally giddy. We broke open the coin rolls and threw everything up into the air, making it rain quarters in front of the café. The sidewalk was covered with coins.

---

20 The Europacenter is an office and shopping center in West Berlin. It had an ice-skating rink until 1979.

We went into a café at Bahnhof Zoo (aka "Zoo" station) that was already open. The whole place was miserable. It gave me the creeps right off the bat. It was the first time I'd been there. It was absolutely disgusting. There were hoboes lying in their own vomit and drunks stumbling around all over the place. I would have never imagined that I'd be spending every afternoon there within just a few months.

At around six in the morning, I finally went home. Lying in my bed, I could feel myself slipping into my first bad trip. On my wall, I had a poster of a girl smoking a joint. In the lower right-hand corner, there was a small blue stain. It suddenly morphed into this grotesque figure, a real crazy monstrosity. I managed to concentrate on something else just in time.

I woke up around noon feeling numb and totally hollowed out. Like I was dead. I thought, what are you, worthless? Why would you let your very first boyfriend dump you like that? I went over to the mirror, took a look, and hated what I saw. Just yesterday, when I looked in the mirror I saw a cool and mysterious girl. I was the epitome of heroin chic—just without the heroin. Now I only looked terrible. There were heavy, dark bags under my eyes. My skin was sallow and oily. I had zits.

I told myself, That's it. No more going to The Sound, no more Atze, no more of that group. Period.

Over the next few days, I tried to kill off all feelings I had toward others. I didn't take any pills, and I didn't take any acid. Instead, I drank tea with hashish all day long and rolled one joint after another. After a few days, I thought I'd more or less recovered my equilibrium. Everything was cool again. I'd achieved my goal: I wasn't worried about what anyone else thought; I wasn't in love with anybody, and the only person I cared about was myself. I thought I had my feelings under control now, and I never wanted to go to The Sound ever again.

The next Saturday night, I stayed at home—and it was seriously the longest night of my life. It had been a long time since I hadn't gone to The Sound on a Saturday night. I couldn't bear to just stay home and watch TV, and I couldn't sleep. I didn't have enough pot to get stoned. When I really thought about it, I realized that I couldn't live without The Sound, and I couldn't manage without the people over there anymore. Without them, my life was meaningless.

I was looking forward to the next Friday even before I really knew that I'd be going back. I fiddled around with my hair for a while, but then I decided that I'd just leave it alone and not even bother combing it. I thought it would give me a more mysterious, dramatic look and make more of an impact.

On Friday, before anything else, I went out to get some Valium. I took the pills, chased them with a beer, and then followed those up with a quaalude. Then I took the subway to The Sound. By that point, I was already totally unconcerned about how I was going to be treated by Atze and all the rest. I wasn't worried about much of anything. I borrowed a big hat from somebody, sat at a table, put my head down, and slept almost the entire night.

I woke up at one point, and Detlef had pushed the hat away from my face and was stroking my hair. He asked what was up. I didn't respond—but I did think it was really sweet, the way he was taking care of me.

All of a sudden, I had a reason to go to The Sound again. By the next weekend, I was spending all of my time with Detlef.

Things moved very slowly with Detlef. It wasn't love at first sight, like it was with Atze. At first, at The Sound, we were just hanging out together. We talked a lot. We got along in a completely different way than I was used to. It wasn't a competition, and neither of us was trying to win. Not in conversation, not anywhere. I could talk to him about anything without having to worry about overexposing myself or regretting it later. There was a lot of give-and-take. And occasionally, we were able to change each other's minds.

I'd liked Detlef from the very beginning, but he wasn't a heartthrob like Atze was. He was too sweet, somehow, and he looked too much like a child. Over time, though, I realized that my friendship with Detlef was a thousand times better than my relationship with Atze ever was. He grew on me, and I started to care for him more and more every weekend, even though I had no intention of becoming dependent on a guy again, like I had with Atze. But at some point, I had to admit to myself that I really liked Detlef. Actually, it was more than that: I was in love with him.

I calmed down, and was generally way more relaxed. Partly because of Detlef, but also because I'd cut out the uppers and was taking a lot of downers now. All my anxiety and restlessness were gone. I hardly ever went on the dance floor now—except when I couldn't find any Valium.

At home it must have been like a dream come true for my mom and her boyfriend. I didn't talk back; I didn't pick fights. I didn't rebel against anything anymore because I'd given up changing anything for myself at home. This, of course, made the whole situation a lot easier.

By Christmas 1975—when I was thirteen and a half—I believed that my relationship with my mom had improved to the point where I could give her at least the partial truth. So I told her that I hadn't been sleeping at Kessi's like I said I was. Instead, I'd spent a lot of nights out at The Sound and was usually still out when the last subway had gone. She reacted exactly as I thought she would: She was angry and couldn't resist lecturing me. I told her that it was better for me to spend the occasional night at a club and still come home when it was over, rather than run away

88

like other kids from Gropiusstadt (who ended up more or less homeless, and who got into even more trouble later on). And I also told her that it was better for her to know the truth, to know where I really was, than for me to lie to her. That much at least she was ready to accept.

By the end of that conversation, I wasn't really interested in telling my mom everything that was going on with me, like I'd originally planned. But the need to be lying all the time got on my nerves. And it was getting harder and harder to make up believable stories. The real reason for my confession was that I wanted to go to The Sound over the Christmas break, and on New Year's Eve, and I couldn't think of a good cover-up story for those nights. And luckily, after our talk, my mom gave me permission to go out over the holidays. That blew me away. But then again, the way I'd described it, my mom thought The Sound was a decent, harmless teenager club—and that all my girlfriends went there. Plus, I reminded her of how much more calm I'd become ever since I'd started going to the club and had the chance to blow off some steam.

Meanwhile, things got more and more extreme at The Sound. Heroin hit like a bomb. It was all we talked about, even though at the time everyone in our clique was against it. We'd already seen enough examples of people whose lives were destroyed by heroin. But then one after another we tried it anyway— "just once," we'd all say—and most of us stuck with it after that. Heroin blew our group apart. Once you did it, it was like suddenly you were part of a totally new group: There were just those who'd tried it and those who hadn't.

I had a deep fear of the drug. Whenever heroin came up, I was suddenly conscious of just how young I was. On the other hand, I had that same weird admiration again for those people who were already shooting up. For me, that was the natural next step, just like pot and LSD had been before. The junkies looked down on us pot smokers and pill poppers with enormous contempt. They called hashish a "baby drug." It was depressing to think that I'd never make it into the junkie group, into the real scene. I had a real feeling of terror when it came to heroin; it seemed like it was the end of the line. And as a result, unless I wanted to go all the way, I didn't have anywhere else to go. My drug career was at a dead end.

It didn't really bother me that heroin seemed to disintegrate all of the old relationships. The others weren't so important anymore because whatever happened to them, I still had Detlef. And things with him just kept getting better. One Sunday in early 1976, I took him along to our apartment. I knew that my mom and her boyfriend wouldn't be there. I cooked a real dinner, and then we sat down and ate our Sunday dinner like husband and wife. I thought it was very cool and kind of magical.

The week after that, I only thought about Detlef; I couldn't stop thinking about that coming Friday and about going to The Sound. When Friday finally arrived, I went to the club almost totally sober but still ecstatic. There was Detlef, sitting with this girl who looked like an absolute disaster. I sat down with them, but Detlef hardly even noticed me; he was fixated on something else. For a second, I panicked and thought that maybe the thing that had happened with Atze was happening all over again with Detlef. But that wasn't too likely with this human wreck of a girl. She was a mess.

At first, the two of them didn't talk, and then when they did, it was only in fragments that didn't make much sense to me. Eventually, I was able to piece the conversation together though: They were talking about heroin. And suddenly, it dawned on me that Detlef wanted to get some H from this girl—either that, or else she wanted to unload some of her stuff to him (which was essentially the same thing). I panicked. I literally screamed:

"Detlef, you're insane! You're sixteen years old! You can't seriously want to start using heroin!?"

He didn't care though. I kept pleading with him: "Go crazy tonight. Take whatever other drugs you want. I'll get the pills for you myself. But please don't fuck up like this." I was literally begging him.

When he didn't react, I made a big mistake—one that I still think about today. I completely panicked and screamed: "If you do this, I don't want to have anything more to do with you. If you do this, you can go to hell! I don't ever want to see you again." After that, I went straight out onto the dance floor.

I'd done everything wrong. I shouldn't have made such a scene. I should have talked to him quietly and calmly as soon as we were alone. After all, he listened to me. But most of all, I shouldn't have left him alone—not even for one second because he was already really stoned when he was talking to that girl.

A couple of hours later, someone told me that Detlef and his best friend, Bernd, had shot up heroin together. They didn't even start by snorting it. They'd shot up right away.

I saw Detlef again that night. He smiled at me, but it seemed like his smile came from very far away. He seemed happy, but like he didn't feel like talking to me. I didn't want to go to him either. That was an even worse night than that Saturday when I'd lost Atze. Detlef was gone. He went off to a world that I didn't belong to. One minute we were so close it was like we were identical—like we were the very same person—and the next moment we were strangers. Like a bolt of lightning, a single hit of heroin had changed everything.

Still, I kept going to The Sound. Detlef had another girlfriend by that time. Her name was Angie, and she was ugly and cold. I noticed that there was no spark between them. I never even saw Detlef talking to her myself. But she was a junkie, so I guess that was the attraction. Sometimes Detlef came over to me, but there was nothing between us anymore. Mostly when he came over, it was because he wanted to borrow some change from me. I already knew he was trying to bum together enough money for his next fix. But still, when I had money, I gave him some.

Sunday mornings were totally depressing. Exhausted and drained, I'd drag myself to the subway station, thinking, What a big, fucking mess. I didn't understand anything anymore. I couldn't understand why I kept going to The Sound or why I was taking drugs, but I also didn't know what else I should be doing instead. I was totally, utterly, absolutely lost. Pot didn't do anything for me anymore. When I got stoned, I usually felt completely isolated and couldn't talk with anyone. But at some point, I'd have to talk to someone, just due to the fact that I didn't have Detlef anymore. As a result, I just kept popping more and more pills.

Then one Saturday, it so happened that I had a little more money than usual, and—since I was feeling depressed, and since drugs were never in short supply at The Sound—I went over-board. I washed down two Captagons, three ephedrines, and a few coffies (caffeine tablets) with some beer. But then I felt way too amped up. So I tossed down some quaaludes and a whole bunch of Valium to balance out the uppers.

I don't remember exactly how I got home after that, but any-way, on the way back from the subway, I collapsed. I crawled onto the stoop in front of a store and sat there, doubled over. After I don't know how long, I pulled myself up and steered myself toward the next object I could hang on to. I went from lampposts to trees and then back to lampposts again. It was an endless journey. I thought I would die if I didn't make it home. The worst was the pain in my chest. It was as if someone had stuck a sword into my heart and was twisting it around.

The next morning, on Monday, my mom couldn't manage to wake me up. When she returned from work that night, I still wasn't moving. She kept forcing honey down my throat. It was Tuesday afternoon before I could get up again. I told my mom that I had the flu and circulation problems. I told my mom that the flu was going around in school. I also told her that the circulatory problems were a normal part of puberty and just a side effect of growing too fast. I wanted to keep her from calling a doctor because I was afraid he would figure out what was going on with me. And luckily that's what happened: My mom didn't call a doctor. She always seemed to calm down and be glad when I gave her any kind of explanation for what was wrong with me.

After that, I'd had it with pills. For the next week, I stayed almost completely sober. I felt like crap.

When Saturday rolled around I made my way back to The Sound and dropped some acid. It turned out to be the worst trip of my life though—at least up to that point. It was just like before. I even saw the same grotesque, monstrous face that I'd seen the last time things started to spiral out of control, when I was staring at that poster on my wall. For hours after that, I was convinced that I was bleeding to death. I couldn't talk, and I couldn't walk. But somehow I made it into The Sound's movie theater. I sat there for five hours, still obsessed with the idea that I was bleeding to death.

After that, everything was out. No pills, no LSD, and pot was useless anyway. So I stayed clean, except for a couple of Valiums here and there. That lasted for about three weeks, I think. It was a pretty shitty time. We moved to Kreuzberg, close by the Berlin Wall. It was a bad neighborhood, but the rent was cheaper. It meant that I had to ride the subway for half an hour to reach my school in Gropiusstadt, but it also meant that I was that much closer to The Sound.

In case it's not clear already, The Sound was nasty—and pretty much unbearable without the aid of drugs. It was also boring; absolutely nothing happened there anymore. But then, one morning on my way to school, I saw that posters were being put up everywhere. Outrageously cool posters that made your eyes pop. I'd never seen anything cooler in my life. "David Bowie is coming to Berlin," they said. I couldn't believe it. David Bowie was our idol. Nobody made better music than him, and absolutely no one was cooler than he was. All the guys wanted to look like David Bowie. And now here he was, coming to Berlin.

Through her work, my mom got me two free tickets to the concert. Strangely enough, I knew right away whom I wanted to invite. His name was Frank, and although it might have seemed a little random, I didn't think twice about it. Frank was someone from our old clique at The Sound. He looked just like David Bowie. He'd even dyed his hair red, using henna. Maybe that's why it had to be him.

But Frank had also been the first one from our group to try heroin. He was also the first one to become addicted. They used to call him "Little Chicken," but now everyone just called him "the zombie" because he looked like the walking dead. He was about sixteen years old, like almost everyone else in our clique. But for his age, he seemed especially wise and worldly. He was superior but not pretentious. He was so self-confident but never condescending, even to me—young pot-smoking girl that I was.

So for my date, I'd chosen a total junkie. This concert was like the biggest event of my life—that's the way I thought about it at the time, at least, even though I couldn't have had any idea how significant it would actually turn out to be. Not when I offered the ticket to Frank, anyway. Somehow my attitude toward heroin must have changed during that time when I began to sour on pills, pot, and LSD. Those solid, impassable barriers between me and the junkies seemed to have vanished.

The day of the concert, I met up with Chicken at the Hermannplatz.[21] He was super tall and impossibly thin. It kind of shocked me; I guess I'd never noticed it before. I told him as much. He said he still weighed 126 pounds. Frank earned part of his dope money by donating blood, and so he was always weighed before he was able to donate. Even though he looked like a corpse and his arms were full of needle tracks, and even though junkies are at high risk for hepatitis, they still kept accepting him as a blood donor.

In the subway, it occurred to me that I forgot my Valium. I told Chicken that I really wanted to have some on hand in case I started to have an anxiety attack at the show. (Even though I'd already taken a few Valium at home, I just wanted to make sure I was able to stay cool at the concert.)

Chicken was suddenly totally fixated on the Valium that I had at home. He wanted to go back and get it. I asked, "Why do you have such a craving for Valium?" He just repeated that we needed to go back. When I took a close look at him, I was able to see why. His hands were shaking—he was going cold turkey, and he totally had the itch. (That was a phrase that we'd borrowed from the Americans. "The itch" is how we generally referred to the withdrawal symptoms veteran junkies got when the effect of a fix was wearing off. Some people also called it "being on the monkey" or "on the hook," but not us.)

I explained to Chicken that we didn't have time to go back because then we'd be late for the show. He said he was out of dope and out of money—he hadn't been able to get anything beforehand because the dealers had been cleaned out by all the concertgoers. It was totally fucked up, he said, lame to go to a David Bowie show without any special assistance—without

---

21 Hermannplatz is a subway station in the Neukölln district of Berlin. It is one of the busiest stations in the Berlin subway system.

even a Valium! And now Chicken didn't seem so cool or confident after all. I'd often seen people who were going cold turkey, but I'd never seen somebody with the itch up close and personal like this.

In the German Concert Hall, where the concert took place, the atmosphere was awesome. Everyone there seemed really cool—of course, since they were all Bowie fans. Next to us, there were some American soldiers who were smoking a pipe. And we only had to look their way for them to pass it on over to us. Everyone seemed ecstatic and high (either in anticipation or on drugs). The overall atmosphere was amazing: It was like falling into an alternate—and better—universe. Frank was sucking on the pipe like his life depended on it. But despite that, he was feeling worse and worse.

When David Bowie came on, he was almost as great as I'd imagined. It blew my mind. But when he got to the song "Station to Station" (with its refrain, "It's too late"), I came down with a crash. All of a sudden, I felt just absolutely miserable. Even a few weeks earlier, when I didn't have a clue what I should do, or where I should go, or why I should even bother, this song got on my nerves. It was just too close to reality for me. And now here it was again, this song, "Station to Station," pulling the rug out from under me. I could've really used some Valium right then.

After the concert, Chicken could hardly walk. He was in the throes of some really bad withdrawal symptoms. Outside, we ran into Bernd, Detlef's friend. He'd shot up before the concert, and he said we really had to do something for Chicken. Anyway, he wanted another fix himself.

Bernd still had two LSD pills. We didn't have any trouble offloading those outside of the concert hall, and we made twelve marks. The rest I was supposed to just bum off of people. I was a real pro at hustling up some money at that point. In The Sound,

I could usually scrape together most of the money I needed for drugs without too much effort. We needed at least twenty marks total. There was nothing you could get for less than that. But begging in front of the venue was a piece of cake. After all, there'd been a lot of people there with plenty of cash, guys who weren't used to being hit up for cash every five feet by random junkies. So I just stood out there and fed people my usual lines about "no money for the subway," etcetera, and in no time, my little plastic bag was heavy with loose change. Bernd quickly scored some H with our new funds. It was more than enough for two fixes. (Dope was still relatively cheap back then.)

And then I had a thought: I was the one scrounging to get all that money together, so at the very least I should try some of it. Let's see if that stuff really is as good as everyone always makes it out to be, with their dreamy expressions and blissed-out looks. That's really all I was thinking. I didn't realize that over the past few months, I'd been subconsciously getting myself ready for H. I wasn't aware that I'd fallen into a deep, dark hole, and that the song "Station to Station" had knocked me down and run me over. No other drug seemed like it could help me get out again, so all of a sudden, the next logical step down my path was obviously heroin. All I could think about was that I didn't want those two junkies to walk away and leave me alone again—stuck in this fucking mess I was in. I told them that I wanted to try some. Chicken was barely coherent. But he got really furious. He said, "Don't do that. You have no idea what you're doing. If you do that, then you'll end up just like me in no time flat. Then you'll be a zombie, too." He knew that we all called him that.

So despite what the newspapers always say, it wasn't like I'd been victimized by some evil dealer or seduced by a junkie. It wasn't at all the case that I'd been turned into a heroin addict against my will. I don't know anyone who'd been forced to shoot up against his will. Most teenagers get into H all on their own, when they think they're ready for it, like I was.

Chicken's earnest but pathetic attempts at dissuading me only made me that much more determined. He was the one in withdrawal. He wasn't cool or in control like he used to be. Instead, he was just a strung-out guy who was more or less dependent on me. I wasn't going to let him order me around. "First of all," I said, "most of that dope is mine because I was the one who got the money. And besides, it's bullshit what you're saying. I'm not going to get addicted. I've got myself under control. I'm just going to try it once, and that's it."

I had no idea yet how helpless you are when you've got the itch. Chicken, at any rate, seemed completely impressed by what I said. He didn't even bother replying. Bernd was going on about something or other, but I didn't listen. I told them that if they wouldn't let me try the stuff with them, then they should give me back my share. We went into a doorway and Bernd divided the dope into three equal portions. Now I was really eager to try it. There was no thinking about it, no feelings of guilt. I wanted to just do it, to finally experience a real high again. The needle scared me a little bit though. I told them, "I don't want to shoot up. I'll snort it." Bernd explained to me how to do it, even though I already knew how from listening to all that talk for so long.

I snorted the powder without hesitation. It tasted sharp and bitter. I had to suppress a quick wave of nausea but ended up spitting out a whole bunch of the stuff anyway. But then the high took over incredibly fast. My arms and legs became insanely heavy but at the same time really light. I was so, so tired, but it felt amazing. All of the aggravation and sadness I'd been wallowing in just fell away, all at once, just disappeared. "Station to Station" didn't bother me at all anymore. I felt great—I felt better than ever before.

That was on April 18, 1976, just a month before my fourteenth birthday. I'll never forget that date.

Chicken and Bernd got into some junkie's car so that they could shoot up. I went ahead to The Sound. It didn't faze me anymore, being alone. It felt good, actually. I felt powerful in a way.

I went over to a bench and sat down. Astrid came over, looked at me, and right away she asked, "Hey, are you on H?" Despite the fact that Astrid was one of my best girlfriends at that time, I went ballistic. "Fuck off," I screamed at her. "Just go away!" I had no idea why I was flipping out like that.

Chicken and Bernd came in, eventually, both totally high. Chicken was back to normal again—totally cool, calm, and collected. Detlef wasn't in The Sound. I was thirsty and got myself a soda. I drank soda all night. I was really scared of alcohol now.

At around five in the morning, Bernd asked if we wanted to come over to his house and have some tea. So off we went. I happily hooked my arm into Chicken's. The soda was sloshing around in my stomach, and I had to throw up. I puked while walking. It didn't bother me at all though, and the other two didn't seem to notice.

I felt like I was part of an awesome new family. I didn't say much, but I had the feeling that I could talk to both of them about anything. Heroin turned us into real brothers and sisters. We were all equals. I would have revealed my most secret thoughts. After those terrible weeks before this, I felt that I'd never been this happy before.

I slept with Bernd in his bed. He didn't touch me though. After all, we were like brother and sister. Chicken lay down on the floor with his head against an armchair. He stayed in that exact same pose until two in the afternoon. Then he got up because he was starting to get the craving again and had to somehow find a way to get his next fix.

Suddenly I was seized with this insane itch all over my body. I ripped off all my clothes and started scratching myself with a hairbrush. I scratched myself bloody, especially on the calves. But that didn't faze me either. I knew that junkies had a tendency to scratch themselves. At The Sound, I'd always been able to tell who was on heroin by how much they were scratching. Chicken's calves were so scratched up that there was hardly any healthy skin left, and in some spots he'd scratched down to raw flesh. Chicken didn't scratch his legs with a brush though; instead, he used a pocket knife.

Before he left, he said to me, "The dope that you let me have today—I'll replace it and give it back to you tomorrow." He was already treating me like I'd become a bona fide junkie, as someone who'd need to re-up soon—the next day at the very latest. Somehow I figured out what he was saying in his matter-of-fact way. I acted cool though, and just said, "No problem. No rush. It's okay if I get it back later."

I went back to sleep again, all calm and happy. And then in the evening I went home. There were moments when I thought, Jesus, you're thirteen and you're already using heroin!? That's so fucked up. But that feeling only lasted for a second, and then everything went back to normal. I was feeling way too good to really think critically about things. When you first start out, you don't have to deal with any withdrawal symptoms. And for me, the high seemed to last a week. Everything went without a hitch; everything was wonderful. There were no more arguments at home. I didn't act out at school. I felt relaxed, and I even participated a little bit and got some good grades. Over the next weeks, I even worked my way up from D's to B's in a few subjects. It seemed to me that I was getting along with everybody and coping with everything. I was floating through life. During the week, I went back to the Center House. In the meantime, four other people from our old group had switched over to heroin. I now sat with them. Within just a few weeks, there were more and more junkies at Center House. Gropiusstadt was just like everywhere else, and when heroin arrived, it exploded.

Jürgen Quandt, Managing Pastor of the Center House

For many years, the basement of the Protestant center, aka the Center House, served as the central meeting place for kids and teenagers from Gropiusstadt and the borough of Neukölln. On most nights, we'd get up to five hundred kids at the youth center, but that ended in December 1976, when we had to close it because of the rapid increase in heroin use among teens. The closing was part of an effort to call attention to the catastrophic situation.

What surprised the teachers and staff was how fast the entire hard drug scene sprang up in Gropiusstadt. Up until then—for instance, during the student movement of the 1960s—our main concern was with the use of so-called soft drugs. Within just a few months in 1976, though, almost fifty teens from our area had started using heroin.

Our attempts up until then had focused on raising awareness through conversation and education, about the dangers of drug use. When it came to heroin, though, those old methods seemed dangerously casual: They amounted to surrender. It was almost like we were admitting that we were too weak to win in a fight against this new, powerful drug.

Our work with teens at the Center House forced us to deal with something that the authorities were still refusing to admit at the time: that the drug problem was actually getting worse. The market for these drugs consisted mainly of working-class teens and other young people who were unemployed, unskilled, and not in college. The only thing that we could do, as educators, was to engage in public protests against official ignorance. The closing of the youth center was supposed to bring to light what many people would've rather kept in the dark. Our strategy was at least somewhat successful. Today in West Berlin there's an intense dispute about the drug problem — as it really exists, instead of how we'd like to imagine it.

In Neukölln, they now have a government-financed drug-counseling center, and in Gropiusstadt there's also a new "Clean-Bus," which is available as a meeting place for at-risk teens. There's also now an expanded availability of therapy and rehab programs. However, the drug problem hasn't gotten any better over the past two years, even though we are now dealing with a new generation of young people. Some of the teens from Gropiusstadt who started using heroin just two years ago have already passed away.

In a high-rise housing development like the housing projects in Gropiusstadt, where approximately 45,000 live, any problem is automatically magnified, just due to the sheer concentration of people in a relatively small area. There's an abundance of the unemployed, of dropouts, of dissatisfaction, and of conflict. Financial hardship, high rents, and a constantly rising cost of living impose a steadily increasing workload and the necessity for both parents to have a job and bring in money. This causes seemingly irresolvable stress: having to come up with more and more energy for the daily grind without reaping the benefits of working harder, such as being happier, more content, and more prosperous. In addition to their parents (or their single parent) having less and less time for them, kids and teens also suffer from overcrowded classes, a lack of jobs and internships, increasing *demands at school and at home, family conflicts, and a lack of recreational opportunities, playgrounds, and open spaces such as parks. Drugs and alcohol have always been a quick, easy way for people to deal with these stresses by numbing the pain.*

In view of the challenging living situation of these teens, we shouldn't be surprised at all about their escalating drug use, increasing criminal activity, and growing brutality. Nobody can seriously dispute that a direct connection exists between the increase in drug abuse among working-class teens and the deterioration of their quality of life.

❋

AFTER THAT FIRST SHORT of heroin, I ran into Detlef at The Sound. He got up in my face immediately: "You've done it now, haven't you! You're completely crazy." He'd already heard about what I'd gotten into from Astrid.

"You started with it, and now you're already a total junkie. But I'm not going to let that happen to me."

That shut him up. He wasn't feeling well enough to put up a fight anyway. He didn't have withdrawal symptoms yet because he wasn't yet physically dependent, but he was clearly craving a fix. After some initial stumbling, he finally made his intentions known: He didn't have any cash, but he wanted to find some way to buy a little dope.

I said, "Well, there you go." And then I suggested that we both go panhandling. He agreed, although he must have known how it would turn out. In twenty minutes, I made about twenty marks. Detlef earned much less. But overall, it did the trick and was enough for both of us (because back then, a very small dose still got us plenty high). We didn't even discuss whether or not I would get some of it. That was just a given. Later that night,

Detlef shot up and I snorted. My resolution to avoid heroin for a month was already shot to hell.

So, suddenly, Detlef and I were back together again, and it was as if we'd never been apart. Neither of us talked about the time when we treated each other like strangers. It just felt right. Things were as good as they'd been when we shared that Sunday dinner together at my place.

Overall, I think I was pretty happy about how everything had turned out. I reasoned that if I hadn't done heroin, then I never would've gotten back together with Detlef. I deluded myself into believing that I would be able to keep on being just a weekend user. Everyone who gets into heroin thinks that way, even though hardly anyone actually manages it. On top of that, I believed I could save Detlef from becoming a junkie. Those were the lies I told myself at the time.

Deep down, I probably knew that I was deceiving myself, even at the very beginning. When someone tried to talk to me about H, I'd freak out. I'd scream at them and tell them to fuck off. I treated people who wanted to talk about it the exact same way I'd treated Astrid when she first confronted me. And I started to hate all the other girls who were my age and looked like they were on a similar path. I could easily pick them out in the subway and at the club, all the little posers with their clumsy attempts at heroin-chic style—twelve- and thirteen-year-old runaways, usually. Even though I was generally very easygoing, seeing those girls really made me aggressive. "That one will definitely wind up on a street corner, begging for a hit," I'd say to myself. I absolutely hated them. It didn't occur to me at the time that the person I actually hated was myself.

After a few weekends of snorting heroin, I did in fact take a short break. I felt pretty good, and so I decided that it hadn't had any real effect on me. Physically I didn't feel worse. But the old attitudes were all coming back. I didn't care about anything, and

I started fighting with my mom again. That was shortly before spring break, in 1976.

The first Saturday of spring break I went to The Sound and sat down on a bench near the stairs. I didn't really know what my agenda was at the time—or if I had an agenda at all. Two girls came down the stairs—they were about twelve years old, but they had on makeup and bras and were all decked out like they were sixteen. (Incidentally, I also told people who didn't know me already that I was sixteen, and I used makeup to try and support that lie.) I instantly disliked these two girls, but at the same time, they were compelling. I didn't let them out of my sight.

I could tell by the way they moved through The Sound that they were looking to make some connections. They wanted in. There was probably nothing they wanted more than to fall in with the hard-core druggies—with the heroin users. It seemed like they already knew Richie, the cook from The Sound's cafeteria. He was in his late thirties, the only real adult working at The Sound, and he got along well with all the kids. He acted as a kind of father figure for a lot of runaway girls. So those two girls kept up a steady stream of chatter with Richie at the bar. They must have noticed that I was watching them because they kept looking over at me—probably because I was their age. One of them eventually came over. Her face was as innocent as an angel's. She said her name was Babsi and asked if I could give her any LSD.

I said, "Come on, give me a break. What would you want with acid?" I enjoyed this sense of superiority. I felt like I was miles above her and years ahead. She should have known that you couldn't just hit someone up for acid—especially if that person was already on to the next big thing: heroin. She apparently thought I was cool, though, just like I used to think all those other guys were cool, a few months ago, just because they'd tried a bunch of drugs that I hadn't. She said she wanted to buy me a drink and would come right back.

After Babsi walked off, the other one came over. Her name was Stella. She asked what Babsi had wanted. I told her.

Stella asked me, "Did she give you any money? I can't find five marks. I bet that bitch stole it from me." That was already classic Stella—the exact same person I'd get to know and come to expect in the days that lay ahead. Babsi and Stella were going to become my best friends—that is, up to the point when Babsi made headlines for becoming Berlin's youngest heroin fatality.

Babsi came back with my soda. I hated her, obviously, but at the same time I also found something appealing about her baby-faced naïveté and her straightforward manner. We started talking. Babsi and Stella'd been kicked out of school because they apparently skipped more classes than they attended. They'd started skipping school because they fell in with a group of regular potheads. So now they'd left home and become runaways; they wanted to experience more than what their little pot-smoking group could offer them. Babsi was twelve. Stella was thirteen.

I invited Babsi over to my house the next morning. Since she didn't have much of anything, I gave her two of my old T-shirts and a pair of underpants. After a minute she fell asleep in my bed, and I cooked something to eat. I'd gotten to really like her. The next day, I became friends with Stella, too. The two of them reminded me of the person I'd been just a short while ago. I felt much more comfortable in their company than with those totally wrecked junkies. They smoked pot and dropped acid, but with them I also managed to gain some distance from the more hard-core drugs and all the junkies. I only had my little snort at the club on Saturdays. The others from my clique made fun of me because I spent so much time with these two teenyboppers. But I didn't care.

The three of us had a lot to talk about. We all had pretty similar home lives. Babsi's dad committed suicide when she was still a child. She said that her mom used to be a dancer in East Berlin and then a model in the West. Her stepfather was supposed to be some kind of pianist. A world-famous artist, she said. She was really proud of her stepfather—especially when, one day, we went into a record store and found a ton of his records. This pianist didn't seem to care very much about his stepdaughter though. As a result, Babsi lived with her grandparents, who'd adopted her. She lived there like a princess. I visited her house later on. She had an awesome room with amazing furniture and a top-of-the-line stereo system, with tons of records. And more clothes than she knew what to do with. But she didn't get along very well with her grandmother, who had a bad temper and a very short fuse. What Babsi really wanted was to live with her mom again. When all the clothes and furniture didn't make up for the way her grandma treated her, she decided to run away.

Like Babsi, Stella had a mom who also happened to be beautiful. Stella loved her, too—but her dad had died in an apartment fire when Stella was only ten. And since then, her mom had had to make do on her own. She didn't have much time for Stella, and she'd started drinking heavily. In those days, Stella was totally obsessed with Muhammad Ali. She was always bragging about how strong he was. In a way, he seemed to replace both her dad and all of her potential boyfriends.

The three of us all came from more or less the same place and were headed in the same direction. Right from the very beginning, I'd known that they wouldn't stop pushing the envelope until they wound up as real, full-blown junkies. But when Stella actually asked me for some H, I was honestly shocked. I couldn't help myself and just started ripping into her: "Stay away from that shit!" I yelled. "Nobody would give you any, anyway. I'm gonna stop using soon, too. It's bad news, trust me."

So I didn't give Stella anything, and I told the others not to give her any either—not under any circumstances. A few days later, she still found a way, via Ralph, one of the guys from The Sound, whom she'd just made friends with. And Babsi got in on the act, too, of course.

But for a while after that, they were pretty limited in terms of what they could do. They were picked up during a drug bust and escorted back home. I didn't see them again for a few weeks.

In the meantime, spring had arrived, and it was getting warmer every day. The first sunny days of the year always carried happy memories along with them. Even when I was a kid, I was immediately reminded of running around barefoot, stripping down to my underwear, splashing around in the water, and watching the flowers open up in the garden. Every new spring, I experienced that same rush of joyful memories. But in the spring of 1976, I waited in vain for that feeling of contentment. I thought it was impossible for life to keep dragging along once the sun came out. But even after the spring came I was still lugging all my old problems around with me. I wasn't even sure what I was worried about, or what was bothering me, or what my problems were. I snorted H, and the problems were gone. But the high didn't last anywhere near as long as it used to.

I celebrated my fourteenth birthday in May. My mom gave me a kiss and fifty marks. She'd cobbled it together out of her household budget. I was supposed to buy myself something that would make me really happy.

That evening, I took the subway to where the dealers hung out at the Kurfürstenstrasse. I spent forty marks for a half-gram of heroin. I'd never had so much all at once. For six marks, I also got a pack of cigarettes. I smoked all the time now, sometimes even chain-smoking one after another. I could go through a whole pack in just a couple of hours. That left four marks for The Sound.

I ran into Detlef right after I got there. He gave me a kiss (which was extra sweet) and wished me a happy birthday. I returned the favor, since his birthday was just two days before mine. He was a little disappointed at the time because his parents didn't even say anything to him on his birthday. Only his grandmother remembered. He had it worse than I did. I tried to console him by saying, "Don't read anything into it, just let it go." It helped that I also had an awesome present for him. I bought him a fix. I had enough dope to keep us high all the way through to Sunday.

After the double birthday party (which consisted of a huge snort for me and a decent fix for Detlef), we started dating seriously. Until then, Detlef had just gone from one casual date to the next, and I'd spent a lot of my time with Babsi and Stella. Now we spent as much time together as possible. Detlef had just quit his apprenticeship as a pipe fitter and was pretty much always free. When we had enough money, we shot up and got high together.

●

SUMMER VACATION HAD FINALLY ARRIVED. On the very first day, Detlef and I and a few others from our group went to the Wannsee public beach, at one of the many lakes in Berlin. We were completely broke, as usual. But it didn't take long for me to learn how to snatch loose-lying valuables and then convert what I'd stolen into cash. We hung around in the back, near the woods, where the older ladies sat. (They were there for the shade because they couldn't handle too much sun anymore.)

First, we started small and just took what we needed. So we'd go to a blanket with a cooler next to it, after the people sitting there had gone out for a swim. Then I'd say, "Where'd grandma go?!" and take a few cans of Coke out of the cooler. Then after that, I swiped a towel and a blanket. And then in the evening, I was able to grab a boom box and some other little things, and Detlef got a watch.

Back at The Sound, I was able to sell the boom box in no time- and made fifty marks on the deal. It was an awesome day. And the way I saw it, it was only going to get better from that point on. When I had the money in my hand I told Detlef, "Enough of this snorting stuff. Today I'm going to shoot up instead."

Detlef put up a weak protest, just like he had before. But it was absurd. Whether you got high by snorting your dope or shooting it into your arm, it made no difference, really. The only difference was that when you were snorting, people didn't con- sider you a real junkie. As long as you were snorting, you could still consider yourself just an "occasional user."

We went to a hot spot just around the corner, on Kurfürstenstrasse. By now our regular dealer was able to spot us from pretty far away. He started walking over as soon as he saw us and then waited until the coast was clear to actually come and meet us. I bought two quarter-gram packets from him for forty marks. I was finally ready to shoot up. When you snort, it takes a while for the high to take effect. But when you shot up, people said it was like a hammer hitting you. I'd overheard some of the guys in our clique saying it was almost like having an orgasm. Without pausing for even a second, and without considering that this next step would also entail a simultaneous drop into wretch- edness, I gave in to my basic, overwhelming desire.

We walked to the public bathrooms near Potsdamerstrasse. It was a really bad area at the time. There were some hoboes and panhandlers hanging out in front, and in return for a pack of cigarettes, we got a few of those guys to let us know if they saw any cops. They knew the drill already and were always dying for cigarettes.

We had someone else with us. Tina, a girl from The Sound. Detlef took a syringe, a spoon, and a lemon out of his plastic bag. He put the junk on the spoon, added some water, and then used a few drops of the lemon juice to help the heroin dissolve more easily (since it was never that pure). Then he held a lighter beneath the spoon until everything was boiling and drew the mixture up into the syringe. (Incidentally, the old syringe was covered in grime, with a point about as blunt as a knitting needle.)

Detlef went first, and then Tina. But then the needle got all clogged up—with absolutely nothing passing through. Or that's what those two told me, anyway. But maybe they just didn't want me to shoot up. But it didn't matter: Now I was more determined than ever.

There was another junkie in the bathrooms who I'd just seen shooting up. He was a total wreck, all fucked up. I asked him if he'd let me borrow his syringe, and he did. But then a wave of utter horror, almost nausea, hit me when I thought about shoving that needle into the vein in my arm. I put the needle where I knew it was supposed to go but couldn't force myself to do it, even though I'd seen everyone else do it a thousand times before. Detlef and Tina pretended that it wasn't any of their business. So I had to ask the junkie for help. It was obvious that he knew it was my first time, and I felt pretty stupid having to ask someone with so much experience to help me out.

He said it was a shame—a fucking shame—but then he took the needle from me anyway. My veins were pretty hard to see, so he had trouble hitting one. He had to jam the needle in three times before he was able to draw any blood (indicating that he'd finally hit the vein). He said again what a fucking shame it was, and then he slammed the whole quarter into my arm.

It really did hit me like a hammer, but at the same time I'd always kind of thought that an orgasm would be different. I was totally numb in the immediate aftermath—I felt like I was dead. I was hardly aware of anything, and I didn't have any thoughts at all. I went to The Sound, slid down into a corner, and just sat there, drinking soda.

So I was finally on par with Detlef—we were at the same level. We were bound together now, just like a married couple, pretty much—except of course for the fact that we weren't actually sleeping together. In fact, we had no sexual relationship whatsoever. I still didn't feel old enough for sex, and Detlef accepted that point without forcing me to explain myself over and over again. That's one of the things I really loved about him. He was an awesome guy.

And anyway I was sure that someday I would sleep with him. And I was glad that I hadn't done that with anyone else yet. There was no doubt in my mind that he and I would stay together. When we'd been together in The Sound, Detlef would always walk me home. That'd take two hours. And then after he dropped me off, he'd hitchhike from Kreuzberg to Lankwitz, where he lived with his dad.

We spent a lot of our time just basically daydreaming together. I'd lost my connection to reality. Reality had become unreal. I wasn't interested in yesterday, and I didn't care about tomorrow. I had no plans, only dreams. I loved talking to Detlef about what we'd do if we ever made a ton of money. We'd buy a big house, a big car, and the best furniture we could find. But there was one thing that never came up in our imaginary futures, and that was heroin.

Detlef came up with an idea. If he could get an advance to buy a hundred marks' worth of heroin from a dealer, then he could divide it into ten packets and sell those for twenty marks each—so that when it was all over, we'd have made a hundred marks from the sale. With the profit, we'd buy another batch and double our take each time. I thought that was a great idea. That's how easy we thought dealing drugs would be at the time.

Detlef really did manage to get that loan. Apparently, a few small dealers had just been busted, and they were looking for fresh new street vendors. But after we'd gotten the dope, we didn't have the courage to go straight out to the streets. Instead, we stuck to The Sound. Detlef (sweetheart that he was) kept approaching people who were already showing withdrawal symptoms—and who were obviously totally broke. He gave out the dope on loan, and they never paid him back (of course). Half of the heroin disappeared just like that, and the other half we shot up ourselves. After all was said and done, we hadn't made a single cent.

The guy who had advanced Detlef the dope was absolutely furious. But he didn't do anything about it. He probably just wanted to test Detlef, to see if he had the guts to deal on the street. And Detlef had proved, beyond a shadow of a doubt, that no, he didn't have any talent for it.

✺

FOR THE FIRST THREE WEEKS of that summer vacation, Detlef and I were in constant contact. We usually got together pretty early in the day, around lunchtime. Then we would spend the rest of the afternoon trying to scrounge up some cash any way we could. I did things that I never would've done when I was younger. I stole anything I could get my hands on—especially if I thought I could sell it at The Sound. Even when I did manage to sell something, though, it was hardly ever enough for two fixes. But we didn't need it on a daily basis yet. We could still do without it for days at a time; we weren't yet physically dependent.

The second half of that summer vacation, I was supposed to go to my grandmother's place in Hessen.[22] She lived in a small

---

22 A cultural region, but also one of the states within Germany.

town. It's funny, but I was really looking forward to it. On the one hand, I couldn't imagine two or three weeks without Detlef, or The Sound, or the glitter and bright lights of the Kurfürstendamm —even for just a couple of days. It was unthinkable to me. On the other hand, I was looking forward to being around the kids over there, who'd never heard of drugs; I was looking forward to outdoor treasure hunts, to splashing around in the stream nearby, and to horseback riding. Between these two conflicting ideas, I couldn't figure out which one should get priority. I didn't know what I wanted.

Without thinking about it, I'd already split myself into two completely different people. I wrote letters to myself. That is, Christiane wrote letters to Vera. Vera is my middle name. Christiane was the fourteen-year-old who wanted to visit her grandmother; she was the good girl; Vera was the druggie. And they fought with each other through these letters of mine.

As soon as my mom put me on the train, I was only Christiane. And when I sat in my grandma's kitchen, it was as if I'd never been in Berlin. I felt instantly at home. My grandma gave me a feeling of comfort just by the way she sat there, all calm and relaxed. I loved my grandma, and I especially loved her kitchen. It was straight out of a picture book—an authentic old farmhouse kitchen with an open hearth, and huge pots and pans that were always cooking something. The whole atmosphere was unbelievably cozy and comforting.

I got along really well with my cousins and all the other kids in the town who were around my age. It was as if I'd never left. They were all still real kids. And I was, too! For the first time since I don't know how long, I felt like a kid again. I threw my high-heeled boots into the corner, and depending on what the weather was like, I would either borrow sandals or rubber boots from the others. I never even touched my makeup because here I didn't have to prove anything to anybody.

I went horseback riding a lot, and together with the other kids, I'd go on treasure hunts both on horseback and on foot. Our favorite playground was still down by the stream. We'd all grown a bit since the last time we were together, so the dams that we had to build needed to be huge. They caused little reservoir lakes to form behind them, and when we cut a breach into the dam at the end of the day, a torrent of water at least ten feet high shot down the stream.

The other kids obviously wanted to know what Berlin was like and what kinds of things I did when I was there. But I didn't tell them much. I didn't want to think about Berlin at all. It was crazy, but I didn't even miss Detlef. I didn't even write him once—even though it was originally my plan to send him a letter every day. Sometimes I tried to think about him at night. But I had trouble imagining what he looked like. He was like someone from another world—a world that I no longer understood.

In my bed at night, I had these weird nightmarish visions—and they only got worse as summer vacation neared the end. I'd see the guys from The Sound like ghosts before me, and the thought that I'd soon have to return to Berlin left me almost paralyzed with fear and anxiety. That's when I considered asking my grandma if I could stay with her. But how could I have justified that to my mom and grandma? I would've had to tell them all about the drinking and the drugs in Berlin. But I couldn't bring myself to do it. I was also afraid that my grandma would drop dead on the spot if I told her that her little sweetie was already shooting dope.

So in the end, I had to go back to Berlin—back to the noise, the lights, and all the frantic activity. But everything that I used to love about Berlin got on my nerves now. I could barely sleep at night because of all the noise. And on the Kurfürstendamm, between the cars and the mobs of people, I started to have these kinds of almost panic attacks.

I didn't even try to get used to things, because I knew that a week after I got back, there was a school vacation planned, and my whole class was going. Although my grandmother had given me fifty marks as a present, it didn't even occur to me to use it for drugs. I didn't look for Detlef either, and the only thing I'd even heard about him was that he didn't go to The Sound anymore. I stayed totally clean until I left for the Black Forest[23] with my class.

I'd been looking forward to the trip, but after a couple of days, I started feeling pretty bad. I got stomachaches after eating and could barely make it through the hikes. As we were sitting in the bus to go take a tour of a chocolate factory, Kessi, who was sitting next to me, suddenly said, "Oh my God, you look completely yellow. Probably hepatitis." She actually moved away from me. I thought the ground was tilting. Sooner or later, every junkie gets jaundice or hepatitis, just because of all the dirty old syringes that keep getting passed around. For the first time in a long time, heroin was back on my mind. I immediately thought about that filthy needle that I'd borrowed from that disgusting old junkie at the public toilets.

But then I realized that Kessi had been just joking—she wasn't serious about the hepatitis thing. And I thought that it couldn't be possible anyway, after just a few shots—and after all, that was months ago now.

From a sausage booth in front of the Suchard factory, I grabbed myself a plastic spoon, and then we entered a crazy, chocolatey, fairy-tale world. I dipped my spoon into any vat that contained anything looking even halfway appetizing. If it was good, I distracted our guide with questions so that I could sample it a few more times. By the end of the tour, I'd also swiped so

---

23 A mountainous, mostly forested region in southwest Germany, part of the German state of Baden-Württemberg.

many bars of chocolate and other kinds of candy that my jacket, which was knotted together into a kind of bag, was overflowing.

Back on the bus, I swore to myself that I'd never touch another piece of chocolate again, and when we got back to the hostel where we were staying, I got really sick. My insides seemed to give out, suffocated by all the junk food I'd been pigging out on.

Now even our teacher noticed how yellow I was looking. A doctor came to see me, and then an ambulance took me, sirens blaring, to the university hospital in Freiburg. The isolation room in the children's ward was spotless and white, but only just about big enough for a bed. No pictures on the wall, nothing. The nurses silently brought me food and medication. Occasionally, the doctor came by to ask how I was feeling. That went on for three weeks. I wasn't allowed to leave the room, not even to pee. Nobody visited; nobody talked to me. I didn't have anything interesting to read and no radio. I thought I was going to go nuts.

The letters from my mom were the only thing that kept me from losing my mind. I wrote to her, too. But more than anything else, I wrote to my two cats—the only pets I had left. After I'd written the letters, I would put them into tiny little envelopes that I folded myself.

Sometimes I thought about my grandma and the kids in that town and the stream and the horses, and sometimes I thought about Berlin, about The Sound—about Detlef and about heroin. I didn't have a clue who I was. When I was feeling really depressed, I'd think: You're just another heroin junkie, and now you've got your first case of jaundice. Congratulations. When I was imagining living at home with my cats and trying hard in school, I'd be thinking about spending every vacation at my grandma's. This went back and forth for days. Sometimes I wouldn't think about anything for hours; instead I'd just stare at the ceiling, wishing I were dead.

After a while, I started to worry that the doctors would figure out how I'd developed my case of jaundice in the first place. But the track marks had healed over the last few weeks, and I didn't have any scars or thromboses[24] yet. Anyway, who would think that the children's ward in Freiburg would have a heroin junkie in its ranks?

After three weeks, I had to practice walking again, a little at a time. Then—finally—I was allowed to take a flight back to Berlin. (The insurance paid for that.) Once I got home, I had to go right back to bed. I was glad to be back home with my mom and my cats. I didn't think about anything else.

My mom then told me that Detlef had stopped by a couple of times and asked about me. My mom told me he'd looked really upset because I'd been gone for so long. After that, I started to think seriously about Detlef again. In my mind, I pictured his beautiful wavy hair and his kind, sweet face. It made me really happy that someone had been worried about me, that I was loved by someone. By Detlef. And I felt really guilty that, for a couple of weeks, I'd almost forgotten all about him.

After a few days, Detlef somehow found out that I was back and came by to visit. I was in for a shock. When he came around to the front of my bed, I was left absolutely speechless.

Detlef had lost so much weight that he was nothing but skin and bones. His arms were so thin that I could easily reach all the way around them with one hand. His face was hollow and white as a sheet—but even so, he was still beautiful. His eyes had somehow become larger and sadder. All the old emotions came rushing back: I was in love with Detlef again. It didn't bother me that he'd become so emaciated. And I definitely didn't want to think about what had caused his physical deterioration.

---

24 Thrombosis is a coagulation (clumping or curdling) of the blood inside the vein or any other part of the circulatory system.

At first it was hard for us to talk. He only wanted to hear about me. But I didn't have anything to tell him that would've interested him. It didn't occur to me at all to tell him about my time at my grandma's or the games I'd played with the kids out there. I finally asked him why he didn't go to The Sound anymore. He said that it was shitty, when it really came down to it. I asked him where he was hanging out instead, and after a minute he told me: at Zoo Station.

I asked him what he was doing there. "Turning tricks," he said.

For some reason, it didn't shock me at the time. I knew from other junkies that they occasionally earned money that way. I didn't have a clear idea of what it really meant to be a prostitute, and I didn't really want to spend any time thinking about it. I only knew that it was a way for some guys to get off, that it was supposed to be separate from any real emotions, and that the guys who sold themselves could make a lot of money doing it. But on that day, I was just happy that Detlef had come over, and that he still really loved me, and that I loved him.

The following Sunday was the first time since my return that I was allowed to leave the house. Detlef picked me up in the afternoon. We went into a café on Lietzenburger Street. Almost everybody there was gay, and almost everybody knew Detlef. They were all very nice to me and had a lot of really nice things to say. They congratulated Detlef on his pretty girlfriend. And I noticed that he was really proud that I was his girlfriend. That was the reason why he'd dragged me to this café where everybody knew him.

I liked these gay men. They were nice to me and didn't try to hit on me like other men did, with their idiotic come-ons. They thought I was cute and liked me without expecting anything in return. All their compliments made me feel really good about myself. I went to the bathroom and looked in the mirror. I thought they were right. I really did look good after having not touched heroin for over two months. I'd probably never looked better.

Detlef said that he still had to go to Zoo Station because he'd promised Bernd, his best friend, that he'd meet him there. Bernd had worked the street for both of them that day. Detlef didn't have time that day because of me. But obviously I was going to come along. I was looking forward to seeing Bernd again.

Bernd had just left with a customer when we got there, so we had to wait around for a bit. The station didn't seem as horrible as I'd remembered. But then again, I was mostly looking at Detlef. At one point, Detlef started talking to another kid, and left me standing by myself for a minute; right away, some foreigners tried to hit on me. All I heard was, "How much?" or something like that. But I just hooked my arm into Detlef's and felt totally safe and secure.

I talked Detlef into going back to The Sound with me. And once we were there, I asked him to let me just have a quick snort. He didn't want to at first. But I told him, "Only tonight. Only as a welcome-back present. I want to be as high as you are. It's either that, or you can't shoot up, either." That did it: He gave me some. But he said that after that, he wouldn't give me any more. I told him not to worry, that he wouldn't have to. After all, for the past two-and-a-half months I'd proved that I wasn't an addict. And in the last couple of weeks, I'd noticed how much better I felt without it anyway.

It seemed like my words had some effect. He said, "Hey listen, I'll quit, too. If you can do it, it'll be a piece of cake for me." After that, he shot up and I snorted. We were both insanely happy and talked about how great our lives would be after our heroin days had ended.

The next day at lunchtime, I went to Zoo Station and met Detlef. He gave me another snort. I started to meet Detlef at that station almost every afternoon after school. I also shot up again. It was as if I'd never left Berlin, as if those two-and-a-half months had never happened. We talked about quitting almost every day, and I kept explaining to Detlef how easy it was.

I'd regularly go straight to Zoo Station from school. In my bag I'd carry a syringe and a big packet of sandwiches. My mom must have wondered how I managed to get skinnier and skinnier when I was taking so many sandwiches to school. I brought them for Detlef and his friends. They were dying for those lunches.

At first Detlef was really pissed about my joining him there. He didn't want me to be around while he was working the street, hustling. He told me directly, "I don't want my girlfriend hanging out at Zoo Station, where you just don't know what's around the next corner. It's a dangerous place, with dangerous people. You can meet me anywhere else. Just don't come here."

It went in one ear and out the other. I just wanted to be with Detlef, and it didn't matter where. Bit by bit, I'd started to feel almost comfortable in that grimy station. Everything had, at the very least, become more familiar. I didn't notice the rotten stench of piss and disinfectant anymore. The whores, the junkies, the human waste, the dispossessed, the beggars, the bums, the cops, the drunks, the vomit spilling over everything: All of that had unquestionably become my natural habitat in the time between school and nightfall. That's where I belonged because that's where Detlef was.

At first it bugged me, the way the other girls at the station sized me up—running their eyes up and down my body like I wasn't even human. Somehow they managed to be even more aggressive than the customers. But then I realized that these girls, who were selling themselves at the station, were also threatened by me. They were scared that since I was younger, fresher, and less spoiled, I would snatch away their best customers. And I guess that much at least made sense: I looked better than they all did. I still took care of myself and washed my hair almost every day.

You couldn't tell that I was using heroin just by looking at me. And I knew that in that respect, I had an advantage over the other girls. That made me feel good. The customers would have just flocked to me. But I didn't have to go selling myself. Instead, Detlef was the one who did it. I was able to get my dope without whoring myself, and it was clear from the way the other girls watched me that they envied me.

At first, the customers drove me crazy. Especially the immigrants in the area, with their constant, "You fuck? You go hotel?" Some of them would only offer like twenty marks. After a while, I discovered I could get some shots in and have some fun with these guys. I'd say, "In your dreams, asshole. For someone like you, it would take five hundred to even start a conversation with me." Or I'd just stare straight through a guy and say, "With you? No chance in hell. Fuck off." It was kind of thrilling to force these pathetic assholes to tuck their tails between their legs and slink away.

I acted superior with Detlef's clients, too. When one of them would get cocky with me or try to get into my pants, Detlef was right by my side. And before Detlef left with a customer, he'd ask his friends at the station to look out for me. They were like brothers to me. They chased away anyone who tried anything funny.

I was pretty much over The Sound I just hung out at Zoo Station now instead. I lost touch with most of my old friends, and just saw the same few Zoo Station people— Detlef of course, and also two other guys; Bernd and Axel.

Compared to Detlef and Bernd, Axel was pretty ugly. None of the features in his face seemed to match. And his arms and legs seemed totally disproportionate to his body. So pretty much not at all who you'd think would work out on the streets. But he got his customers and even had some regulars. Detlef could insult his customers and scream at them whenever they pissed him off, but they always came back to him, whining for more. Axel on the other hand, because of his looks (or lack thereof), always had to swallow his pride and really cater to his customers. But who knows, maybe he did something special for those guys, something kinky that really drove people wild. Otherwise there was no way he could've kept up with the competition.

But he still found ways to revenge himself on the customers whenever he could. Once he got his hooks in someone, he would lie, cheat, and steal for all he was worth. Axel was a cool, strong guy. If you made fun of him or humiliated him in some way, he would never let it show. He always remained sweet and friendly. He was always willing to help out someone else—a quality that was rare among the other junkies. In fact, there was nobody else really like him. It was as if he didn't deserve to live in this shitty world. A year later, he was gone.

Axel's story was familiar by now. His parents were divorced, and he lived with his mom until she moved in with a boyfriend of hers. At least his mom was generous. She left him a two-room apartment with a few pieces of furniture and even put in a TV for him. Once a week, his mom would visit him and gave him a little money to live on. She knew that he was an addict. And she probably told him several times to quit. In her own view, she did more than a lot of other parents. She gave him an apartment with a TV.

I spent one weekend in Axel's apartment. My mom thought I was staying with a girlfriend.

It was an absolute dump—a real junkie's place. I could smell the odor from inside as soon as they opened the door. Inside, there were empty sardine tins everywhere. And cigarette butts had been stuck in oil, tomato sauce, or mustard—whatever was handy. And then there was the issue of the cups. They were absolutely everywhere—glasses and other small containers, each one with a little grab bag of water, ashes, tobacco, and rolling papers inside. When I tried to move a few yogurt containers over to the only table in the place, a couple of sardine cans at the other end clattered onto the floor. The sauce soaked into the carpet. Nobody cared.

And that was the worst part: the carpet. When I watched Axel shoot up, I saw why it stank so much. He pulled the syringe with the little bit of blood out of his arm, filled it with water, and then squirted the pink brew directly onto the carpet. That's how he cleaned his syringe. After every fix a few more drops of blood were added to the threadbare Persian patterns. And that's what caused the sickly sweet musty smell—that, and the fish sauce. Even the curtains were yellow and smelly.

In the midst of this stinking chaos was one dazzlingly white bed. I fled to it immediately. As I pressed my face into the pillows, it smelled like my favorite laundry detergent. I thought for sure that this was the cleanest bed I'd ever been in.

Axel said, "I changed the sheets just for you." And the bed had fresh sheets on it every Saturday for the next few weeks, whenever I was there. I never slept on the same sheets twice, while the guys probably never changed their sheets.

The boys bought me whatever I wanted to eat or drink. It seemed like all they wanted was to just treat me well and make me smile. And best of all, they only bought me the best dope. My liver was still giving me trouble back then. When I shot up anything dirty, it made me feel horrible. They really worried about me when I started to look run down and sickly. So they only bought the purest stuff for me, even though it was expensive. The three of them were always there for me. Somehow, they only had me to care about. Aside from Detlef, Axel, and Bernd, I didn't have anyone.

I felt real happiness—a happiness that was almost totally unknown to me otherwise. I felt protected and safe. In the afternoons at Zoo Station, and on the weekends at Axel's heroin den, I felt at home.

Detlef was the strongest in the group, and I was the weakest. I felt physically inferior to the boys, but I also felt like I was of lesser stature otherwise, too—probably just because I was a girl. But for the first time in my life, I enjoyed that feeling of dependence. I enjoyed the fact that Detlef was in the driver's seat. And I savored the way Detlef, Axel, and Bernd were always there when I needed them.

I had a boyfriend who did what no other junkie would ever do: He always shared his dope with me—every little bag. He earned money by doing pretty much the worst job there was—and now that I was using more, he had to take on one or two customers more a day. Everything was different with us. With us, it was the guy who did the hustling. I used to think we were special that way—that maybe we were the only couple in the world with that kind of an arrangement.

It never really occurred to me, during those weeks in the fall of 1976, that I should go earn money that way myself. I mean, every once in a while the thought would pop into my head—usually when Detlef had to go off with a scumbag customer—but I knew that Detlef (who never threatened me) would've slapped me if I so much as hinted at working the streets myself.

I still didn't really understand what it was, exactly, that the prostitutes did for their money. I didn't want to think about it, and I didn't really want to know anything. Detlef didn't talk about it. From various conversations, I just knew that, one way or another, they got their customers off. But in my mind, all that stuff had nothing to do with Detlef and me. I didn't feel repulsed by what Detlef had to do. If he had to touch the customers, that wasn't so bad. That was his dirty job, and that was the only way we were able to score more dope. I just didn't want those lowlifes to touch my Detlef. He was mine and only mine.

At first, I thought some of the customers were okay guys, more or less. The boys around the station sometimes pointed out this one or that one who was supposed to be all right, and then they'd say that someone should try to keep him hot so he'd come back. That's where I got my start. Some customers were really nice to me when they saw me with Detlef at the station. They thought I was sexy. That was kind of weird, the fact that these guys—who I thought were all gay—liked me like that. Sometimes one of the boys gave me twenty marks and said it was from a customer who thought I was really nice. Detlef never told me that some of these guys were already badgering him to have him involve me in a three-way.

I watched the other girls; almost all of them still just kids like me. And I saw the horrible shape they were in. Especially the ones who were addicted to H and who had to sell themselves to fund their habit. I saw the disgust in their faces when a customer came over to talk business (although they still tried to smile nicely). I hated the customers. They were a special breed of assholes, perverts, and pigs—skulking through the corners of this grungy station on the hunt for desperate, underage hookers. What was so much fun about going off with these strange girls—girls who were so clearly disgusted by them and who were so clearly miserable?

Eventually, my attitude toward Detlef's work soured. Over time, I began to realize what Detlef had to go through with these guys. Sometimes he had to really force himself to do a job, using every little bit of willpower to overcome his nausea and disgust. If he wasn't doped up, he often couldn't do it.

When he was going into withdrawal, so just when he needed a job the most, he had a tendency to just run away from the customers. Axel or Bernd would usually step in at that point, so that the money wasn't lost. But it really took it out of them. Axel and Bernd also had to be doped up in order to make it work.

It really bugged me that these guys all ran after Detlef like that. They stammered their funny confessions of love for him and slipped him love notes while I was standing right there next to him. They were all so pathetic and lonely. But I couldn't feel sorry for them. It made me want to scream. "Don't you get it?" I wanted to yell, "Detlef belongs to me, and no one else . . . and definitely not some sad, old asshole like you!" But I knew I couldn't because we needed those guys: They supplied us with cash, and we could take it from them like candy from a baby.

Then I noticed that some men at the station appeared to know Detlef pretty intimately—much more intimately than I did, anyway. It made me want to puke. And when I heard a rumor that some of the customers wouldn't pay until the hustler also had an orgasm, I just about lost it.

I saw less and less of Detlef. He was always off with some client asshole. I was worried about him. Somebody told me once that a lot of male hookers eventually become gay themselves. But I couldn't blame Detlef. We needed more and more money. And half of it was spent on my dope. Since I was part of this group, I wanted to become a real junkie, just like them. I shot up every day. But I always made sure that I had enough H left over for my fix the next morning.

Nevertheless, neither Detlef nor I were physically addicted yet. When you start to use heroin, it takes a while before you're completely dependent on the stuff. We could usually manage to go cold turkey for one or two days, using other stuff to get high. We hadn't really gone down the rabbit hole yet. And since we were able to take some time off, we talked ourselves into believing that we were different from all the addicts, all the junkies, all the human wrecks. We could quit any time we wanted to.

I was still feeling pretty good, I think. Every Saturday I found some happiness in Axel's apartment. Detlef would crawl under the clean sheets with me, give me a good-night kiss on the lips, and then turn around. We slept back-to-back, with our butts snuggled against each other. And when I woke up, Detlef would give me a good-morning kiss.

That was as far as we'd go for the first six months of our relationship. When I first met Detlef, I'd already had some experience with male brutality. And I told him right away, "I'm still a virgin, you know. And I want to take my time. I want to wait until I'm a little older."

He understood immediately and didn't make a big deal out of it. I was his girlfriend, of course, and we could talk together about anything and share everything, but at fourteen I was also still a child. He was always so sensitive and understanding. He was able to sense what I wanted, and without my saying so, he could tell what I could and couldn't do. Sometime in October, I asked my mom to put me on the pill. She got a prescription for me because by that time, she knew that Detlef and I were sleeping in the same bed, and she didn't believe that there was nothing going on between us.

So I took the pill but didn't let Detlef know about it. I was still afraid. When I got to the apartment one Sunday at the end of October, Axel had put fresh sheets on his bed. He said that it was silly that he stretched out in that big bed while the two of us squished onto a small cot. So we should take his bed.

All of a sudden, the apartment seemed to kind of lighten up. Detlef proclaimed that the apartment could use some housecleaning for a change. The rest of us immediately agreed. I started by tearing open every single window in the apartment. When some fresh air started to come in, I realized once again what a horrible stench we'd been living in. Any normal person would have been knocked out by the stink of blood, ashes, and moldy sardine cans before he even set one foot inside.

Two hours later, the apartment was in a state of utter chaos. We gathered up these huge piles of trash—each one a kind of garbage dump unto itself—and stuffed everything into plastic bags. At the end, I even started up the vacuum cleaner and cleaned out the birdcage. A sleepy parakeet looked down from his perch at all this activity. Axel's mom had given the bird to him along with the TV, since her boyfriend didn't like birds. But the thing was, Axel hated it, too. When it was lonely and started to chatter and tweet, Axel banged his fist against its cage, which made the poor creature start thrashing all around in there. None of the guys did anything for the bird. But Axel's mom brought it some food once a week, and I gave it enough birdseed on Saturdays to last through the whole week. I also bought a little glass water dispenser for the bird, which was able to hold enough clean water for six days.

That night, when we went to bed, everything was different. Detlef didn't give me a good-night kiss and he didn't turn around. He started talking to me. Softly, and lovingly. I felt his hands on me, easy and gentle. I wasn't anxious at all. I touched him, too. We caressed each other for a long time without saying a word. It was wonderful.

Probably an hour went by before Detlef said something again. He asked, "Will you sleep with me next Saturday?"

I just said okay. I'd always been afraid of this question. But now, when Detlef asked, it made me happy.

After a while I added, "Under one condition. We have to both be sober. I don't want any H involved. I mean, otherwise

I might not like it. Or I might love it and think it's incredible but only because of the dope, and then maybe I won't be able to appreciate it when I'm sober. I want to be totally sober. And I want you to know what it's like when you're sober with me."

Detlef said okay, and then he gave me my good-night kiss. We turned around and fell asleep, like always, with our backs pressed against each other.

We really did stay sober that next Saturday. The apartment was dirty and stinking again, but our bed had fresh white linens on it. As we were taking our clothes off, I started feeling a little anxious. At first we just lay side by side without moving. I thought of the girls in my class who told stories about when the boys got on top of them for the first time. How they'd forcefully rammed their thing inside them and wouldn't stop until they were finished. The girls said that it hurt like hell the first time. And a few of them didn't even keep dating the guy who took away their virginity.

I told Detlef that I wanted to have a different experience from the girls in my class. He said he understood.

We stroked and caressed each other for a long time. He entered me a little bit, and I almost didn't notice. Detlef could sense when it hurt without me having to say anything.

I thought, If it winds up hurting a little, that's all right. After all, he's already waited for half-a-year.

But Detlef didn't want to hurt me. After a while, it was like we were one person. I loved him intensely right then. But still, for some reason I couldn't do much more than just lie there, completely motionless and stiff. Detlef didn't move either. He must have sensed what I myself couldn't think or express just then. I was totally consumed by the conflicting emotions of fear and happiness.

Detlef pulled away and put his arms around me. I felt almost high, with this intensely warm and magical feeling. I thought,

How did you ever find such a great guy? He only thinks about you and never himself. Even when you sleep together, he only cares about making you feel good—he doesn't even finish. I thought of Kathi, how he'd just grabbed me between the legs in the movie theater. I was so glad that I'd waited for Detlef—that he was the one I belonged to. I loved this guy so much that I suddenly got scared: scared of dying.

I kept thinking the same thing over and over: I don't want Detlef to die. So while he was caressing me I said to him, "Detlef, we should stop shooting up."

He said, "I agree. You should never become a junkie."

He kissed me. Then we slowly turned around, and with our butts pressed against one another, we fell asleep.

I woke up because I felt Detlef's hands on me again. It was still very early, but there was some gray light coming through the curtains. We started making out, and then we made love for real. It had more to do with what was going on in my head than what was going on with my body. But now I knew how really good it was to sleep with Detlef.

On Monday after school, I went straight to Zoo Station. Detlef was already there. I gave him my lunch sandwich and my apple. He was hungry. I was hungry, too, but in a different way. After having gone clean for three days, I really needed a hit. I asked Detlef if he had a shot for me.

He said, "Nope. And you also won't get any more from me, either. I don't want that. I love you too much. I don't want you to turn into a junkie."

I flipped out. I had a real craving, and I ripped right into him: "Oh, please, don't put on this holier-than-thou act. Your pupils are like pinpoints. You're totally doped up. And meanwhile you've got the nerve to tell me that I should stay clean. If you quit, I'll quit, but don't act like you're doing me any favors when you're just hogging all the dope for yourself!"

I really let him have it. And didn't have any reply because of course I was right: he'd been high for days already at that point. He finally gave in and promised me that later on we'd quit together. Then he serviced another customer for my next shot.

Having slept with Detlef changed a lot of things for me. I didn't feel that comfortable at the station anymore. I suddenly had a much better idea of what Detlef and his friends did to earn their money. Now I knew exactly what those scumbags wanted when they hit on me. They wanted to do with me what I had done with Detlef. They wanted sex.

That wasn't news to me, of course, but up to that point, it had all been very abstract to me. Now it was something real and wonderful and intimate. It was something that Detlef and I shared. The customers disgusted me. What went on at this station was almost unimaginable. How could I ever think of going to bed with one of those desperate foreigners or let some drunk asshole, or some bald, sweaty fat guy actually have sex with me? How could anyone? The thought turned my stomach. It wasn't funny anymore when the johns used their stupid pickup lines on me. I didn't want to return fire with any clever replies anymore. I just turned away, repulsed; sometimes I even went after them with kicks. I also felt a completely new hatred for the guys who went after Detlef. I could've killed them. And in order to just keep my cool, I had to keep suppressing the thought that Detlef was acting affectionate toward them.

But despite all that, I kept on returning to the station after school every day. I went because that's where Detlef was. When he'd finished with a customer, we'd go to the Zoo Station café, and I'd have a hot chocolate. Sometimes business was pretty bad, though, and even Detlef had a hard time making enough cash for dope for the both of us.

By hanging out in the Zoo Station's café, I got to know some of the other prostitutes through Detlef, although he'd always tried to keep me away from them. They were much more fucked up than we were, and had a much harder time attracting customers. They were older, the kind of experienced street veterans that I used to admire for some reason, not so long ago.

Detlef said that they were all friends of his. And he warned me to watch my back around them because after all they were longtime addicts and would do just about anything for a little extra cash or another fix. They were always craving a hit, but they never had any money. As a result, you could never let on that you had any money or dope on you. Otherwise you risked getting knocked out and waking up with empty pockets. Not only did they rip off their customers; they also robbed each other.

I began to see what this "glamorous" drug scene was really like. I was almost in it now. Once upon a time, the only thing that I wanted was to be a part of this world.

Friends of Detlef would occasionally tell me, "Girl, you gotta quit. You're too young. You can still do it. You just have to get away from Detlef. He'll never get off the stuff at this point. Don't be stupid. Break up with him."

I gave them all the finger. Breaking up with Detlef—that was the last thing I wanted. If he was going to die, then I would, too. I didn't say that though. Instead I just told them that they were crazy. "We're not addicted," I'd say. "We can quit whenever we want."

●

NOTHING CHANGED MUCH FROM one day to the next in the month of November. From two until eight, I was at the station. Then we'd go to the Hot House, a club at the top of the Kurfürstendamm. The Hot House was the place where Detlef liked to hang out. It was even trashier than The Sound, and the people who went there were worse off, too. I often stayed till the last bus left, at 12:20 a.m. I basically just lived for the Saturdays when I slept with Detlef. Sleeping with him got to be more and more amazing—as long as we didn't do too much dope.

Then December came. It kept getting colder. I was freezing. I never used to feel the cold before. And now I was always freezing. I was a wreck, and I knew it. I'd known ever since one Sunday ealier in the month when I woke up next to Detlef at Axel's apartment.

When I woke up, I was freezing. Across the room there was a box and when I looked at it, the writing suddenly jumped out at me. The colors were glowing, and they were so bright that they were hurting my eyes. That was especially true of this one shade of red, which was scaring me. I'd always been afraid of red when I was tripping. But when I was on H, red became a soft, gentle color. Like all colors, red was beautiful when you were on H, as if it was coming at you through a soft veil.

And now the old red was back. My mouth was full of saliva. I swallowed, but right away it was back. It kept coming back up somehow. When it did finally stop, I had a really dry, sticky mouth. I tried to drink something but couldn't manage it. I shivered from the cold for a while, but then I got so hot that the sweat was literally pouring down my body. I woke Detlef up and told him that there was something wrong with me.

Detlef looked at my face and said, "You've got pupils as big as saucers." He paused for a minute, and then he said quietly, "Well, it's finally happened to you."

I was shivering again. "What?" I asked him. "What's happened?"

Detlef said, "You're having withdrawal symptoms. You're at the point now where you have to have it."

I thought to myself, That's it, then. That's what it's like. You've got the hunger now for real.

But they're really not so bad, the withdrawal symptoms. Everyone was always making such a big deal about them, but at least I wasn't in any actual pain. In the end, it just turned out to be some nausea, some shivering, and some weird experiences with colors.

Detlef didn't say anything else after that though. He picked a small packet out of his jeans pocket and then grabbed some ascorbic acid and a spoon and cooked the stuff over a candle. Then he gave me the syringe, ready to go. I was shaking so much that I had trouble hitting the vein. But I managed it after a second. Then I felt fine again. The colors turned soft and gentle, and the saliva in my mouth was gone. All my problems had vanished, and I fell back asleep next to Detlef, who'd also shot up while he was at it. When we got up around noon, I asked Detlef how much dope he still had.

He said, "Of course you'll still get a shot before you go home tonight."

"But I need something for tomorrow morning, too."

"I don't have that much anymore," he replied. "And I'm really not in the mood to go to the station today. It's Sunday and there's nothing going on there, anyway."

I was furious, and in a panic I yelled at him: "Don't you get it?! If I don't have a fix tomorrow morning, then I'll go into withdrawal again and won't be able to make it to school."

"It was always going to happen like this," he said, "and now it has."

We went to the station in the afternoon. I had a lot of time to think things over. My first withdrawal symptoms. I was now physically dependent on H, and I was financially dependent on Detlef. In all honesty, it was my dependence on Detlef that was more worrying. What kind of love was that, when one person was totally dependent on the other? What if I have to beg and plead with Detlef to give me dope some night? I knew how junkies could get when they were going into withdrawal. I had seen how they humiliated themselves and how they let other people humiliate them, too. How they shrank down to nothing. I couldn't beg. And I definitely couldn't beg Detlef. If he allowed me to beg, then it was over with us. I'd never been able to beg anyone for anything.

Detlef finally found a customer, and I had to wait a really long time for him to get back. From then on, I'd have to wait for Detlef to get my morning hit.

I was in a dark mood that afternoon. Without thinking about it, I'd started a long conversation with myself—a kind of self-examination—which went more or less like this: "So, Christiane, now you've done it. You got what you've always wanted. Is this what you imagined? (No, it wasn't.) But this is what you wanted, right? For some reason, you always admired those old heroin fiends. Now you're one yourself. You're not a little girl anymore, and nobody can make you feel like one ever again. You don't have to wonder what it's like to go into withdrawal anymore. You know enough now to stay away from cons. Now you can be the one doing the conning."

I wasn't very good at making myself feel better. I kept thinking about the craving, the withdrawal. I remembered how I'd always laughed at the junkies in withdrawal. I never really understood what was going on with them. All I knew was that they seemed helpless, so easily hurt; they had no strength. Junkies in withdrawal would never talk back to anyone, so everyone walked all over them. They were almost subhuman.

Sometimes I'd use them as an aid to my own ego or to release some pent-up anger or frustration. If you knew how to do it, you could reduce them to absolutely nothing, give them a real wake-up call. You just had to tease out their weaknesses, their sore spot, and keep hammering away at it, until they collapsed.

After all, when they were in the pain of withdrawal, that's when they had the insight to see what miserable losers they really were. These were the same people who generally acted like they'd been everywhere, done everything, and were over it. But when they were in withdrawal, the act was over. They didn't feel superior to anyone anymore.

And now that's exactly what they'll do to you, I thought. They'll tear you to pieces. They'll see how pathetic you really are. But you knew this all already, didn't you? Funny how it only occurred to you today.

These little talks with myself didn't really help much though. I should've talked to someone else. I could've simply gone up to one of those junkies at the station. But instead I crawled into a dark corner near the train station's post office. I already knew what other people would say to me. Detlef, too. Detlef could only come up with clichés when it came to our drug habit.

"Don't take it so hard," they'd say. "Just pull yourself together. It'll all work out in the end. If you really want to, you can quit. There's methadone[25] available if you need it."

The only one I could maybe talk to was my mom. But that wouldn't work, either. I couldn't do that to her. I thought, She loves you and you love her, too, in a way. She would freak out if you told her all this. And she couldn't help you anyway. Maybe she'd put you into an institution. And that wouldn't really accomplish much. Nobody can quit if they don't want to. And least of all you. You'd really dig your heels in then; maybe you'd even break out and run away. That would only make things worse.

---

25 Methadone is used to prevent withdrawal symptoms in people addicted to opiate drugs who want to stop taking the drugs. It works as a substitute for drugs such as heroin by producing similar effects and preventing withdrawal symptoms in people who have stopped using these drugs.

I found myself talking under my breath again: "Just stop it. This is something you can handle with your hands tied behind your back. When Detlef comes back, you'll tell him: 'I don't want any dope. I'm quitting. And either you quit right now also, or it's over between us. You've got two halves in your pocket? Okay then: We'll shoot up one more time and tomorrow we're done.'" I noticed how, while I was talking to myself, I was working myself into a craving again. Then I whispered as if I was revealing a big secret to myself: "Detlef isn't going to buy it. He won't do it. And you—would you really break up with Detlef? Come on, stop telling fairy tales. Be real for a minute and tell the truth. This is the last station. The end. It's over. Really the end. You didn't get much out of it, did you? But this is the life you wanted."

Detlef came back. Without saying a word, we went to the Kurfürstenstrasse and found our regular dealer. I bought a quarter, took the subway home, and holed up in my room.

●

TWO SUNDAYS LATER, DETLEF and I were alone at Axel's apartment. It was the afternoon. We were both incredibly, incredibly sick. We hadn't found our regular dealer on Saturday and were ripped off by somebody new. The dope he'd sold us was so bad that we had to shoot up twice as much as usual just to get by. So that was all we had, and it was still only the morning. Detlef had already started sweating, and I noticed that I wasn't that far behind.

We looked everywhere in the apartment for something that we could turn into cash. But we already knew there was nothing left. From the coffee machine to the radio, everything was gone, everything had been used to pay for dope. Only the vacuum cleaner was left. But that thing was so old that there was no way we'd get even a single mark for it.

"We've got to get some cash," Detlef said, "and we've got to get it now. In a couple hours we'll be sober and have the itch, and we'll be worthless. There's no way I can get enough money on a Sunday night all by myself. You've got to help. Best thing to do is for you to go to The Sound and hit some people up for cash. You've got to get forty marks. If I do a customer for another forty or fifty marks, then we'll still have some left over for tomorrow morning. Can you do it?"

I said, "Of course I can. You know I've got a talent for it." We agreed to meet again in two hours at the latest. I'd done a lot of mooching in my days at The Sound. Often just for fun, and it had always worked. But not this time. Not at all. I was in a hurry, but for the art of mooching you need time. You have to watch the guys closely and watch them for a while before you approach them. You have to adapt yourself to their ways of communicating, maybe talk to them for a while, and be cool. You had to enjoy it.

I started going into withdrawal and didn't have my usual touch. After a half-an-hour I only had around seven marks. I thought, You'll never make it. I thought of Detlef, who was at the station now, where there were probably just a bunch of families getting back from a Sunday afternoon at grandma and grandpa's. He was also going into withdrawal. He wouldn't attract any customers while he was in that state anyway. I started to panic.

Without a definite plan in mind, I walked out onto the street. I was still hoping that the pickings might be easier out in front of the club. A flashy Mercedes stopped in front of the entrance. There were often big, fancy cars pulling up or driving slowly past because The Sound was the one place where you were guaranteed to find pretty young boys and girls. There were some girls who didn't even have enough money for the cover charge because their allowance was all gone. They got inside those big fancy cars just for the price of admission and a couple of Cokes.

The guy in the Mercedes waved me over. I recognized him. He was often in front of The Sound, and he'd hit on me before. Did I want to earn a hundred? I'd asked him once before what he wanted for that, and he said, "Nothing really." I'd laughed at him and walked away.

I don't know exactly what I was thinking. Probably not much. Maybe I just thought I'd go over and find out what he really wanted. Maybe get a few singles off of him. In any case, he was waving like wild, and suddenly I was standing next to the car. He said, "Why don't you get in?" He said he couldn't stay there much longer. I got in.

I knew exactly what was going on. That this was not about mooching anymore.

Johns weren't alien beings to me anymore. From my time at Zoo station, and after hearing all the stories that the guys told over there, I knew how this scene would unfold. I also knew that it wasn't the customer but the hooker who set the price and conditions. I tried to be cool about it. I wasn't trembling, but I kept gasping for air when I was talking and had trouble finishing my sentences in the same tone that I started them. "So, what's up?" I said.

He said: "Not too much. A hundred marks. Do we have a deal?"

"Well, sex or something like that is out of the question for me."

He asked why, and I was so flustered that nothing came out of my mouth—well, nothing at first, and then the truth: "Listen. I have a boyfriend. And he's the only one I've ever slept with. And I want to keep it that way."

He said, "That's fine with me. Then give me a blow job."

I said, "No way; I won't do that either. I'll puke."

Then I was back to being cool.

He didn't let himself get rattled at all. He said, "Okay, a hand job then."

I said, "Sure, no problem . . . for a hundred." I wasn't registering anything right then. Later I realized that this guy must've been really into me. A hundred marks for a hand job—and at the Kurfürstenstrasse, where the cheap baby hookers hung out? That was unheard of. He must have gotten off on my fear, which I couldn't really hide. He knew that I wasn't pretending, the way I sat there, squeezed against the door, my right hand on the door handle.

As he was driving away, I was scared out of my mind. I thought, I'm sure he wants more; he will force me to give him more—a hundred marks' worth. Or maybe he won't pay at all. He stopped at a nearby park. I'd walked through this park a thousand times before, but it was pretty sketchy, with condoms and tissues everywhere.

I was really shaking and starting to feel a little sick. But the guy stayed very calm. And that's when I got up my courage and said what I was supposed to say, according to the old rules: "First the money." He gave me a hundred-mark note. I was still scared. I'd heard enough stories about customers who took the money back by force, after it was all over. But I knew what I had to do. The boys in our clique had lately exchanged a lot of stories about their experiences with customers because there wasn't much else to talk about.

I waited for the moment when he was undoing his pants and opening his fly to slip the money into my boot. I knew he wouldn't be paying attention to me then. All of a sudden, he was ready. I was still sitting on the farthest corner of my seat, trying not to move. Without looking at him I groped my way over with my left hand. My arm wasn't long enough, so I did have to slouch over toward him a bit. And I ended up having to glance over once before I had his thing in my hand.

I felt so nauseous I wanted to throw up. It was also freezing. I looked through the windshield and tried to concentrate on something else—on the headlights shining through the bushes, or the one neon advertisement that was lit up and that I could still see. It didn't take very long.

The guy took out his wallet again. He held it so I could see what was in it. There were a bunch of five hundred- and one hundred-mark notes. I guess he wanted to either impress me or bait me for the next time. He gave me another twenty, as a tip.

Once I was out of the car I managed to calm myself down, and took stock of the situation: So that was your second man, I thought to myself. You're fourteen years old. Barely four weeks ago you lost your virginity. And now you're walking the streets as a hooker.

But that being said, I stopped worrying about the john, and what I'd just done. I actually felt pretty good. I mean, I had 120 marks in my boot. I'd never had so much money all at once. I wasn't thinking about Detlef and what he would say. I was already in major withdrawal and was crazy for a fix. I couldn't think of anything except shooting up. I was lucky. I found our regular dealer right away. When he saw the money, he asked, "Hey, where'd you get that? Did you go whoring?"

"Shut the fuck up," I told him. "Me and whoring? Before I'd do that, I'd stop using. Nope, my dad happened to remember that he's got a daughter. He gave me some spending money."

For eighty marks I bought two little packets, each containing a quarter. It used to be that a quarter gram was enough for three of us. But these days, Detlef and I could manage on that amount.

I went to the public bathrooms at the Kurfürstenstrasse and shot up. The dope was first-class. The rest of it (along with the leftover forty marks) I stuffed into the plastic cover of my student bus pass.

Doing the job and scoring dope had only taken about fifteen minutes. I'd left the apartment about a half an hour before that, so I was sure that Detlef would still be at the station. I took the subway to the Zoo, and sure enough, there was Detlef. A little pile of misery. It was just like I thought: He hadn't been able to get a customer—not on a Sunday evening, and definitely not while looking so strung out. I went over and said to him, "Come with me, I've got some."

He didn't ask from where. He didn't say anything at all. He just wanted to get to the apartment, fast. We went straight into the bathroom. I got out my student bus pass. He opened one of the little packets and emptied the stuff onto a spoon. As he was cooking it up, he stared at the plastic cover of my bus pass, whichstill held a quarter and two twenty-mark notes. Then he asked the question: "Where'd you get the money?"

I said, "Mooching didn't work. It was impossible. There was a guy there with tons of cash, so I gave him a hand job. Seriously, just a hand job. What else could I have done? I did it for you."

Even before I'd finished Detlef started freaking out. He looked like he was going to go insane. He screamed, "You're lying! Nobody pays a hundred for a hand job. You're lying to me. And anyway, what do you mean by 'only a hand job'?"

That was it—he didn't have any strength left. He was in full-blown withdrawal. His whole body trembled, his shirt was wet with sweat, and his legs were cramping up.

He tied off his arm while I sat on the rim of the bathtub, sobbing. I thought that Detlef was entitled to freak out. I waited for his shot to take effect, still crying. I was sure that once he'd recovered himself, he'd punch me in the face. I wouldn't have even tried to defend myself.

Detlef pulled out the syringe and said nothing. He left the bathroom and I followed. Finally he said, "I'll take you to the bus." I wrapped some of the second quarter for him and gave it to him. He stuck it in his jeans without a word. We walked to the bus stop. Detlef still didn't say anything. I wanted him to yell at me, to hit me, to do anything or make any kind of sound. I said, "Hey, c'mon, say something." But from him there was nothing: silence.

When the bus arrived at the bus stop, I didn't get on. After it drove away again, I said, "What I told you was the honest-to-God truth. I just gave him a hand job, and it wasn't so bad. You have to believe me. Or don't you trust me anymore?"

Detlef said, "Okay, I believe you."

I added, "You know, I really only did it for you."

Detlef's voice went up a notch. "Stop kidding yourself. You did it for yourself. You had the itch, and you found a way to scratch it. Congratulations. You would've done it even if I hadn't been in the picture. Wake up and smell the coffee—you're a junkie now. You're totally addicted. At this point, anything you do, you do for yourself."

I said, "Okay, you're right. But listen: This is the way we have to handle it from now on. You can't do it all by yourself anymore. We need too much dope. And I don't want you to be the only one who works the street. From now on, we'll do it the other way around. I can probably make a pile of cash, especially at first. And I can do it without having real sex. I promise you that I won't be fucking any of the customers."

Detlef didn't say anything. He put his arm around my shoulder. It had started to rain, and I didn't know if the drops running down his face came from the rain or were tears. Another bus came by. I said, "There doesn't seem to be any way out of this mess. Do you remember when we were still just taking pills and smoking pot? We were free. We were totally independent. We didn't need anybody or anything. That's how we felt. I guess things have changed."

Another three or four buses passed while we just talked. It was all sad stuff. I cried and Detlef held me. Finally he said, "It's going to get better. Someday soon we'll just quit. We'll be able to do it together. I'll get us some methadone. First thing tomorrow morning, I'll ask someone about methadone. We'll be together when we quit."

Another bus came and Detlef pushed me up the steps.

At home I did what I did every evening, as if I was on auto-pilot. I went into the kitchen and got myself a yogurt out of the fridge. I only took the yogurt into my room when I went to bed, so that it wouldn't look weird that I was also taking a spoon. I needed that in the morning to cook up my dope. Then I also got a glass of water out of the bathroom. I could use that to clean the syringe the next morning.

When I woke up, everything was the same as ever. My mom woke me at a quarter to seven. I stayed in bed and pretended I didn't hear her. But she popped in every five minutes or so until I finally said, "Fine, yes, I'm up, I'm up!" She came back in and nagged me, and I counted the minutes till quarter after seven. That's when she needed to leave the house for work if she didn't want to miss her subway. (And she never missed her subway.) Actually, I should have left the house at a quarter after seven, too, if I wanted to get to school on time.

When I finally heard the front door slam shut, I sprang into action almost automatically. I fished the foil packet out of my jeans (which lay in a heap at the foot of the bed) and then grabbed the plastic bag that lay beside them. Inside the plastic bag was my makeup, a pack of Roth-Händle cigarettes, a small bottle of lemon juice, and a syringe wrapped up in toilet paper. The syringe was almost always clogged, and this time was no different: The damn cigarette tobacco had gotten loose in the bag and plugged up the syringe. I cleaned the needle in the water glass, put the dope on the yogurt spoon, dribbled some lemon juice on it, cooked it up, tied off my arm, and so on. For me, all of this was as natural as a morning cigarette is to other people. After that first shot, I usually fell asleep again and didn't get to school until the second or third class of the day. I was always late when I shot up at home.

Sometimes my mom was able to drag me out of bed in time to take me to the subway with her. Then I had to shoot up in the public bathrooms at the Moritz Square subway station. That was pretty unpleasant since the bathrooms there were especially dark and disgusting. The walls had all these little peepholes in them, and on the other side of the wall, there were all these bums and other perverts crouched down, hoping to catch a glimpse of some girl peeing. They got off on it. I was always afraid that they'd call the cops on me—just out of spite because all I ever did was shoot up.

I almost always brought the syringe to school with me, too. Just in case. In case someday we had to stay longer for some reason—like maybe for some last-minute event in the auditorium—or if I wasn't able to go home right after school. Occasionally I had to shoot up in the school bathrooms, but the doors to the stalls were all broken. My girlfriend Renate had to hold the door shut for me while I shot up. Renate knew what was going on with me. Most of the kids in my class knew, I think. But they weren't bothered by it. In Gropiusstadt, it wasn't a big deal if you got hooked on drugs. Not anymore.

During the classes that I still attended, I daydreamed my time away, staring into space. Sometimes I was even able to fall into a deep sleep, with my head on the desk. If I'd had a lot of dope in the morning, I could barely get a few words out. The teachers must've noticed what was going on with me. But only one of them addressed the topic of narcotics with me and asked me about my problems. The others just treated me like a lazy, narcoleptic student and failed me. We had so many teachers—and they had so many students—that most of them were happy just to know our names. There was hardly any personal interaction. They didn't even bring up the fact that I never did homework anymore. And the only time they took out their grading ledger was when during exams all I'd write was, "Can't do it." (After that, I'd hand in the blank exam and then just sit there doodling.) I think most of the teachers weren't any more interested in school than I was. Like me, they'd become totally resigned. Their only goal was to just get through each class period without provoking a riot.

After that first night with the guy in the car, everything went back to normal. At least for a while.

Every day I bugged Detlef to let me help him bring in some more cash. I wanted to have access to more than just the few odd marks I could scramble together by "borrowing." Detlef was jealous, and it showed. But he'd realized a while ago that we couldn't keep going on that way and suggested that we do it together, as a team.

He'd gotten to know the regular Zoo Station clients pretty well and knew that there were a few bisexuals and even some homosexual guys who would want to try it with a girl for a change, as long as a guy was there also, just in case. Detlef said he'd pick out some customers who wouldn't need to touch me and who definitely wouldn't want to have sex with me. In other words, customers who had a kink—who wanted something done to them. Those were the ones Detlef liked best, anyway. He thought we could make about a hundred marks a pop working together.

The first customer that Detlef settled on for us was this guy Max—who we called Stutter Max. He was a regular customer of Detlef's, and I'd gotten to know him pretty well, too. Detlef said that all he wanted to do was have someone whip him. I just had to take my top off. That was fine with me. I even thought the whipping was a good idea because it would give me a chance to release some of the anger that I felt in general for Detlef's customers. Stutter Max was totally into the idea of me coming along when Detlef suggested it. Of course, it would cost him twice as much. We made a date for Monday at 3 p.m. at the Zoo.

I was late, as always, and Stutter Max was already there. Detlef wasn't, but that was no surprise. Like all junkies, he was totally unreliable. I had a suspicion that he'd gone off with another customer before our appointment at the Zoo, and that turned out to be exactly what had happened. This other guy apparently paid well, and so he had to spend some extra time with him. Stutter Max and I waited for almost half an hour, but Detlef still didn't show up. I was terrified. But Stutter Max was even more scared than I was, and it showed. He explained that for more than ten years he hadn't done anything with a girl. He could barely get a word out, but that didn't keep him from trying. He normally stuttered pretty badly, but now he was almost unintelligible.

I couldn't stand going over all this right there at the station. Somehow I had to put an end to it. And anyway, I was out of dope and worried about going into withdrawal before this thing with Stutter Max was over. The more nervous he got, the more self-confident I became. I realized that I had a better handle on the situation than he did. Finally I just said to him flatly, "Let's get out of here. Detlef stood us up. You'll be happy with just me alone. But the price is still the same: a 150 marks."

He stuttered out a yes. His willpower was just gone. I hooked my arm through his and actually had to lead him away.

I'd heard all about Stutter Max's sad story from Detlef. He was originally from Hamburg, and now he was in his late thirties and employed as an unskilled laborer. His mom was a prostitute, and he'd been bullied and beaten up a lot as a kid. By his mom and her pimps, and then later on in all the various foster homes in which he'd been placed. They battered him so badly that he developed a stutter, and now he also needed to be beaten to be able to satisfy himself sexually.

We went to his apartment. I asked for the money up front, even though he was a regular, so you didn't really have to take those precautions. He gave me the 150 marks, just like he'd said he would, and it made me feel almost proud—proud of the fact that I was worth that much money to him.

I took my T-shirt off, and he gave me the whip. It was like in a movie. I was someone else, not myself. At first I didn't hit him very hard. But he whined and whimpered and begged for more. So at a certain point I just let it rip. He screamed, "Mommy!" and God only knows what else. I didn't listen. I tried not to even look. But I saw how the welts swelled up more and more on his body, and then the skin even split open in some spots. It was so, so gross—and it lasted for almost an hour.

When he finally came, I threw on my T-shirt and ran. I ran out of the apartment door and down the stairs and just barely made it. Once in front of the house, I couldn't control my damn stomach any longer and puked. It was all over after I'd vomited. I'd stopped crying and feeling sorry for myself. It had become crystal clear to me that I was the one who had gotten myself into this situation— that I'd fucked up, and now I was stuck in this shit. I went to the station. Detlef was there. I didn't say much. Just that I'd done the job with Stutter Max by myself. I showed him the 150 marks. He fished a hundred-mark note out of his jeans, too—the compensation from his customer. We walked arm in arm to the corner where we were usually able to score first-class stuff from our regular dealer. It was turning into a pretty good day.

From that point on, I usually earned the cash for my dope on my own. I was a big hit at the Zoo with almost all the customers, and could pick and choose the guys I went with, and also decide on the terms of the agreement. Everyone stayed away from the foreigners because we thought they were pretty sketchy and would cheat you if you weren't paying attention. A lot of the time, they would only pay twenty or thirty marks, but they still wanted to have actual intercourse, and without condoms, too. Like all of the other girls at the station, I stayed away from the foreigners, as a general rule.

Fucking the customers was still out of the question for me. That was the thing that I hung onto—that I reserved for Detlef. I stuck to hand jobs and blow jobs. It didn't make me feel too upset, as long as they didn't do anything to me. Under no circumstances were they allowed to put their hands on me. If they did, I would freak out on them.

I always tried to negotiate the conditions right there at the station. Guys who pissed me off, right off the bat, didn't even get a chance to negotiate. Preserving my last bit of pride, however, cost me a lot of time. It often took all afternoon to find a customer who'd agree to all my conditions. And we hardly ever had as much money again as we did on that day when I was with Stutter Max for the first time.

Max became the first regular customer for Detlef and me as a team. Sometimes we both went to see him, and other times it was just one of us. Max was actually a pretty okay guy. He loved both of us. Of course, he couldn't keep on paying 150 marks on his worker's wages. But forty marks—enough for one shot—was an amount that he could always scrape together. Once he even smashed his piggy bank, fished some change out of a bowl, and counted out exactly forty marks for me. When I was in a hurry, I could stop by at his place and get twenty marks on loan. I told him that I'd be back the next day at a certain time and do it to him for twenty. If he still had a twenty, he was game.

150

Max was always game, always expecting us. He always kept some of my favorite drink, a kind of peach juice, on hand for me. And for Detlef he maintained a steady supply of tapioca pudding. Max made the pudding himself. In addition to that, he always prepared a selection of yogurt and chocolates for me because he knew that I liked to eat those after a job. The whippings had become totally routine, and afterward I'd hang out for a while, just eating, drinking, and talking with Max.

He was getting skinnier and skinnier. He really spent his every last cent on us, to the point where he couldn't buy himself enough to eat anymore. He'd gotten so used to us and was so happy that he hardly stuttered at all when we were with him. He bought himself a couple of newspapers first thing every morning, just to check if there was another notice about someone having died from heroin. Once, when I stopped by his place to borrow another twenty from him, he was stuttering like crazy and pale as a ghost. The newspapers had reported that someone named Detlef W. had become the umpteenth victim of heroin that year. He pretty much cried with joy when I told him that I'd just seen my Detlef, and he was very much alive. He blubbered at me (not for the first time) that Detlef and I should quit heroin, or we'd follow all the other kids to the grave. But I told him, cold as ice, that if we quit heroin, then we wouldn't have any reason to come and see him anymore. After that he let it drop.

Detlef and I had a funny relationship with Max. We hated all the johns, without exception, so we also hated Max. But if we really thought about it, we couldn't deny that, all in all, he was an okay guy. Our response to him probably did have a lot to do with the fact that he was always good for forty marks. But then again, I'm also positive that we really did feel sorry for him. He was using us for his own sexual satisfaction, but he was also worse off than we were. He was so lonely. We were the only people with whom he had any kind of relationship. But we didn't care enough to really think that deeply about him at the time. It wasn't going to be the only time that we ruined one of our customers.

Sometimes we'd get comfortable watching TV in Max's apartment and then wind up staying the night. He let us use his bed and slept on the floor himself. One night we got a little wild. Max put on some crazy music that he liked, and pulled on a long wig and a ridiculous fur coat. Then he danced like a crazy person, which made us all laugh hysterically. But then, out of nowhere, he tripped, fell, and hit his head on his sewing machine. For a few minutes, he was out cold. We were scared to death and called a doctor. It turned out that Max had a concussion and had to stay in bed for two weeks.

Shortly after that, he was fired from his job. He was a wreck—completely devastated and hopeless. Without his having ever tried dope, it had still ruined him. We had ruined him. He begged us to visit him at least sometimes, just as friends. But friendly visits like that just weren't possible. Not for us.

At this point, Detlef was incapable of caring about anyone else. That was the first thing. But also, he was busy all day trying to scrape together enough cash for his next fix and didn't really have any time for that sort of sentimental stuff. Detlef laid this out for Max in pretty stark terms after Max promised to give us plenty of cash as soon as he had some again. "A junkie's like a businessman," Detlef said. "Every day he has to take care of his bottom line so that he doesn't end up in the red. He just can't afford to extend credit out of friendship or sympathy."

Shortly after I started working the street, I had a nice little reunion. It happened at the station. I was waiting for some customers, and suddenly Babsi was right next to me. Babsi, my friend—and that same little girl who had hit me up for some acid just a few months earlier. Babsi, just twelve years old back then and already on the run because of some trouble back in school. The same girl who'd tried a few quick snorts of H before she was picked up and taken back to her grandparents' place.

We looked at each other, recognized immediately what was up, fell into each other's arms, and kissed. She was overjoyed and so was I. Babsi had gotten crazy skinny. No boobs and no butt. But she almost looked more beautiful. Her shoulder-length, blond hair was healthy and sleek, and her clothes were chic and polished. I knew from first glance that she was also an addict. I didn't even have to look into her pin-size pupils. But I could still believe that, if you didn't know what heroin did to people, you would've never in a million years guessed that this pretty girl was already an addict, already a junkie.

Babsi was almost unbelievably calm. She wasn't at all like the other junkies—hectic people like me, who chased after money and dope all day. And right away, she told me that I didn't need to do a customer right then, that she'd buy me a shot and something to eat.

We went upstairs to the Zoo Station café. We didn't bother talking about how we were both doped up all the time or what our lives were like now, as prostitutes. But at the same time, I was really curious about how Babsi got so much cash and dope—and she wouldn't tell me. She only said that ever since she'd been brought home again she'd been under a strict watch. She had to be home before eight every night and also go to school regularly. Her grandmother kept an eagle eye on her.

I finally asked her about her money more directly, and she said, "Yeah, I have a regular customer. He's kind of old but very cool. I take the taxi to him in the afternoons. He pays me in dope, not cash. I get three quarters from him each day. He's got other girls, too, and they also get their dope directly from him. But for the moment he only likes me. I'm done in an hour. No sex, of course. Only stripping and talking. I let him take pictures of me, we talk, and, well, blow jobs. But sex is out of the question for me."

The name of her regular was Heinz. He owned a stationery store. I'd heard of him before. He was cool because he paid directly with H, so that you could save yourself the trouble of running around, finding a dealer, and buying the dope. I was jealous of Babsi, who was home by eight at the latest, always got a good night's sleep, and lived without all this stressful, hectic running around.

Babsi had everything. Even a stash of syringes. Although syringes were actually supposed to be thrown away after one use, back then they were so hard to get that you had to hold onto them. Mine had become so dull that I had to constantly sharpen it on the rough surface of a matchbox so that it was still possible to slam the thing into my vein. Babsi had plenty of syringes. Without a second thought she promised me three of them.

Then a few days later, I ran into Stella—Babsi's girlfriend and old couch-surfing buddy. She'd started using H even before Babsi did. Hugs, kisses, and another round of real happiness. Stella was also hooked, of course. But she wasn't doing as well as Babsi. Her mom had opened a bar together with her Italian boyfriend and started drinking. Stella had always swiped cash from the bar for her dope. Then when she stole fifty marks directly out of her mom's boyfriend's wallet, it all came out. She couldn't go home anymore and had started just bumming around the city again.

In the station café again, it didn't take long before we started talking about customers. Stella first of all enlightened me about Babsi. She was already scraping the dregs and was in a pretty fucked-up situation. This guy Heinz turned out to be a real scumbag. A filthy, mean, old, fat, sweaty guy, whom she was definitely having sex with. Stella said, "That would be the absolute worst for me. To let someone like that actually fuck you. To let any customer fuck you. I mean, at that point you've got no standards: You'll go away with anyone. A blow job here and there—well, okay. But sex for pay is the final frontier—that's when you know you're at the end of the line."

I was really shocked to hear how bad things had gotten with Babsi. At the time, I didn't really think to ask why Stella knew all these details and why she was telling me. But later on, Babsi told me that Heinz used to be Stella's regular. That's why Stella knew exactly what he demanded in return for those three quarters. I'd eventually learn that for myself, too, later on.

Stella then told me how disgusting she thought it was to be a hooker at Zoo Station: "That's only for the real fuckups. I'd never want to deal with those assholes over there."

Stella worked the Kurfürstenstrasse, where cars passed by slowly and picked up child prostitutes. Most of the girls who waited around there were thirteen- and fourteen-year-olds, all hooked on heroin. I had an overwhelming fear of getting picked up via car because then you couldn't really check out beforehand who your client was. "Now that's where things are really bad. That's where the girls do it for twenty marks. Two customers for one shot? No way."

We kept at each other for almost an hour, arguing about whether it was worse to be a child prostitute at Zoo Station or on Kurfürstenstrasse. In the meantime, we did at least agree that if Babsi was really fucking that filthy old man, then she was in a very bad way.

So our reunion began with a fight over our honor as hookers. This was a fight that Babsi, Stella, and I continued to have almost every day over the next few months. The central question was always which one of us had it the worst. And none of us could ever admit—either to ourselves or the others—how low we were sitting on the food chain. When only two of us were together, we always talked shit about the third.

The best thing to do, of course, would be to find a way to get by without having to deal with the customers at all. On the first day of our reunion, Stella and I convinced ourselves that we could do just that. We'd get the cash we needed by begging, borrowing, and stealing. Stella had a whole arsenal of tricks up her sleeve.

We went straight to the Department Store of the West[26] to try out her new trick. It involved the women's restroom. To pull this off, you had to wait until a couple of old ladies disappeared into the stalls. After they went in, they'd usually hang their handbags on the inside door handles. Then, once they'd peeled themselves out of their corsets and pantyhose and plopped down onto the toilet seat, you'd yank down the outside door handles. The handbags would drop down and then you could easily pull them out through the gap beneath the door. The old ladies wouldn't dare come out with their pants down, so to speak. And by the time they'd reassembled all their clothes and put everything back on, you'd be long gone.

So, there we were, hanging out in the ladies' room at the department store. But every time Stella whispered, "Now!" I got scared. It wasn't something that she wanted to do on her own. And besides, you really needed four hands for this job. So the great ladies' bathroom robbery was off. I was pretty anxious about stealing from the outset, and the longer it dragged on, the worse my nerves got.

After a few more misadventures in petty larceny (with supplemental small-time loans), Stella and I decided to go back to working the street, but this time around we were going to be a team. I insisted that we work Zoo Station—but we'd only go with

---

26 The Kaufhaus des Westens, or Department Store of the West. At the time, it was the largest department store on the European continent.

a customer if he agreed to take on both of us. That had several advantages: Although we'd never admit it, this arrangement provided us with a sense of security because we'd be able to see exactly how far the other was willing to go—and stop ourselves short accordingly. We'd always be at the same level. But we also felt safer. With two of us involved, it was harder to rip us off, and we could defend ourselves better if a customer didn't want to stick to the agreement. And it was quicker with two. One of us kept the guy busy up top, the other down below, and the whole thing was over and done much faster.

On the other hand, it was way harder to find customers who could afford to pay for two girls. And there were also all the experienced johns who were simply afraid to deal with two junkie brides at once because it was also easier for us to rip off a customer if we were double-teaming him. While one of us kept him busy, the other could get at his wallet. Stella was the one who liked the arrangement the best—whether it was with Babsi or me. She had more trouble attracting customers by herself because she didn't look as young as we did anymore.

It was the easiest for Babsi. Even when she still had Heinz, she earned some money on the side just to be able to treat us to dope. She never put makeup on her innocent baby face. Without a butt or boobs, and just barely thirteen, she was just the kind of "baby prostitute" the customers were looking for. Incredibly (to us), she once made two hundred marks in just a single hour, with five different customers.

Babsi and Stella blended right into our social group, which of course still included Detlef, Axel, and Bernd. So now we were three girls and three boys. When we went out together, I went arm-in-arm with Detlef, and the other two boys each grabbed one of the girls. There was nothing going on between them. We just all really liked each other. Each of us could still talk about his or her life and problems with any of the others—despite the many fights we had over little things, just like any other group of heroin friends. During this phase of our lives, heroin simultaneously caused all our problems but also kept us all together. I'm not sure that this sort of friendship, the kind we had in our little group, could exist among kids who weren't addicted to drugs. And in all honesty, that kind of desperate closeness seemed like it impressed a lot of other young people. People looked up to us.

My relationship with Detlef started to get rocky when the two girls joined our group. We still loved each other, but we got into a lot more fights. Detlef was often irritable, so I spent a lot of time with Babsi and Stella, and he didn't really like that. But what really pissed him off was the fact that he didn't have any control over which customers I was going with anymore. I was now picking them on my own, or together with Stella or Babsi. Detlef started to accuse me of having sex with the customers. He was really jealous.

I now had a more relaxed view of my relationship with Detlef. I loved him, of course, and would always love him. On the other hand, I wasn't dependent on him anymore. I didn't need his dope or his protection. Actually, our relationship had become similar to a modern marriage—with no one holding power over the other. We were equals. We girls got used to treating each other to dope when one of us had a little extra, and the guys did the same thing.

But our friendships were still entirely dependent on heroin, when it really came down to it. We all became more and more aggressive from one week to the next. The dope and our frantic lifestyle, the daily struggle for money and H, the constant stress at home, the cover-ups and the lies that we used to fool our parents—it all wreaked havoc on our nerves. It was also getting harder and harder to manage all the little grudges that we'd developed toward one another over time.

I got along best with Babsi, who was still the calmest one of us. We worked together a lot. We bought ourselves the same tight black skirts, with long slits in them. Underneath we wore black nylon stockings with black lace garters. That really turned the customers on.

Shortly before Christmas 1976, my dad went on vacation, and he let Babsi and me sleep in his apartment, along with my little sister. On the first night there, we got into a huge fight. Babsi and I were so nasty to each other that my sister, who was only a year younger than me, started to cry. We really had that street talk down, and it came out in a fight. And my sister of course had no clue about our double lives.

The next morning, Babsi and I were best friends again. It was always the same: After we'd had some sleep and started to come down again, we were usually in a pretty peaceful mood. Babsi and I made a deal to postpone shooting up that morning for as long as possible. We'd tried this out a few times already. It had become a kind of sport, to wait until you couldn't wait any longer to shoot up. However, we couldn't talk about anything else except the awesome high we were about to get, any time we wanted to, with this great, first-class dope. We were like kids on Christmas right before our parents let us open our presents.

My sister knew that something was up. It didn't take her long to figure out that we had some kind of drug. But she didn't have any idea that we were addicted. She thought we were just experimenting. She sincerely promised not to tell my dad or mom, and to keep her mouth shut if someone from Babsi's family came by unexpectedly. Babsi's family was very strict with her, and neither her grandparents nor her parents had the slightest inkling that she was a heroin junkie and a hooker to boot.

Babsi reached into her purse and took out her strawberry-flavored powder called Quarkfein. She had a real addiction to this stuff, which is a kind of powdered flavoring you can mix into dairy products like cottage cheese. She pretty much lived on cottage cheese with Quarkfein. My diet wasn't much more varied than that: Besides cottage cheese, I also ate yogurt and pudding and Viennese rings, a pastry you could get in the Kurfürstendamm subway station. By that point my stomach would reject pretty much anything else.

So Babsi was mixing up her strawberry-flavored cottage cheese in the kitchen, which was like a religious ritual for her. Meanwhile, my sister and I sat and watched her with appropriate reverence, all of us in happy anticipation of our huge, pink, cottage cheese breakfast. But obviously we weren't going to be able to eat until after Babsi and I had shot up.

When Babsi had whipped the cottage cheese into a really creamy confection, we couldn't stand it anymore. We told my sister that she should go ahead and set the table, and then we went and locked ourselves into the bathroom. We hadn't been there for more than two seconds when the drama started up between us because we were starting to go into withdrawal.

We only had one useable syringe left, and I said that I wanted to shoot up first, just real quick. But Babsi already had an edge on. "Why do you always get to go first? Today I should start. After all, I was the one who got the dope."

That really rubbed me the wrong way. I couldn't stand it when she tried to gain an advantage like that. There were a lot of times when she'd have more dope than the rest of us, and she would always get like this. I said, "Jesus, don't freak out. It just takes you forever!" It was true. This girl needed like half an hour before she was done. She hardly had any veins left. And when she'd get the needle in and couldn't draw any blood, she'd freak out. She'd slam the needle into her skin again and again, getting more frantic by the minute. The only thing that she could hope for then, that would put a stop to her frenzy, was a lucky hit.

It still went pretty smoothly for me back then. If Detlef didn't do the shot for me—he was the only one I'd let near my veins— then I'd always aim for a spot in the crook of my left arm. That worked well until the day I got a thrombosis there, which ruined that vein for me. But later on, I also got to the point where I didn't know where to stick the needle anymore.

I got my way though—for that morning anyway. Babsi was totally pissed. I got the syringe, immediately hit a vein, and was done in a little over two minutes. It was a really fucking awesome shot. My blood was rushing like a river through my body. I got really hot. I went to the sink, let water run over my face, and then happily, absentmindedly fussed with my hair and clothes.

Babsi sat on the rim of the bathtub, plunging the thing into her arm again and again, and freaking out. "Shit!" she screamed. "Why's there's no air in this dump? Open that damn window!"

I said, "You'll just have to get used to it. Get off my case, will you?" I didn't care at all about what was going on with her. I'd had my shot and everything was okay.

Babsi was squirting blood everywhere, but she wasn't hitting any veins. She was seriously freaking out now. She screamed, "There's no light in this fucking bathroom! Get me some light. Get that lamp from the kid's room."

I was too lazy to go out and get the lamp for Babsi. But eventually, after she kept going on about it, yelling and generally making a racket, I got worried that my sister would notice and went out to grab the stupid lamp. Then, finally, Babsi did it. She immediately calmed down. She cleaned the syringe and wiped the blood out of the bathtub and off the floor. She didn't say another word.

We went into the kitchen, and by that point, I was really looking forward to the Quarkfein. But Babsi grabbed the bowl, wrapped one arm tightly around it, and started to shovel it in. She actually forced down the entire bowlful of cottage cheese. The only time she even looked up was to say, "You know why."

We'd both really looked forward to those days together in my dad's apartment, and the first morning had started with the fight of the century. And all of it over nothing. But we were heroin addicts, after all. And all heroin addicts turned out like this sooner or later. Dope destroys relationships among people—even with us. Despite how young we were, and how close we'd been. Despite the fact that, even then, I still believed that no one could ever be as close as we had been.

My fights with Detlef got nastier also. Both of us had physically deteriorated a lot already. I was about 5'5", but I was down to under a hundred pounds, and Detlef, who was 5'9", was down to 119 pounds. We felt sick all the time, and then everything got on our nerves, and we were deliberately vicious to one another. When we insulted each other, we always went for the jugular and tried to say whatever would hit the other person at the deepest level. Since we were both so ashamed of what we did with our bodies (and even though we both pretended that hooking was just a part-time thing), prostitution was usually the topic that we focused on.

Detlef would say something like, "Do you really think I want to sleep with someone who sleeps with such nasty scumbags all the time?" And then I'd respond with something like, "I'm not the one who gets buttfucked." And so on.

Most of the time, one or both of us would end up crying. And when one of us was going into withdrawal, then the other could really tear him or her down—until there was almost nothing left. It didn't make things any better that at some point we'd inevitably huddle together, clinging to one another like two little kids. Things had gotten so bad, between us girls and now also between Detlef and me, that we could see our own miserable, shitty selves reflected in the other. Each one of us hated the rotten mess he or she had become, and therefore attacked that same rotten mess in everyone else. It was all part of a feeble attempt to prove that we weren't as bad off yet as everybody else.

This aggressiveness would of course also get vented on strangers. I already lost my mind whenever I walked onto a subway platform. They were packed full of old ladies holding onto their shopping bags. To start things off, I'd usually get into a nonsmoking car with a lit cigarette. When the old ladies started muttering under their breath, I told them to switch to another compartment if they didn't like it in this one. I especially enjoyed stealing a seat right out from under one of their noses. The stunts that I pulled would sometimes set off pandemonium in the entire train compartment, and occasionally wound up with me being removed from the train and forced to get some "fresh air." The way I behaved even got on my own nerves. It also got on my nerves when Babsi and Stella behaved like that. I didn't want to have anything to do with those drab, tedious old people. I didn't even want to be fighting with them. But I couldn't help myself and kept doing it.

I didn't give a shit what strangers thought of me. When I got the itch, when it was bad and I itched all over, then I scratched the itch—no matter where I was at that moment. It didn't matter whether it was under tight clothes or even beneath my makeup: I got at it. It didn't bother me to take my boots off in the subway or lift my skirt up to my belly button if I needed to scratch myself. The only people whose opinion mattered were the people in our clique.

There comes a time when junkies don't care about anything anymore. That's when they start to turn solitary. I knew a few of the old junkies who'd been shooting up for five years or longer and had somehow survived. We had a mixed relationship with the old veterans. To us, these loner types were almost celebrities—but not in a good way. Everybody knew them though, and it made an impression on other people when you could tell them that you knew one of those guys. On the other hand, I despised them because they were all totally wrecked, ruined, fucked up. Above all, all of us kids were absolutely terrified of them because they didn't have any morals, conscience, or compassion left. They would hit their best friend over the head with a rock if he was standing in the way of a fix. The most infamous one of them all was Rip-Off Man. Everybody called him that because he was the absolute worst and was always on the hunt. When the dealers saw him coming, they scattered quicker than during a police raid. When he got hold of a small-time dealer, he took everything— all of his dope. Nobody dared put up a fight. Least of all some young junkie.

I'd once seen Rip-Off Man in full action. I'd just locked myself into a public toilet stall and was about to shoot up when somebody leaped over the dividing wall and landed right on top of me. It was him. I knew from the stories the others told that this was his M O: He'd wait in a bathroom until a girl with H came in, and then he'd pounce. And I knew how brutal he could be. So without any resistance, I gave him my syringe and my dope. He walked right out of the stall and stopped in front of the mirror. He wasn't afraid of anything or anybody anymore. He slammed the shot right into his neck. He didn't have a single spot left on his body that he could shoot into. He bled like a stuck pig. I thought maybe he'd hit the main artery. But he wouldn't have cared if he did. He just said, "Thanks a lot," and left.

I was sure that I'd never get to that point at least. In order to survive as long as Rip-Off Man had, you had to be a really tough, ruthless character. And I just wasn't. I couldn't even get myself to swipe some old ladies' handbags in the department store bathroom.

The world of our clique revolved more and more around our shared profession. The boys had the same problems that the girls had. We still had mutual interests and could help each other out by exchanging information. We girls swapped stories about our experiences with customers. The field of customers that we had contact with was very limited. So when a customer was new to me, it was still likely that Stella or Babsi had already been with him. And then it was to my advantage to know what their experiences had been like.

There were recommended customers, less recommended customers, and then there were the problem clients. We never bothered with personal feelings. We also didn't care about his job or if he was married, etcetera. We never talked about the personal nonsense the customers unloaded on us. All we cared about was what they were able to pay.

A customer was considered advantageous if he was terrified of STDs and wouldn't do anything without a condom. Unfortunately, those guys were few and far between, despite the fact that most girls working the streets caught a disease sooner or later, and even then they were afraid to go to a doctor, especially if they were drug addicts.

Another advantage was if you found a guy who knew what he wanted and asked for it, right from the start (especially if he only wanted a blow job). Then you didn't have to spend hours haggling over everything. We also gave points to a customer who was relatively young and not disgustingly fat, and also of course if he didn't treat you like a piece of meat but like an actual human being and remained somewhat friendly, possibly even invited you to an occasional meal.

The most important criterion in determining the quality of a customer was, of course, how much money he paid and for which services. The ones to be avoided were the guys who didn't keep up their end of the agreement or who suddenly tried to threaten or bribe you into doing more stuff with them.

What we really kept an eye out for though, and warned each other about, was the kind of sleazy guy who would ask for his money back afterward, or sometimes even force us to give it back, because he supposedly wasn't satisfied with us. The boys, though, had more trouble with scumbags like that than we did.

Somehow or other, the year 1977 finally rolled around. Time didn't seem to compute in my brain anymore. Whether it was winter or summer, whether the rest of the world was celebrating Christmas or New Year's, to me one day was just like the next. The only good thing about Christmas was that I got some money, and so I didn't have to do as many customers. That was especially important over the holidays, when business was slow. I was totally numb in this phase. I didn't think about anything. Nothing at all. I didn't feel anything and didn't notice anything around me. I was totally preoccupied with myself. But I didn't know who I was. Sometimes I didn't even know if I was still alive or not.

I can hardly remember any specific details from that period. There probably wasn't anything worth remembering anyway— that is, until one Sunday at the end of January. I came home sometime in the early morning hours. I was feeling pretty good, actually. I lay in my bed and drifted off, imagining that I was a young girl who'd just gotten home from a dance. At this dance, my alter ego had just met a super-cute boy, and she already had a huge crush on him. I only felt good when I was dreaming, and in my dreams I became a completely different person. My favorite dream was one in which I was just a happy, carefree teenager. The teenager in that dream reminded me of someone in a Coca-Cola advertisement.

My mom woke me up around noon and brought me some lunch. When I was home on Sundays—that is, on the Sundays when I wasn't with Detlef—my mom always brought me lunch in bed. I choked down a couple of bites. It was almost impossible for me to get anything down anymore, except for yogurt, cottage cheese, and pudding. Then I grabbed my white handbag. It was already pretty shredded: no handles anymore and with holes everywhere. That shouldn't have been a surprise, though, because in addition to syringes and cigarettes, I'd also stuff my jacket in there. It didn't even occur to me to get a new handbag; that's how little I cared about everything. I was so far past caring that I didn't even think twice about shuffling past my mom to the bathroom, shredded bag in hand. I locked the bathroom door behind me. Nobody in our family locked the bathroom door. I looked in the mirror, just like I did every day. A totally strange sunken face stared back at me. It had been a long time since I'd been able to recognize myself in the mirror. That face wasn't mine. Neither was this emaciated body. It was a body that was totally foreign to me. I couldn't even feel it when I was sick. It just went its own way. The heroin made me numb to any pain or hunger, even to a high fever. The body only registered one thing: withdrawal.

I stood in front of the mirror and prepared the shot. I was pretty anxious about it because I had M-powder. In contrast to the white or tan dope that you usually got on the market, this was a gray-green speckled powder. It's generally very impure,[27] but it gives you an incredible kick—it's supposed to be like a flash. It goes right to the heart, and you have to be really careful with the dosage. Too much of it, and you're a goner. I knew the danger, but I still wanted it. I needed it. I was dead set on experiencing that kick from this M-powder.

I pushed the needle into the vein, pulled back, and immediately drew blood. I had filtered the M-powder a couple of times, but it was still extremely impure. And then it happened. The needle clogged. That's about the worst thing that can happen, if the

---

27 Street heroin may be very "impure," containing a variety of other chemicals like calcium oxide, ammonia, chloroform, etc., that may cause unexpected side effects.

needle gets plugged up right at that moment. Because then there's nothing else for you to do. You have to throw away the dope.

So I couldn't pull out anymore. I pushed as hard as I could to get this shit through the needle. And I was lucky. I got the shot to go in. I drew back once more in order to get the rest of it into the vein, but then the needle clogged again. I was furious. I only had eight or ten seconds before it hit me. So I pushed with all my strength. The syringe popped out of my hand and blood squirted everywhere.

The flash was insane. I had to hold onto my head. I felt an unbelievable cramp in my chest, right where my heart was. There was a roaring in my head, as if someone had hit it with a sledge-hammer, and my scalp tingled as if pricked by a million needles. My left arm was virtually paralyzed.

When I could move again, I grabbed some Kleenex to wipe up the blood. It was everywhere—in the sink, on the mirror, and all over the walls. Luckily our whole bathroom was covered with an oil-based paint, so the blood came off pretty easily. While I was still wiping up the blood, my mom banged on the door. She immediately started in on me: "Open the door! Let me in! Why'd you lock the door, anyway? That's unacceptable, Christiane."

"Shut up," I called back. "I'm almost finished."

I was super pissed that she was bugging me now, of all times, while I was wiping frantically at the walls with the tissues. In my panic, I missed a few bloody spots and even left a bloody tissue in the sink. I unlocked the door and my mom burst past me into the bathroom. I was totally unsuspecting and just thought she had to pee. I went into my room with my handbag, lay down on my bed, and lit a cigarette.

No sooner had I lit it than my mom came running into the room. "You're taking narcotics!" she screamed at me.

I said, "What? What gave you that idea?"

She then practically threw herself on top of me and forced my arms straight. I didn't put up any resistance. She saw the fresh needle marks immediately. She took my handbag and dumped everything out onto the bed. Out came the syringe, some loose tobacco from the Roth-Händle cigarettes, and a whole pile of small foil squares—which used to contain my heroin. When I'd go into withdrawal and didn't have any dope, I'd use a nail file to scrape the last bits of dust from the paper to get one more shot out of it.

The stuff that fell out of my bag was proof positive that I was an addict. It had already become clear to her in the bathroom though. Not only did she find the bloody tissue and blood splatters, but also some soot from the spoon in which I cooked up the dope. She had already read a lot about heroin in the papers, and she'd put two and two together now.

Denying it was useless, so I gave up trying. Although I'd just given myself a really awesome shot of M-powder, I broke down and cried. I sobbed so hard that I couldn't get out a single word. My mom didn't say anything either. She was shaking. She was totally shocked. She left my room, and I heard her talking with her boyfriend, Klaus. Then she came back. She seemed a little calmer and asked, "Can't anything be done about this? Don't you want to get off that stuff?"

I said, "Mom, there's nothing I'd rather do. Seriously. You have to believe me. I really want to get away from all this."

She said, "Good. Then we'll try it together. I'll take vacation days so that I can be with you the whole time, while you're going through withdrawal. We'll start today, right now."

"That's great. But there's this one thing. Without Detlef I can't do it. I need him and he needs me. And anyway, he also wants to get off the stuff. We've talked about it for a while now. We were just waiting for the right time to do it. Together."

My mom was completely stunned. "Oh, Detlef? Him too?" she asked, in a weak voice. She'd always liked Detlef and was proud that I'd found such a nice boyfriend. "Of course, Detlef too," I said. "Do you think that I would've done this all by myself? Detlef never would've let me. But he also won't let me suffer from withdrawal without him either."

I suddenly felt much better, almost cheerful. The thought of Detlef and me getting clean together really made me optimistic. After all, we'd been talking about it for a long time. But my mom was completely devastated. Her face turned a pale-green color, and I thought she was going to have a nervous breakdown. The news about Detlef had given her another shock. She was probably stunned by her own naïveté and gullibility over the last two years as well. And now there were more doubts haunting her. She wanted to know how I came by the money for the heroin. Of course, she immediately thought working the street, prostitution, etcetera.

I couldn't bring myself to tell her the truth. So I lied: "Oh, I'd just asked people for a few marks here and there. And most of the time it worked. Then I also cleaned people's apartments or offices, off and on."

My mom didn't pry any further. Once again she seemed very relieved that she got an answer that didn't confirm her worst fears. What she'd already found out on this particular Sunday was enough to totally devastate her. I felt truly sorry for my mom. It made me feel very guilty.

We drove off immediately to look for Detlef. He wasn't at Zoo Station, and he wasn't at Axel and Bernd's either.

In the evening, we went to see Detlef's dad. Detlef's parents were also divorced. His dad was a government official. He'd known for a long time what was up with Detlef. My mom criticized him for not telling her about what was going on. That's when he almost broke down and cried. He was incredibly embarrassed about the fact that his son was a drug-addled prostitute. But he was glad that my mom wanted to do something about it. He repeated over and over, "Yes, we've got to do something."

Detlef's dad had a whole bunch of sleeping pills and sedatives that he kept in his desk drawer. He gave them all to me because I told him that we didn't have any methadone, and that it would be absolute hell to try and get clean without any chemical assistance.

On the subway ride back home, I tossed down a whole handful of pills, because I could feel the withdrawal symptoms coming on. And then with all those pills in my system I felt pretty good and slept through the night.

The next morning, Detlef showed up at our doorstep. His dad had found him right away, and he was already in full withdrawal. I thought that was pretty courageous of him that he hadn't tried to give himself one last fix and arrived in the same state I was in. He must've known that I didn't have any more dope. And he said he wanted to be at the same level as me when we started going clean. He was a genuinely good and considerate guy.

So Detlef definitely wanted to get off the stuff just as bad as I did. And he was also glad that it was happening this way. Both of us were, like our parents, ignorant of just how stupid it is to have two addicts, who are also friends, trying to quit together. Because at some point one of them will get the other one going again, and they'll work each other up to the next shot. Well, maybe we did have some idea, just from the stories we'd heard. But then again, we were living within our own world of illusions. We always believed that whatever applied to other drug addicts somehow didn't apply to us. And anyway, we couldn't imagine doing anything of importance without the other.

Over the course of the morning, we were able to keep our heads above water with the pills from Detlef's dad. We could still talk to each other. We painted a fantastically upbeat picture of our future after we'd gotten clean, and we promised each other to stay tough and brave through the next few days. Despite the pain that we were starting to feel, we were still pretty happy.

In the afternoon though, we were in the thick of it. We kept popping those pills and chasing them down with wine—lots of wine. But it didn't help. I lost control of my legs. There was this huge pressure on the back of my knees. I lay down flat on the floor and stretched out my legs, trying to alternately tense and relax the leg muscles. But they were beyond my control at that point. I pressed the legs against the dresser, and that's where they stayed. I couldn't move them after that. I was rolling around on the floor, but my feet somehow stayed glued to the dresser.

I was soaked through and through with an icy cold sweat. I was freezing and shaking, and the cold sweat ran down my face into my eyes. I reeked. I thought, This is that nasty, evil poison that's coming out of your body.

It seemed to me like I was going through my very own exorcism.

Detlef was even worse off than me. He was almost going berserk. He was shivering with cold, but then he suddenly took off his sweater. He sat down on my chair by the window. His legs were in constant motion. They were running while he was sitting. His pencil-thin legs twitched like they were possessed, up and down, up and down. And he kept wiping the sweat from his face, his whole body shaking terribly. This wasn't your run-of-the-mill shivering anymore. Again and again, he doubled over and screamed. It was stomach cramps.

Detlef smelled even worse than me. That whole tiny room was full of our stink. I thought about what I'd heard, that friendships between heroin addicts always fall apart after a successful withdrawal. I also thought that even now I still loved Detlef—even though he smelled absolutely horrible.

Detlef got up, somehow made it over to the mirror in my room, and said, "I can't take it anymore. I can't do it. I just can't do it." I couldn't answer. I didn't have enough strength to bolster him up or give him courage. I tried not to think those thoughts. Instead, I tried to focus on a stupid story, frantically turning the pages of a newspaper over and over again and tearing it apart in the process.

My mouth and my throat were totally dry. But in a weird way, my mouth was also full of saliva. I couldn't swallow and started to cough. The harder I tried to swallow it, the more violently I coughed. I got a coughing fit that just wouldn't stop. Then I started throwing up. I threw up all over my rug. It all came out as white foam. I thought, Just like my dog used to do after she ate some grass. The coughing and the puking went on and on and wouldn't stop.

My mom was in the living room through most of this. When she came into our room, she was completely helpless. She kept running to the shopping center to get something for us, but we couldn't swallow anything anyway. At around this time though, she brought me some cough drops, and these did actually help a little bit. The coughing stopped. My mom cleaned up the vomit. She was so sweet. And I couldn't even say thank you.

At some point, and I don't know when, the pills and the wine started to work. I'd swallowed five Valium and two quaaludes, and on top of that downed almost a whole bottle of wine. Any normal person would have slept for a few days after that. My body, however, was so thoroughly poisoned that it hardly reacted. But at least I was able to calm down enough so that I could lie down on my bed. We'd set up a cot, too, for Detlef, and he lay down on that. We didn't touch. We were each way too preoccupied with what was going on with ourselves. I drifted off into a kind of waking sleep. I slept but at the same time was aware that I slept, and was also fully aware of my pain. I dreamt and thought things over. It was all muddled together. I thought that everyone, especially my mom, could see right through me. That everyone could read my horrible, evil thoughts. That everyone had to see what a revolting piece of shit I really was. I hated my body. I would've been glad if it had simply died on me right then.

At night I took a few more pills. Again, any normal person would have probably been dead at that point, but I just fell asleep for a couple of hours. I woke up after a dream about my life as a dog. I'd always been treated kindly by people before, but now I was being thrown into a kennel to be tortured to death.

Detlef was flinging his arms around and hitting me. The light was on. Next to my bed was a large bowl of water and a wash-cloth. My mom had put it there. I washed the sweat off my face.

Detlef's whole body was in motion, even though he seemed to be out cold. His body was bucking up and down, his legs were kicking, and sometimes his arms would shoot out, too.

I seemed to be a little better off than he was. I could at least manage to wipe Detlef's forehead down with the washcloth. He didn't feel a thing though. I still loved him like crazy. Later, after I'd dozed off again, I was half aware of Detlef reaching out to me and stroking my hair.

The next morning, we both felt better though. Apparently, the old rule about the second day of withdrawal being the worst didn't hold true for us. But of course, this was our first time going cold turkey for any extended period of time, and your first time was supposed to be much less difficult—by half, even—than all the later attempts. Around noon, we even started talking again. First about trivial stuff, but then, later on, about our future as well. Our plans lost their domestic theme from earlier. Now we swore to never, ever do heroin again—no LSD and no pills either. We wanted to live a peaceful life with peaceful people. We agreed that pot was okay, just like during that time when everything seemed so wonderful. We also wanted our friends to be from pot-smoking circles, as those kinds of people were mostly very laid-back. We thought that we'd avoid the drinkers, though, because we didn't want anything to do with those aggressive boneheads. So our overall plan was to get out of the H scene and dive back in among the potheads.

Detlef wanted to look for work again, too. He said, "I'll just go back to my old boss and say that I kind of fucked up, but that now I've got my head screwed on the right way again. He's always been really understanding. I'll start my apprenticeship as a pipe fitter all over again."

I said that I wanted to totally focus on school again and maybe even finish high school and, after that, go for the college entrance exams.

Then my mom came back in with a surprise for us. She'd been to her doctor, and he'd prescribed a bottle of methadone for her to take home. Detlef and I took twenty drops each, just as the doctor had instructed. We didn't take any more because we knew it had to last all week. With methadone in our system, we felt even better. The withdrawal symptoms were much less intense now. My mom kept feeding us a steady supply of pudding, ice cream, and anything else we needed or had a craving for. She brought us piles of stuff to read, too. Tons of comics. I used to think that comics were boring. Now I read them together with Detlef. We didn't just skim over them like we used to. We read every panel carefully and only stopped when something really got to us and made us laugh hysterically.

We were still improving on the third day, too. That being said, we were also always on something. Methadone, Valium, and a lot of wine, too. We felt pretty good, even though our poisoned bodies sometimes still revolted against their lack of heroin.

On the night of the third day, after what had been a long time, we slept together again. When you're on heroin, your sex drive really takes a hit. It was the first time—since the first time—that Detlef and I had slept together without any heroin. It was unbelievable. We realized that we hadn't experienced anything like that in a long, long time. We lay in bed together for hours, sweating still, but happy just to be able to touch each other. We probably could have made it out of bed on the fourth day, but we didn't bother trying. We stayed in bed an extra three days, sleeping together, drinking wine, taking Valium when we needed to, and leaving all the other details to my mom. Going through withdrawal wasn't that bad, we thought. We were happy to have finally made it to the other side.

On the seventh day, we got up again. My mom was so, so happy that we'd recovered and that it was all over. She kissed us both.

My feelings about my mom had started to change over the course of the previous week. I felt something like genuine friendship and gratitude toward her. And of course I was also very happy about having Detlef back in my life. I thought that he was just about the best boyfriend ever. I mean, I loved the way he decided to join up with me in getting clean. He didn't even think twice about it. And the fact that all the stress and pain of withdrawal didn't break us up—as happened with most other couples—was also unbelievably cool. In fact, if anything, our connection was even deeper now.

We told my mom that we wanted to get some fresh air. She agreed that it would be a good idea since at that point Detlef and I had spent an entire week holed up in a tiny room.

"So, where to?" Detlef asked. I looked at him, clueless. I really didn't have any idea. It just now occurred to us that we didn't have anywhere to go anymore. All of our friends were heroin junkies. And all the places we knew, where we somehow felt at home, were part of the heroin scene. We didn't even know where the potheads hung out anymore.

After Detlef asked where we should go, I suddenly didn't feel so good anymore. We were out of methadone. That must have been the reason why we'd gotten so restless and wanted to go outside. Not having a destination in mind, however, made things even worse. I suddenly felt really drained, really empty. We might have gotten off H, but now we didn't know what to do next.

We walked to the subway without talking about a destination. It was like we were on automatic pilot. There was an invisible thread pulling us along, without us being aware of it. And then we were standing at Zoo Station. Detlef finally said something: "We really should say hi to Axel and Bernd. Otherwise they'll think we're dead or in jail or something."

"Of course!" I said—full of relief. "We have to at least tell them what it's like to go absolutely cold turkey. And maybe we could talk them into getting clean, too." It only took a second to find Axel and Bernd. They had a lot of dope, after a good day with customers. Detlef told them about what we'd been through, and both of them said how awesome it was that we'd actually done it. After that, though, Axel and Bernd said that they were going back to their apartment to shoot up.

Detlef looked at me, and I looked back at him. We caught each other's eyes and started grinning. Looking back I remember thinking, Already—on the first day! That's crazy! But Detlef said, "We can still shoot up every now and then, you know. Heroin's still a great time, in moderation. We just have to be careful. We have to watch it, so we don't get hooked again. Because I'm not about to do a total withdrawal all over again."

"Sure, a shot every once in a while. I'm cool with that. We just can't let ourselves get hooked again."

We had absolutely no ability to take stock of what we were actually getting into. It was like the reasoning parts of our brains had been shut down. The only thing I could think about was that next shot of heroin.

Detlef said to Axel, "Can you spot us some? You'll get it back soon, no problem." Axel and Bernd told us we should really think about it first. Then they said that they'd get clean next week, too, just like we did. They just had to get some methadone lined up first. They thought it'd be cool to be able to go to work again and just shoot up every once in a while.

Two hours after we'd left my mom's apartment, Detlef and I were using again—and totally doped up. Arm in arm we strolled down the Kurfürstendamm. It was such a good feeling, to be high and not have to worry about getting anywhere. Instead, we could just walk around. We didn't even have to worry about getting a supply for the next morning. "Well," Detlef said to me, with a smile on his face, "tomorrow morning we'll wake up, do a few stretches, and start our day off right: without any H."

We actually seriously believed we had recovered. Our first mistake was in thinking that over the course of the past week at my mom's, all that pain and puking had been proof of a real, complete withdrawal. And sure, the poison had left our bodies— the heroin at least. But we'd been busy replacing one drug with another. With lots of others, in fact: with methadone, Valium, and whatever else was on hand. And we hadn't wasted a single thought on what we would do afterward. My mom was similarly naïve. She felt optimistic that we'd gotten over it once and for all. And how could she have known any better?

Actually, we should've known better because we'd already heard stories from a lot of other people about the process of withdrawal. But we weren't that interested in what was really going on with us. We were still incredibly naïve. We didn't care what other people had been through, or what other people thought they'd learned. We knew best.

For the next month or so, it looked like we were actually pulling it off. Neither one of us had to do any hustling. We only shot up when someone treated us or when we had some extra cash. At the same time, we were getting more and more impatient every day about finding someone who'd treat us to a shot or who had a few extra dollars to loan us. We were anxious for our taste—but not ready to admit it.

It was a good time for us. I didn't have to go back to school yet, because my mom wanted me to be happy and relaxed during my first few weeks off heroin. She even let Detlef stay over with us. I got to know a totally new side of Detlef and fell deeper and deeper in love with him—if that was even possible. He was carefree and happy and full of ideas. It seemed like we were always having fun. And if we weren't, at least we pretended.

We went into a giant park nearby called the Grunewald[28] and took long walks. Sometimes we took my two cats with us and let them climb the trees there. We made love almost every night. Life was awesome. Sometimes we were clean for a couple of days, and sometimes we stayed doped up for three days running. If we got our hands on a big enough stash, we left the nasty heroin scene behind as fast as we could. We liked to head over to the Kurfürstendamm and mix in with all the normal nine-to-fivers over there. It was fun to feel like we were part of that world but also . . . different. That was the way we had of proving to ourselves and to others that we weren't junkies; we just shot up sometimes. We could still join in and be a part of real, everyday life.

We also liked to get high and go to the lame clubs that the teenagers and tourists loved. We sat there, totally high, thinking we were just like everybody else. Sometimes we would decide to just stay home for the whole day instead. We'd sit by the window, looking out, and telling each other stories. We'd also try to pick the leaves from these sickly old trees that were growing in front

---

28 The Grunewald (German for "green forest") is a quarter within the Berlin borough of Charlottenburg-Wilmersdorf.

of our house. Detlef would hold onto my legs, and I'd lean way out of the window and see how many I could grab. We made out, ran around, read, and were mostly just kind of silly. Our future was never a serious topic. But every once in a while, I had these pangs of real anxiety. It was almost like a sickness that attacked me whenever a dark reality seemed to intrude on our little fantasy lives. It would happen whenever I had an argument with Detlef. It didn't matter how trivial the fight happened to be—I just couldn't deal with it. I had to push everything serious far away from me, and I was always worried about freaking out about some stupid little thing. Whenever I started to have these feelings of anxiety or insecurity, I'd start to have the hunger again. Because with one shot of heroin, the problem would be gone.

Eventually, we had a real problem. My mom's boyfriend, Klaus, was upset about Detlef. He said that the apartment was too small for a fourth person—especially if that fourth person was a stranger. It was hard for my mom to argue with that, and there wasn't anything I could say to change his mind. It made me feel so powerless. It was just like the time when Klaus ordered me to give up my dog. In a flash, my peaceful, awesome, easy life was over with. I had to go back to school, and Detlef wasn't allowed to sleep over anymore.

Back in school, it felt like I'd never left. It didn't seem like I'd missed anything, anyway—but I'd given up on school a long time ago. I had one new problem though: smoking. When I wasn't on H, I smoked four to five packs a day, chain-smoking one cigarette after another. And now I couldn't even make it through the first class of the day without a smoke. I had to leave and go to the bathroom now. That first morning at school I literally smoked until I threw up. I puked into a wastebasket. I could hardly spend any time in class.

For the first time in weeks, I didn't see Detlef. The next day, after school, I started to get nervous and took the subway over to Zoo Station. There was my Detlef, waiting for his next customer.

It was sickening to see him back at the station, looking out for customers. But Detlef said that he was completely broke. And anyway, he had no idea what else he should do. He was sleeping at Axel and Bernd's again and working the streets at Zoo Station and shooting up again, every day. If I wanted to see Detlef, that's where I needed to be. He was the only person I had. I didn't believe I could live without him. So I went back, too, every day—back to Zoo Station.

Christiane's Mom

On the Sunday when I came across the bloodstains in the bathroom and checked Christiane's arms for track marks, the light bulb finally went on. It felt like someone had kicked me in the stomach. In a way, I guess, it was just time for me to pay the piper. I'd raised Christiane a certain way, and I'd been proud of my parenting skills. But in the end, it was all wrong. I wanted to avoid the mistakes my own dad had made, but I'd made my own mistakes instead.

When Christiane started to go to The Sound, I wasn't exactly happy about it, but her friend Kessi and the other teens from the Center House all seemed to go there pretty regularly. So I told myself, Okay, so why shouldn't Christiane go there too? The kids all raved about The Sound. I thought back on all the harmless things that my dad prohibited when I was a girl, and that was enough for me.

I was still sticking with that permissive style of parenting when Christiane introduced me to her boyfriend Detlef. She'd met him at The Sound, and he made a really good impression on me. He knew how to be polite, he had good manners, and he just generally seemed like a well-meaning kind of kid. Just a really sweet guy. And I thought it was normal for Christiane at her age, that she would be so head over heels in love. More than anything else, I was just glad that she'd hooked up with a decent guy. I could see that he really cared for Christiane.

If you had told me back then that they were already using heroin, I would've said you were crazy. The fact was, aside from Christiane's crush, I didn't notice anything at all unusual going on with her. On the contrary, she seemed to be calmer and better adjusted after a phase of real defiance. She even seemed to be doing better in school.

After she'd finished with her school day, she would usually call me and tell me what she was up to. She'd say that she was going to see friends or picking up Detlef from work. And I had no problem with any of that. On weekdays she was usually home for dinner. And when she was running late, she'd call and even then generally arrive home in an hour or so. When she was late, she told me it was because she'd stopped at the Center House or met up with friends.

She started lending a hand around the house again, and when she did I'd try and give her something in return, like a snack, or a record, or a little increase on her allowance. Klaus didn't think that was a good idea though. He thought I should focus more on myself and said that Christiane was just taking advantage of me. Maybe he was right, in retrospect. But I always felt a little guilty for what Christiane had already been through at that point and was just trying to do something nice for her. I wasn't seeing things clearly back then.

Klaus also thought it was a bad idea for me to let Christiane stay overnight at her girlfriends' places. He never thought she was telling the truth about that stuff. But it wasn't my style to go spying on her or checking out her stories. That was the kind of thing my dad would do, even though I was never really up to anything.

Then one day Christiane told me that she had slept with Detlef. "Mom," she said, "he was so sweet to me; you can't even imagine." When she told me that, I thought that was the reason why she always wanted to stay overnight at her girlfriends' houses.

And really, so what, I thought. I didn't think it was a huge deal. From that point on, I occasionally allowed her to sleep over at Detlef's. I mean, how could I have prevented them from sleeping together anyway? Everyone in the media is always talking about how kids mature earlier these days, and it seems like the general feeling is that their sexuality shouldn't be suppressed. I agree with that.

Christiane at least had a steady boyfriend. Other girls in the neighborhood seemed to just go from one guy to the next. So her steady relationship with Detlef was reassuring to me. It showed some maturity.

On the other hand, if I really wanted to be honest, I sometimes got the feeling that something was really wrong. Especially when it came to her other new friends from The Sound. She told me that they sometimes did drugs, but she didn't talk about hard stuff like heroin. But I knew they'd smoke pot and had even taken acid. She described some really horrible things to me—like the fact that her friend Babsi was already an addict. But she talked about it all as if she was disgusted and turned off by it—I never would've thought that she herself was involved in any way.

When I asked her why she was hanging out with these kinds of people, she said, "Oh Mom, I feel so sorry for them. Most people don't want anything to do with them. So when someone does take the time to listen to them, they're so grateful and happy. They really need help."

Christiane had always been altruistic, so that made sense to me. But now I can see that she was actually talking about herself.

One night, in the middle of the week, she didn't come home until 11 p.m. When she got back she just said, "Don't be mad at me. I went to a release center with some of my friends." I asked her what a release center was, and she told me, "Well, it's where we go to try and get all the druggies to lay off for a while!" Then she added, "God, if I ever got addicted . . ." and suppressed a laugh. I stared at her, shocked. But then she broke in again with, "I'm just kidding, Mom. Everything's okay."

"And what about Detlef? Is he okay?" At that point, Christiane seemed offended: "Of course!! That would be the last thing on his mind! He doesn't care about drugs."

That was in the winter of '76. From then on I was seriously concerned that there was something very wrong, but I was trying to ignore that feeling. I didn't listen to my boyfriend either. By that point, he was absolutely convinced that Christiane was taking some serious drugs. But I wasn't ready to accuse her of anything yet. What kind of a mother wants to admit that she's failed? That everything she's done was for nothing? As a result, I just kept insisting that my daughter would never do that.

Still, I tried to rein Christiane in a little. But there were many times when she wouldn't show up for dinner, even though I'd told her we'd be expecting her—and I didn't know quite what to do at times like those. Where could I have gone looking for her? Even without my impressive talent for self-deception, I never would've suspected that she was hanging out at Zoo station. I was always glad when she called to let me know that at least she'd be home soon. I just didn't know how to handle her anymore.

But sometimes she'd respect my rules. Sometimes when her friends called, she'd tell them proudly, "No, I'm not allowed to come out today. I'm staying home." It didn't seem to bother her. That was the contradictory thing about her: On the one hand, she was infuriatingly rude and disrespectful—refusing to talk to me and doing whatever she wanted—and on the other hand she respected me when I set clear limits. But by then, it was already too late.

I got my wake-up call in late January 1977. It was horrible. I wanted to go into the bathroom, but the door was locked. That was unusual for us. Christiane was inside and wouldn't open the door. All of a sudden, I just knew. And for the first time, I faced up to my history of self-deception. Otherwise, how could I have known what was going on in the bathroom?

I started banging on the door, but she wouldn't open up. I was absolutely fuming. I began yelling at her, demanding that she open the door. Finally she burst out past me. I caught a glimpse of a blackened spoon and blood spatters on the wall. That was it. I knew all the signs from reading the newspaper stories. All my boyfriend said was, "So, do you believe me now?"

I ran after her. "Christiane," I said in a shaky voice, "what have you done?" I was devastated—completely at a loss. My whole body was shaking. I didn't know whether to break down and cry or scream at her. I had to talk to her first. She was crying her heart out and didn't want to answer. I asked, "Did you shoot up?"

She didn't answer. She was sobbing so hard she couldn't talk. I grabbed her arms, forced them straight out beneath her, and saw them: track marks on both her arms. But it didn't look too bad. Really it didn't. She didn't have any bruises, and I could only see two or three needle marks, one of them fresh. That one was still red.

And then, through her tears, she confessed. I wanted to die. I really wanted to just leave it all behind and die. I was so distraught that I couldn't think. I didn't know what to do. "What are we going to do now?" I asked. I actually asked Christiane, as if she had the answer. Because I myself was completely at a loss.

So this was the nightmare I had wanted to avoid. This was the truth that I couldn't face up to. Couldn't accept. But I didn't know the signs to look out for. I hadn't noticed any apathy in Christiane. She was mostly cheerful and perky. The only thing that stood out over the previous few weeks was that sometimes, when she came home late, she'd go straight into her room. I just thought it was because she felt bad about coming home late though.

After I'd calmed down a bit, we talked about what to do next. As we considered the various options, Christiane revealed that Detlef was also addicted to heroin. It made sense for both him and Christiane to get clean together. Otherwise, whoever hadn't quit would keep pulling the other one down again. That made sense to me. We decided that both of them should clean up their act together at our place.

Christiane seemed very open and honest about the whole situation. She confessed that Detlef had also been involved in the prostitution scene at Zoo station in order to earn the money they needed for the drugs. I was stunned. It didn't occur to me that she might be doing the same thing; at the time, I thought her love for Detlef would have precluded it. She said that he was always able to earn enough on his own for both of them.

Christiane kept insisting that she "really, really" wanted to get off the stuff. So that same night we went off looking for Detlef. That's when I saw, for the first time, all of these sad, emaciated figures, walking up and down between the trains. And Christiane said, "That's not how I want to end up. Just look at them all!" She still looked relatively good. That almost reassured me.

After a couple hours of searching, we gave up and went to Detlef's father's house. He was aware of Detlef's heroin addiction, but he didn't seem aware that Christiane had reached the same point herself. I jumped right down his throat. "Why didn't you tell me anything?" I asked him. He said that he was too embarrassed.

Detlef's dad seemed relieved. He wanted to help financially. Until now, he'd tried in vain to get help for his son. It must have seemed like a real blessing to him, our interceding like this. I was so self-assured I even surprised myself. It felt good to take some control of the situation—even if I had no idea what actually lay ahead of me.

The next day I went out to get some professional advice. The first place I tried was the youth welfare office. I told them that my fourteen-year-old daughter was a heroin addict and asked what I should do. They weren't very helpful. "Put her in a home for other kids with the same problems," they said. I told them that that was totally out of the question. Christiane would feel like I just wanted to get rid of her. And besides, they couldn't even recommend an appropriate place. They would have to do some research, and it would take a while. "It's hard to find a good spot for kids who aren't very well-behaved," they told me.

"That's not what this is about," I replied. "She isn't hard to manage! She's just addicted to heroin." They just kept looking at me and shrugging their shoulders. Their final advice was to take Christiane to a family counselor.

When I suggested this to Christiane, she just said, "That's ridiculous, they don't have a clue. What I need is rehab therapy." But the authorities and bureaucrats didn't offer anything like that. I went from one clinic to another—I went to the technical university, to the Caritas[29] office, and I forget where else. I just didn't know how to deal with this problem myself.

The advisors didn't think a home withdrawal would work out well. Without therapy, they said, just taking the heroin away from her wouldn't make a big difference. But because Christiane was still so young, it wasn't viewed as totally hopeless. The point

29 Caritas International is a confederation of 165 Catholic relief, development, and social service organizations operating in over 200 countries and territories worldwide.

turned out to be moot anyway: They didn't have a spot for her in any of their therapy programs. Maybe in three months, they said. Before I left, they gave me some dietary advice to counteract the nutritional deficiencies that she had probably developed.

At the end of a week, both Detlef and Christiane appeared to have gotten over all their withdrawal symptoms. Neither of the two tried to con me, and neither tried to run away. I dared to hope. After the eighth day, I was sure that it was over. Thank God, I thought to myself, she's made it. Christiane went back to school again a few days later and supposedly participated regularly as well.

But then she started to roam again. I was comforted somewhat by the fact that she would at least tell me where she was going. She gave solid, detailed information. When she called at 8 p.m., she would say, "Mom, I'm in this or that café. I met up with this or that person. I'll be home soon!"

I'd now been warned. I kept checking her arms, but didn't find any new needle marks. I told her that she couldn't stay at Detlef's over the weekend anymore, but I wanted to show her that I trusted her, so I let her stay out a little later on Saturday nights. I was suspicious, but I still didn't know exactly how to act. I tortured myself, agonizing over what to do.

❋

I WAS TERRIFIED ABOUT BECOMING physically addicted again. But when Detlef was doped up and I was sober, there was no connection between us. We were like strangers. That's why I started shooting up with Detlef again. And yet while we were driving the needles into our arms, we kept telling ourselves that we would never fall back into our old ways ever again. Once again, we convinced ourselves that we weren't addicted and could stop whenever we wanted—while at the same time, we were frantically making sure that we'd have enough dope left over for the morning.

The whole fucking cycle started up all over again. Strangely, even though we'd been through it all before, we couldn't tell just how badly we were in deep shit again because of our delusion that now we had things under control.

Just like before, at first, Detlef was the only one working Zoo Station. It wasn't very long, however, before I joined him there. Things went well at the beginning though. I ran into a lot of my old regulars, and so the jobs weren't too revolting.

On the first day that I was back on the streets, Detlef took me along to meet this new guy, Jürgen. Jürgen was pretty well-known in the Berlin business world. He was loaded and lunched with senators—so he was very well connected—and even though he was over thirty, he still seemed kind of young. He talked the way we talked and seemed to understand the issues we were dealing with. He wasn't just your ordinary businessman or your usual stuffy manager type.

So this was my first time in Jürgen's apartment. When we got there, there were about a dozen people. They were all gathered around a giant wooden table that had candles in silver holders and expensive bottles of wine. Everyone was relaxed, and the conversation seemed to be flowing easily. It was immediately apparent that these people were pretty smart. Jürgen was leading the discussion, and I thought, man, this guy is sharp. It was also hard to ignore the fact that he was living in such an amazing apartment, packed with first-class stuff. And despite everything, he was still so laid-back, easygoing, and generous.

We were treated like we really belonged—despite the fact that we were obviously the only junkies there. After a little small talk, one of the couples asked if they could go take a shower. Jürgen said, "Of course, what else are they here for?"

The showers were right next to the living room. The first couple went in, and a few other people followed after them. A short while later, they came back in, naked and asking about towels. It seemed like a pretty cool environment to me, where everyone seemed to get along with everybody else and be up for anything. I felt like Detlef and I could live like this someday, in a first-class apartment, and invite totally cool friends like this.

A few people were already naked or with just small towels around their waists, and they were walking around and touching each other and starting to make out. One couple went into the bedroom, onto the huge bed there. The bedroom happened to be connected to the living room by a wide passageway, so you could look right in. This couple undressed and began to kiss, and soon they were joined by a number of the other guests, who crawled right into the huge bed with them. There were guys with guys, and guys with girls—everything. Some of the people there didn't even make it to the bed: They were going at it right at the table. But I'd realized that I was attending a certified orgy well before things had gone that far.

The guests obviously wanted Detlef and me to join them, but I wasn't into it. I didn't want to be groped by just anybody. I wasn't necessarily opposed to what was going on or grossed out by it. In fact, I was even a little turned on by how they were all having fun together and how chill everything was. But that's exactly why I wanted to be alone with Detlef.

Detlef and I went to a separate room and started making out. Suddenly Jürgen appeared next to us, watching. It didn't bother me though, because, for starters, I felt so safe, but also because I knew he was paying us for this. I only hoped that he wasn't going to join in.

But Jürgen just watched. While Detlef and I had sex, he jerked off. And then, when we left later on (my mom was still expecting me at home), he casually slipped Detlef a hundred-mark note.

Detlef R., Christiane's boyfriend, outside of Zoo Station.

Lutz F., "Lufo," died on January 25, 1978.

Stella, who lived with Christiane from time to time. At 14, Stella was incarcerated in the Women's Prison at Lehrter Strasse in Berlin.

Andreas W., "Atze," died of an intentional heroin overdose on April 7, 1977. He was Christiane's first love.

Babette D., "Babsi," died
on July 19, 1977. She was
Christiane's best girlfriend.
The stepdaughter of a famous
pianist, she made news as the
"youngest heroin casualty"
in Berlin.

Gropiusstadt, as viewed the roof of one of its many highrises.

The Center House was the meeting place for many of the Gropiusstadt teens. Its director, Pastor Jürgen Quandt, watched helplessly as the youth club turned into a drug scene.

The Sound operated as a gathering place for many young Berliners.

A neglected, overgrown lot near The Sound. This area served as a destination for men looking to pick up young, heroin addicts.

176

Young addicts working the Kurfürstenstrasse in Berlin.

Werner H., 21, and Michael S., 21, at the Kurfürstendamm subway station. Werner H.: "I started shooting up at 16. I was sentenced to three years in jail, and after that no one had time for me any more…. I don't stand a chance anymore, I'm in way too deep.

Michael S.: "I started when I was 15. But I don't want to lose hope. I just have to find something that I can hold on to, that I can believe in, and then maybe I'll be able to get clean. "

A typically desolate apartment in the Beusselstrasse (Beussel Street), Berlin.
Almost every heroin addict sells off anything valuable he owns right away—from
the iron (and ironing board) to the stereo system—to help buy himself heroin.

Rudi H., 17, and Dirk L., 18, selling themselves at Zoo Station. Rudi says: "I've been shooting up for three months now, and prostitution is the only way that I can get the money I need." Dirk had been shooting up for a year and a half: "Once I went into detox and got a job, but then my boss found out about my past and fired me. I'm not afraid of the physical withdrawal, only of what comes after."

Bärbel W., 21, at the Eisenach youth hostel. "I shot up for the first time when I was 13 years old. Working as a hooker is disgusting, but for girls it's the only way we know to get the money we need. If you want to quit, you need to have a reason. And right now I just don't."

Karin S., 17, in front of the public bathrooms at Bülowbogen: "I started shooting up when I was 13. When my mom realized what was going on, she called the police. She really thought that I would stop using in jail. But it was just as easy to score dope in there as it was on the street. When you start as early as I did, you don't really have a chance."

Detlef R. in pre-trial detention
at Moabit Prison.

Jürgen became a regular. He was bi, and most of the time we visited him together. I would entertain him up top and Detlef would attend to things down below. We always got a hundred marks for that. Sometimes one of us would go alone, too, for sixty marks. It goes without saying that Jürgen was, on the one hand, a john like any other—not the best, but not that gross either. At the same time, he was the only customer for whom I felt something like friendship. I respected him. I liked talking to him. He was interesting and often had some real insights. He lived in the real world, and he lived well.

I especially admired the way he handled money. That was the thing about him that interested me the most. He told me once about how, once he'd invested in something, the money almost seemed to grow by itself. He was incredibly generous. He didn't pay anyone else who attended his orgies, but once I was around when a younger guy asked him for a couple thousand marks, for a Mini Cooper. Jürgen didn't get into a big discussion about it. Instead, he just wrote out a check and said, "Here." Jürgen was the only customer who would sometimes have me over without asking for anything from me. I sometimes watched TV with him at night. When I did, it seemed like all was right again with the world, at least while I was there.

MEANWHILE, IT DIDN'T TAKE very long for Detlef and me to settle right back into our old routine. We never went to the clubs anymore—they were for kids. So when I wasn't hanging around Zoo Station; I was at Kurfürstendamm. Sometimes there would be like a hundred junkies just on the small subway platform there. That's where the dealing happened. There were a lot of johns there looking to take advantage of some desperate junkie, but that didn't bother us. It was just the place where we met up.

When I was there, I'd walk from group to group, talking with the others. I felt like I really mattered when I was making my rounds on that platform, right below the Kurfürstendamm. I felt like a star. I'd see the old ladies heading back from the department stores with their bags full of junk, staring at us with this disgusted, frightened look in their eyes, and I'd think, Oh my God, we have it so much better than they do. Our lives might be hard, and it might not be the safest way to live—the prognosis wasn't good, anyway—but at the same time, we wouldn't have it any other way.

For me at least, I liked it like that. I mean, think about the money I was making. Just for the heroin alone I needed a hundred marks a day. With all the other expenses included, an average month cost about four thousand marks. That's what I had to bring in, and it was a lot, but I still managed it. The way I looked at it was: I'm making more than a lot of my clients do, and I'm only fourteen years old.

Working the streets and turning tricks was pretty shitty work, obviously; but when I was on dope it didn't bother me that much. And anyway, I kind of ripped off my customers because they didn't get much for their money. I still called the shots. Sex was out of the question.

But I was a pretty small player in the overall scene. I was in awe of the guys who said they needed four grams of dope every day. That worked out to 500 to 850 marks' worth of heroin every day, but they almost always managed to get what they needed. So they were making more than almost anyone in Berlin at the time, and they were doing it without getting caught by the cops. And even if I wasn't at their level yet, I could still walk up to them at Kurfürstendamm, and they would talk to me.

Anyway, that's what I was thinking at the time, back in February and March of 1977, when I was still okay. I didn't feel great, but still, I hadn't hit rock bottom yet. I still believed the lies I was telling myself. I'd slipped right back into the life of a junkie. I thought I was really cool. I wasn't afraid of anything.

Before heroin, I was afraid of everything: of my father, and then later of my mom's boyfriend; of my shitty school and the teachers there; of landlords, traffic cops, and even subway ticket checkers. Now I felt untouchable. I wasn't even scared of the undercover cops who prowled around the station. And I had a reason to be cocky: At that point, I'd gotten through every police raid without so much as a scratch.

Back then I was also hanging around with some other users—junkies, really—who I thought were somehow still in control. Atze and Lufo were like that. Atze was my first boyfriend. The only guy I'd had a close relationship with before Detlef; I used to be crazy about him. In 1976, Lufo—like Atze and Detlef—was part of our pot-smoking clique at The Sound. Atze and Lufo got stuck on dope right before I did. They got an apartment, and it looked like they'd made it: The apartment had a French bed, a matching couch and recliner set, and wall-to-wall carpeting. Lufo even had a totally legit, minimum-wage job at Schwarzkopf.[30]

Both of them claimed that they'd never been physically addicted to heroin, and that they could go for weeks or even months without shooting up. I believed them, but at the same time, they were always high whenever I hung out with them. Atze and Lufo were my idols. At the time I was worried about sinking back to the state I was in before my first purge. I thought that if Detlef and I could be as cool as Atze and Lufo were when it came to our habits, then we could also make it like they did and live in an apartment with a French bed, matching couch and recliner sets, and wall-to-wall carpeting.

---

30 Schwarzkopf was a well-known hair product store.

Also, neither of them was aggressive like the other junkies were, and Atze had a really cool girlfriend, too—Simone, who didn't shoot up at all. I thought it was awesome that they were so in love and accepting of each other even though one of them was a user and the other one wasn't. I liked spending time at their place, and sometimes, when I'd had a fight with Detlef, I slept on Lufo's couch.

But one night I came home, and since I was in a good mood and felt like things were going pretty well overall, I stopped in the living room to sit down with my mom. Right away she got up and went to get the paper without saying a word. I could sense what was coming next. She always handed me the paper like that when there was a report about a heroin death. I hated it. I didn't want to read whatever she wanted to show me.

But I read the obituary anyway: "Glassblower's apprentice Andreas W. (17) wanted to get off drugs. His sixteen-year-old girlfriend, a nursing student, wanted to help him: but to no avail. The young man died of an overdose in an apartment in Tiergarten, which his father had furnished for the young couple for several thousand marks."

The story didn't sink in right away, because I didn't want to believe it. But all of the elements were there: apartment, glass-blower's apprentice, girlfriend, Andreas W. . . . It was Andreas Wiczorek—Atze!

At first all I could think was, Shit. My throat was dry and I felt like I was going to puke. I couldn't understand how Atze could have overdosed. Atze, of all people—who knew just how much dope he could handle and was always cool and in control. I didn't want to let my mom see how upset I was. She had no idea that I was using again. So I took the paper and just went back to my room.

I hadn't seen Atze for a long time, but the paper filled me in on his last few days. According to the news story, he'd already been shooting up way too much during the previous week and had eventually landed in the hospital. His girlfriend, Simone, slashed her wrists right after that, but both of them survived.

Then, the day before Atze died, he went to the police and ratted on all the dealers he knew, even these two girls who were known as "the twins" and who always had first-class heroin. Then he wrote a suicide note, which the paper reprinted in full:

> I'm ending my life because an addict only brings anger, anxiety, bitterness, and despair to his friends and family. He drags everyone else down with him. Please tell my parents and my grandmother that I'm thankful for all they did for me.

> I'm an absolute zero. To be a junkie means you're the worst of the worst—the bottom of the shit pile. Why do so many kids—so many young people who enter this world so full of life and hope—fall into this kind of self-destructive cycle? I hope that my life can at least serve as a warning to someone else who may at some point ask himself the question: Well, should I try it, just this once?

> Don't be an idiot. Just look at me, and you'll have your answer.

> You don't have to worry about me anymore, Simone. Take care.

I lay on my bed and thought, That was your first boyfriend, and now he's in a coffin. I couldn't even cry. I was totally numb.

When I hit the scene the next afternoon, no one was thinking about Atze. It makes sense: Nobody cries on the street. But on the other hand, some people were definitely pretty angry. Atze had ratted on some good dealers who sold first-class dope, and now they were all sitting in jail. Also, Atze still owed a lot of people a lot of cash.

The craziest thing about this whole story is that a week after Atze died, his girlfriend, Simone, who'd never used before and who always tried to convince him to get off the stuff, started shooting up, too. A few weeks later, she quit her internship in the nursing program and started working the streets.

Lufo died from an overdose about a year later, in January 1978.

ATZE'S DEATH COMPLETELY OBLITERATED this crazy fantasy that we all shared. We all used to believe that we could shoot up and still live normal lives. But now that dream was dead. Everyone in Atze's old crowd began to fear and mistrust each other. Before, when there weren't enough needles to go around, everybody wanted to be first. Now, all of a sudden, everybody wanted to go second. Nobody talked about how scared they were, but everyone was worried that the stuff would be too pure, too strong, or that it would be cut with strychnine or some other poison. You could die from an overdose, but you could also die from shit that was too pure or too dirty.

So there it was. Everything was all fucked up again. It was just like Atze said in his suicide note. In the meantime, I was making life hell for my mom. I came home whenever I wanted, just like before, but whenever I got back my mom would still be up, no matter what time it was. It's funny, but the first thing she would do as soon as she knew I was back was take some Valium so that she could finally get some sleep herself. In fact, I think the Valium is the only reason she made it through that period.

I was getting more and more freaked out by the thought that I was going to end up like Atze. But I'd find little things to cling to still—things that would give me some degree of hope for the future. Even at school. There was one teacher I really liked:

Mr. Mücke. In his class, we'd have to act out certain situations from a normal adult life. So we'd pretend to be going to a job interview, for instance. One of us would have to be the employer, and the other one would have to play the role of the applicant. When I played the job applicant, I wouldn't let the employer get a word in edgewise. Instead, I turned the tables on him, so that he felt intimidated and quickly backed down. I thought that maybe I could learn to assert myself like that in real life, too.

We also went to the career services office with Mr. Mücke. But that meant that we also had to watch an Allied Forces military parade.[31] The guys were all really into it. They couldn't shut up about the tanks and all the new technology. But I had the opposite reaction because the tanks made a hellish, head-splitting noise, and their only purpose was to kill people anyway.

But then I got another boost in the career services office, when I read about the job of animal caretaker. I read through everything I could find about it, and the next day I went back with Detlef and asked them to make me copies of everything they had on that kind of work. Detlef, for his part, found some information on a few jobs that he was really excited about. He was looking for something to do with animals or farming. We were so into it that we almost forgot that we still needed to get the cash for our next fix. So next thing you know we're back at Zoo Station, waiting for customers, but still holding our bags full of photocopies from the career services center. It made everything seem so unreal again. If I kept on going like this, I felt like I probably wouldn't even make it through high school.

On my way to school the next morning, I bought a copy of *Playboy* at one of the subway stations. Detlef loved *Playboy*,

---

31 West Berlin, as an "island" within Communist East Germany, had a strong presence of American, French, and British troops (known as the Allied Forces), which regularly held military parades in order to maintain a high military profile.

and I bought it for him as a present for him (although I always read through it first myself). I don't know why we both liked *Playboy* so much. Today, looking back, I just don't get it. But back then *Playboy* seemed like a cleaner world. Clean sex. Beautiful girls who lived problem-free lives. No perverts, no pedophiles, no "clients" at all. The guys in the magazines smoked pipes and drove sports cars and were rich. And the girls had sex with them because they wanted to, because it was fun. Detlef said that that was all bullshit, but he still loved those magazines.

While I was in the subway that morning, I read a short story from that issue. I didn't understand all of what it said because I was already pretty messed up from my morning hit. But I liked the mood of the story. It took place somewhere far away under a blue sky and a hot sun. I got to this spot where a pretty girl is waiting around for her boyfriend to get back home from work, and I just started to cry. I couldn't get ahold of myself and kept crying all the way to my stop, where I had to get out.

When I was in school, all I could do was daydream about leaving with Detlef—going someplace far, far away. And that afternoon, when I met Detlef at the station, I told him about my daydream. At that point, he told me about his aunt and uncle in Canada.

They lived on a huge lake with nothing but forests and cornfields around them, and he was sure they would take us in. He said I should finish school first, since that would be the smart thing to do. He would go ahead first and find himself a job (apparently they had lots of jobs available), and when I followed after him a bit later, he would have already found a log cabin for us to live in together.

I wanted to finish school first anyway. Things were already getting a lot better. I could feel it. I was determined not to talk back anymore; instead, I would focus on my schoolwork and getting good grades.

Detlef went off with a customer, but I was still standing around and waiting. Suddenly there were these two guys behind me. "What are you doing here?" they asked me, and I knew right away they were cops. I'd never been arrested before, and the cops didn't scare me because up to now they'd always left me alone. I'd been turning tricks for a few months now at Zoo Station, along with a bunch of other girls my age. There were daily raids by the cops, but usually they were just looking for people who had smuggled cigarettes or schnapps over from East Berlin.

So I stayed real cool and just told the cops I was waiting for my boyfriend. One of them asked me if I was working as a prostitute. "No way," I said. "Why? Do I look like one?" Then they asked me how old I was, and I said I was fourteen. They wanted to see my ID, but you can't even get an ID until you're sixteen. (I made sure I explained that to them).

One of them, apparently the leader, jumped in then and said, "Why don't you hand over that plastic bag there?" Right away he found the spoon. He asked what I used it for. I said, "I need something to eat my yogurt with, don't I?" But then he pulled out the toilet paper with the needles and everything, and at that point I had to go with them. They brought me to the police station near the Zoo. I wasn't scared though; I knew that they couldn't throw a fourteen-year-old in jail. I was just pissed that these two shithead cops had ruined my day.

They locked me in a cell right next to the chief asshole's desk. I was still so sure of myself, somehow, that I didn't even try to get rid of the dope that I still had in a little plastic bag in my jeans. I just couldn't get myself to do it, to throw away good heroin. But then a woman cop came in. I had to take off everything, even my underwear; she examined everywhere, every orifice, before she finally thought about checking my jeans pockets, where she found the drugs.

One of the cops typed up the whole incident—all insanely complicated and tedious—on a sheet of paper, and when they were done they put a copy in a big fat binder. I was now on the record as a registered heroin user. But the cops were pretty nice about everything in the end, except for the fact that they kept coming back to me and asking, "God, sweetie, what the hell are you doing? You're only fourteen; you're young, you're pretty, but you're killing yourself with this stuff."

I had to give them my mom's work phone number, and one of them went out of the room to give her a call. My mom got to the station after work, totally stressed out, around five thirty. She actually got into a conversation with these cops, who seemed like they were only capable of stupid jokes, and after, they asked her the same thing they kept asking me; she said, "I know, I know, it's hard with these kids now. I don't know what to do with her anymore. I helped her quit once. But she actually doesn't want to quit."

That was the last straw: "Doesn't want to quit"? My mom didn't have the slightest clue about me or about heroin. Of course I wanted to stop. But how? That was what I'd like her to tell me. Once I was outside, she started to ask me all these questions. What had I been doing? Where had I been hanging out? And so on.

"Jeez, Mom, I was just at the station."

"You know you shouldn't go there."

"I was waiting for Detlef—but maybe I'm not allowed to do that anymore either."

She thought I shouldn't be hanging out with that "unemployed, antisocial loser" anymore. Then she threw a question at me: "Are you selling yourself?!" And I screamed at her, "Are you crazy? I dare you to say that again. Why on earth would I ever sell myself—can you explain that to me? So you think I'm a prostitute, huh?"

She backed down pretty quickly. But now I was really afraid I'd lose my freedom. And it was kind of scary, how cold my mom seemed to act toward me all of a sudden. It seemed like she'd given up on me now and would just let me fall on my own, wouldn't bother helping me anymore. But then I realized that she wasn't helping me anyway by just nagging about not "going to that train station" or hanging out with "that loser Detlef."

I had to go home with my mom, and I didn't have any junk for the next morning either. When my mom got me out of bed the next morning, she looked at my face and said, "What sort of eyes are those, sweetie? They're so blank. I see nothing but fear and despair in them."

When she left for work, I looked in the mirror, and for the first time I saw what happened to my eyes when I went cold turkey. They were 100 percent pupil. Completely black and dull. Totally blank.

I felt hot and washed my face. But then I was freezing, so I took a hot bath. I couldn't bear to get out of the tub because it was way too cold out there. I kept adding more and more hot water. Somehow I had to make it to noon. There was no way I'd find a customer at the Kurfürstendamm station or someone who'd give me a hit before then. Nobody had any junk until the afternoon. As things stood, it was pretty hard to find anyone who would share some with you. I could forget about asking Axel and Bernd, as they watched their stash like hawks; they needed every quarter-gram for themselves. They could barely make enough money to buy only that much. Even Detlef was getting selfish with his supply. And the others on the street would have rather thrown their junk down the toilet than share it.

As the withdrawal symptoms got worse, I forced myself to get out of the tub so that I could try to find some money in the apartment. The living room was locked, as always. Klaus, my mom's boyfriend, did that because he was worried that I would ruin his LPs. But I'd figured out how to pick the lock with a wire hanger. Unfortunately, the living room was broke: It didn't have a dime. But then I remembered the beer can on top of the kitchen cabinet. My mom used it as a container for all her shiny, five-mark coins.

My hands shook as I grabbed the heavy beer can—partly due to the fact that I was going into withdrawal, but also because I was about to steal from my mom, and I'd never sunk that low before. I wouldn't have even considered it. That's why I was different from the other junkies—from people like Bernd, who'd taken everything from his parents' apartment, piece by piece: the TV, the coffee maker, the electric bread slicer—anything that could be turned into cash for dope. I'd sold my jewelry and almost all my LPs, but at least that stuff was mine.

So now I was dumping my mom's five-mark coins out of the beer can. The street price of a quarter gram had just gone down from forty marks to thirty-five. So I needed seven of the five-mark coins. I figured that since I usually charged my customers forty marks, I'd get a fiver back in change. So I could easily replace one five-mark piece every day. In a week I would have repaid the money, and my mom probably wouldn't even notice. So I took my seven fives and went to my morning hookup spot outside the dining hall of the technical university, picked up some heroin, and shot up in the university bathroom. I was already in full withdrawal at that point.

My mom checked my arms for fresh needle marks every night, so I shot into my hand—always in the same spot. It turned into a scab, but I told my mom that it was just a scrape that wasn't healing well. Eventually she noticed that I had a fresh needle mark. "Give me a break," I told her when she found out. "What's the big deal? It was just today. I only do it once in a while; it's nothing to worry about."

But nevertheless, she gave me a pretty good spanking. I didn't resist. It didn't really bother me much anymore. She treated me like a piece of shit anyway and was always yelling at me for something or other. Instinctively, she was doing exactly the right thing. An addict has to lose literally everything and feel like the last piece of shit on earth before she'll think seriously about changing something. Then she'll either kill herself, or she'll hang her hat on whatever slim chance she has to ditch the dope. But back then I didn't have that kind of insight yet.

My mom still believed in me, though, and thought I could get better. She made plans for me to go and visit my grandma and cousins over spring break. She said that it was possible I could even stay longer. I didn't know if I should be happy or worried about the separation from Detlef and the inevitable withdrawal symptoms I'd experience over there. But by now I was doing whatever anyone wanted anyway, I only insisted that Detlef sleep over the last night before I left.

During that last night in Berlin, I came up with yet another plan. After Detlef and I had sex, I told him, "We've always done everything together. I really want to cut this shit out while I'm gone. I'll never get this kind of an opportunity again. You should do it, too. Then when I get back, we'll both be clean, and we can start a new life."

Detlef said that yeah, of course he wanted to quit with me. But that was no surprise. (He already had a source for methadone.) By the time I got back to Berlin, he'd have a new job, and starting tomorrow or the day after that he'd stop working the streets.

The next morning I took a really big hit before I went off to grandma and my new life. When I arrived, the withdrawal symptoms hadn't started yet. But I felt like an alien in that idyllic farmhouse kitchen. Everything got on my nerves. It annoyed me that my little cousin wanted to get on my lap, even though I'd always loved playing with her when she was as a baby. The old outhouse—the one that I'd found so romantic last time—was also irritatingly outdated.

The next morning, the withdrawal symptoms started up with a vengeance. I slipped out of the house and went into the woods, but the birds wouldn't stop their stupid twittering, and a little rabbit made me jump right out of my skin. I eventually climbed up into a tree stand. I couldn't even smoke. I wanted to die up there. At some point though, I don't know when, I crawled back to the house and got into bed. I told my grandma that I had the flu or something. She was a little concerned but not too worried, despite the way things looked.

Above my bed there was a poster that showed a skeleton hand holding a needle. Below the hand it said, "Curiosity was the beginning. This is the end." (My cousin insisted that she got the poster in school.) I didn't realize that my mom had already told my grandma that I was an addict. Now I was staring at the needle on the poster—only the needle though. I didn't pay any attention to the letters and the skeleton hand anymore. I just imagined that that needle held a quarter gram of first-class heroin. The needle seemed to peel away from the poster and float toward me. For hours I stared at that fucking poster and almost went insane.

My cousin came into my room a lot and pretended not to notice what was going on with me. She kept playing these annoying cassette tapes of teenybopper music, probably thinking that they could distract me somehow. In retrospect, of course, it was touching how they were trying to help me and pretending not to know what was happening with me.

That first day of withdrawal seemed like it would never end. Once, when I dozed off, I had a dream about this junkie I knew from the streets of Berlin. He was so messed up from shooting up that his skin had started to develop these open, oozing wounds all over. He was literally decomposing while he was still alive. His feet had already decayed and turned black. He could hardly walk anymore. He stank so badly—even from two yards away—that nobody could stand to be near him. But when anybody suggested that he should check into a hospital, he just grinned this deathly grin. He was just waiting to die. I couldn't get this guy out of my mind—that is, when I wasn't too busy staring at the needle in the poster or delirious from the pain. It was just like the first time, with all the same sweating and stinking and puking.

The next morning I couldn't take it anymore. I dragged myself to the phone booth in town and called my mom. I was crying and blubbering snot into the receiver. I begged her to come and bring me back to Berlin.

My mom was unfazed. She said coolly, "So you're sick again? I thought that you only used heroin sometimes. Well, in that case it can't be that bad."

Finally I wound up begging her to send me some sleeping pills via express mail. I'd heard that in the next town over there was an active H scene. I figured that out during my last visit. But I didn't have the strength to get there. Also, I didn't know anyone over there. When a junkie is separated from his own scene he's totally helpless and alone.

Thankfully, the withdrawal period only lasted four days, just like before. When it was over, I felt empty, depleted, sucked dry. It didn't even give me a sense of triumph to know that the poison was finally out of my body. I felt nothing but disgust for Berlin again, but I didn't belong in this town either. Actually, I felt like I didn't really belong anywhere. I tried to just not think about it.

All I had for entertainment were the sleeping pills that my mom had sent (way too late) and a bunch of hard cider that was stored in my grandma's basement. I was starving though, and I ate everything. In the mornings I would start with four or five rolls, and in the afternoons, in between meals, I'd eat like a dozen pieces of flatbread with jam. At night I'd go into the giant pantry and binge on the canned plums, peaches, and strawberries (with piles of whipped cream on top). I could never go to sleep before two or three in the morning anyway.

In no time, I'd put on over twenty pounds. My butt got big, and I developed a serious potbelly. My relatives were delighted. Only my arms and legs stayed as skinny as they were before. But I didn't care. I couldn't stop eating—it was almost like I was addicted to food. It didn't take long before my skintight jeans didn't fit anymore. That's when my cousin gave me a pair of baggy pants like the kind I wore when I was eleven. It didn't bother me though. I was becoming part of the community here again. But I didn't think it was for real. That was a trip, a nice little movie, and it would all be over again soon.

●

I KEPT DRUGS OUT of my conversations with other people, and I also did a pretty good job of keeping them out of my mind entirely. I didn't want to ruin this pretty little movie I was taking part in. There was one exception though: Right after I arrived at my grandma's place I wrote a letter to Detlef asking him to send me some dope (for which I also included twenty marks). It showed just how hollow my earlier lectures about quitting were, but I couldn't help myself. I managed not to mail the letter, though, because I figured that Detlef would just spend the money on himself anyway.

I let my cousin show me around like I was a tourist and visited castles and other fortresses in the area, and I also went horseback riding almost every day. I went down into the quarry (which had once belonged to my grandpa), too, along with the other kids. My grandpa had literally sold the quarry and used the proceeds to fund his drinking habit. He drank himself to death eventually. That's the environment my mom grew up in.

My grandma told me that somewhere in the quarry there was a room, locked up behind an iron door, that contained all the old family documents. And so we spent almost every night searching for that door. Sometimes the workers would forget to take the key out of the backhoe. Then we would drive all over the quarry with that thing.

I got along really well with my cousin who was the same age as me. I told her about how much I loved Detlef, and she reacted as if it were a completely normal teenage romance. I also told her that we'd already slept together, and she didn't see anything wrong with that—she thought that was totally okay.

My cousin said that there was a boy from Düsseldorf that she had a crush on. He always came up to where she lived on camping trips in the summer. He had wanted more from her, but she had stayed firm. She asked me if I thought that was dumb.

I told her of course not. It was absolutely her decision, and if she didn't want that camper to touch her, then she shouldn't let him. She should wait until she found someone who she really wanted to do those things with.

Everyone up there came to me for help with their problems. I turned into a regular "Dear Abby" for my cousin and her friends. I didn't mind though. I felt pretty comfortable doling out advice, especially when it came to adding some perspective to their trivial little issues and concerns. In fact, almost all their problems seemed ridiculously insignificant to me. But I always listened, and I always had some ready advice. There was nothing I was afraid to confront with these kids, but when it came to my own problems, I was helpless.

Detlef called me one night—and I was so excited and happy I could hardly stand it. He said that he was at a john's place—that's why he was able to call me. We talked for a really long time, thanks to this guy's generosity.

I told Detlef about my awful withdrawal experience and about how this time I'd almost gone insane. He said that he hadn't quit yet. It was just so sad. I was looking forward to seeing him again. I asked him if he could write me once more like he promised. Detlef said that he really didn't feel like it. But he'd call me the next time he came back to this john's apartment.

After our phone call, I felt reassured that I was as good as married to Detlef. We belonged together—no matter what sort of shit he got himself into. At night, before falling asleep, I'd spend several silent minutes sending good thoughts to Detlef. Praying almost. And I counted down the days until I'd be with him again.

My grandma gave me a regular allowance, and I saved every penny. I wasn't sure why. Saving money had never been my thing. But once I'd saved up forty marks, I couldn't deny what I was up to anymore. I was really proud of having saved so much and put it away in a safe place. Forty marks was the price of a shot. Forty marks was what I charged my customers. Forty was the magic number for me.

Once I'd realized what I had in mind, I reprimanded myself for stockpiling drug money even while I was working to stay clean. And then, to drive the point home, I went into town and bought myself a T-shirt for twenty marks, just to get away from that damned number forty! I'd come to my grandma's house with the sole intention of getting clean. I never wanted to shoot up again. That was the whole point—to get away from that life for good.

As the month came to an end, my mom called and wanted to know if I wanted to come back or stay a while longer. Without a second thought I told her I was ready to come back. Maybe if she had asked if I wanted to spend the rest of my life out there, I would have thought more about it. But since I knew that it was only a temporary state of affairs one way or the other, it just seemed like it had all been a kind of a dream—a nightmare at the beginning, but in the end a sweet, gentle, beautiful dream. But now it was over. After four weeks, it was time for me to get back to Detlef.

The first thing I did on the day that I was supposed to head back was to change back into my old set of clothes. My grandma and my cousin tried to convince me to stick with that old pair of checkered kids' pants (which at that point fit me perfectly again), but that was never a real possibility. Instead, I squeezed myself into my skinny jeans. The seams could hardly handle it, and there was no way in hell I could get the zipper up all the way. I slipped on my black men's blazer, and my favorite pair of high-heeled boots. So before I'd even left my grandma's house, I was already looking heroin chic. Or at least the best I could manage. I took the train back to Berlin with my pants undone.

The next afternoon I went straight to Zoo Station. Detlef and Bernd were both there. Axel, however, was not. I figured he was off with a customer.

The two boys gave me a huge welcome. They were genuinely happy to see me. Especially Detlef. I said, "So, you got a good job and dropped the dope?" All three of us laughed. I asked, "How's Axel?"

The boys looked at me kind of strange, and after a while Detlef said, "Haven't you heard? Axel's dead."

That knocked the wind out of me. I couldn't breathe for a while. "You're joking," I said between gasps. But I already knew that it was true.

Axel.

I'd spent most of my weekend nights with Detlef over at Axel's place. He always put clean sheets out for me, even though the rest of the house was always a mess. He kept up a steady supply of yogurt for me, and I always brought him his beloved canned tuna. He was always willing to hear me out whenever I had any problems or whenever I had a fight with Detlef. He was never angry or aggressive with anyone in our clique, and even though I was pretty guarded with everyone else, I could even cry in front of him. And now he was gone. "Why?" I asked.

Detlef said, "They found him in some public toilet stall with a needle in his arm." For the two boys, Axel's death was already old news. But they seemed uncomfortable talking about it.

I couldn't stop thinking about the goddamn tuna fish. Suddenly I realized that Detlef might have also lost his place to sleep, so I asked him if he was still staying at Axel's place.

"His mom has already sold the apartment," Detlef answered. "I'm staying with one of my customers."

"Oh, shit," I said. I just blurted it out because at that moment I thought that I'd lost Detlef to one of his customers for good. The fact that Detlef was living with a john hit me almost as hard as Axel's death.

"The guy I'm staying with is pretty all right. He's still young, in his mid-twenties, and he's still kind of in shape, too. I've already told him about you. You can sleep over there, too."

We took the subway over to where we knew some dealers would be selling since Detlef needed a hit. We kept running into people we knew, and whenever we did I would say to them, "Doesn't that just fucking suck about Axel." But the others didn't react at all. So I just kept muttering the same thing over and over to myself.

After scoring some dope, we went to the public bathrooms on Bülow Street.[32] Detlef wanted to take care of business right away. I came along to help, but I was also hoping Detlef would offer me some—I wanted to turn it down, just to show him that I was strong enough to do it. But I didn't get my chance because Detlef never offered me any.

The thing with Axel shocked me to the core, and I was having a problem processing it. When Detlef was cooking up his dope, I suddenly got this insane craving. This is some serious shit with Axel and with Detlef, I thought, and a shot will help you out—plus it's not like one little shot means anything. You don't become an addict again just like that.

Detlef said, "Are you serious?! You want to get high? I thought you'd quit."

"Course I did," I replied. "But that's not a big deal. It's easy to quit. After all, while I was away getting clean, you did the same thing, right? But whatever. I'm just freaking out a little bit after hearing what happened to Axel. I just want a little shot."

"Yeah—quitting's not a big deal. I could have done it, too, I just didn't feel like it. But I'm just saying, if you're clean now, you should stay clean and not start up again now."

While we were talking—and despite what he was saying—he finished shooting up himself and left a little bit for me, too. After being clean for so long that little shot was enough to get me a little high. I almost forgot all about Axel. Almost.

I went from sobriety to full-blown addiction way faster than I did the last time. My mom was clueless though. It took me a while to lose those extra pounds, and she was happy about how healthy I looked.

---

32 The public bathrooms on Bülow Street were one of the many places in Berlin that Christiane F. made famous because of her life story.

If I wanted to see Detlef now, then I had to head over to Rolf's house. That was Detlef's client—the guy he was staying with. There was nowhere else we could go to sleep together anymore. I didn't like Rolf though. He was totally in love with Detlef, and as a result he was really jealous of me. He loved it when we'd fight, and he always took Detlef's side. That drove me crazy. Detlef treated Rolf like his own personal servant—like a submissive wife or girlfriend. He sent him shopping and let him do all the cooking and cleaning. That pissed me off too, because I would've liked to do some of those things for Detlef myself.

So one afternoon I told Detlef that it just wasn't working out. The three of us just didn't make a good team. It was like Rolf was the third wheel on the wagon. But Detlef said he didn't have anywhere else to go. He said that Rolf was basically an okay guy, and it was nice to work for someone who wasn't a huge asshole.

Detlef did what he wanted with Rolf. And when he was angry or annoyed, he'd tell him bluntly, "Just be grateful that I stick with you." And Detlef only slept with Rolf if he needed money really badly.

Detlef and I slept in a bed in the same room as Rolf. When we had sex, Rolf would watch TV or just turn away from us. He was gay and didn't want to see us together. I guess all three of us were pretty fucked up.

I couldn't shake the idea that Detlef was going to "become gay" if he kept sleeping with men. There was one night in particular when I thought that it had finally happened. Detlef needed money, so he had no choice: He had to sleep with Rolf. I lay in the other bed. Detlef had turned off the light just like he always did when I was there and he had to satisfy Rolf because he needed to earn some money. The whole thing seemed to take a really long time. And at one point I thought I heard Detlef moaning. I stood up and lit a candle. Both of them were going at it under the blanket. It seemed like they were both touching each other. (That was against the rules. Detlef and I had an agreement: No one was allowed to touch us.) So I was insanely pissed off. So pissed off that I wasn't even able to articulate what I actually wanted. I just said, "You guys seem like you're having a lot of fun over there."

Detlef didn't say anything, but Rolf was furious. He blew out my candle and kept Detlef with him for the whole night. I cried silently into my pillow all night because I didn't want the other two to hear how much this affected me. The next morning, I was so upset that I honestly considered leaving Detlef. The heroin was undermining our relationship at every turn, but we weren't even aware of it. We couldn't see what it was doing to us.

It was clear to me now that as long as we were on H, Detlef would never be totally mine. I would have to share him with his customers—especially Rolf. In my case, of course, it was different. I sold myself at Zoo Station every day, and since I was under more serious time constraints, I didn't have the luxury of picking and choosing all my customers. At this point, there were a lot of times when it was the clients—and not me—who set the terms of our agreement.

In order to keep away from Rolf, I started to spend more time again with the other people in our clique—especially with Babsi and Stella. But it was getting to be more difficult to get along with them as well. Everyone wanted to just talk for hours about themselves; nobody cared what was going on with anybody else. Babsi, for example, was going on and on about the weird punctuation on traffic signs, while Stella and I wanted to talk about how a dealer ripped us off (he gave us flour instead of dope). We told Babsi to shut up, but after Stella and I had gotten control of the conversation we wound up fighting with each other over who would get to tell the rest of the story.

Most of our conversations ended with someone yelling, "Shut up!" We were all desperately in need of someone who could listen to us. But that person just didn't exist—at least not in our circle of friends. There was no real communication amongst us anymore. The only time anyone paid any attention was when we were talking about the cops. We were all united in our opinion against the fucking cops. I was actually a bit more developed than the others in that respect because in the early summer of 1977 I'd already been arrested for the third time.

It happened at Zoo Station. Detlef and I were just coming back after an encounter with a customer. He'd given us 150 marks just to watch us. So we were pretty happy, each of us with a quarter of dope in our pocket and plenty of cash left over. I saw them first, the cops pouring onto the platform. It was a drug raid. A train was just pulling in, and I was running down the platform in total panic. Detlef, not thinking clearly at that moment, ran after me. As I jumped onto the last car of the train, I ran right into an old man. He said, "Fucking zombie hag! Watch where you're going!" He really said that. Thanks to the newspaper coverage, almost everyone seemed to know what was going on at Zoo Station. So even the drones in the subway realized quickly that this was a drug raid in progress.

Detlef was right behind me—and behind him, of course, were two undercover cops. After all, we'd behaved suspiciously enough. The cops didn't have to work very hard to catch up with us, despite our head start. Even before they'd arrived on the scene, a bunch of geriatrics in the subway had grabbed hold of us, gripping our clothes and screaming hysterically: "Here they are! Police! Police!" I felt like an outlaw in an old Western, and it seemed like the next scene was going to show Detlef and me dangling from some tree.

I clung tight to Detlef, but when the cops took us away, one of them just said, "That Romeo and Juliet act isn't going to cut it, so hurry it up; let's go!"

We were loaded into a VW bus and taken to the police station. The cops were mean, but they didn't bother taking down any additional information on me. They just told me that since this was the third time that they'd picked me up, they already had a binder on me. One of them typed up the usual statement, and all I had to do was sign it. They didn't even take the time to notify my mom. In their eyes, I was just another hopeless case. They'd keep filing away these statements and filling up the binder until the day when they could finally put a cross next to my name and forget about me.

Detlef and I were released about an hour later. Since they'd confiscated our dope, we had to go straight back to the hot zone to score two more quarters. Luckily for us, we still had some cash.

The undercover cops all knew me by then, and they generally left me alone. One of them—a young guy, with a cute, friendly Bavarian accent—was even kind of nice to me. The first time he saw me he snuck up behind me and shoved his badge in my face. I was obviously freaked out and worried, but then he laughed and asked me if I was working the streets. I answered innocently, like I always did, "The streets? Me? Are you serious?"

But he wasn't buying it. Still, he didn't even bother to go through my bag. He just told me to stay out of the area for a few days so that he wouldn't have to take me into the station. I bet the other officers at his station must have appreciated that, too, since taking me in would require that they write up yet another statement about a zombified fourteen-year-old addict.

After getting arrested, we couldn't find our old dealer, so Detlef and I had to buy our dope from this new guy whom we'd never heard of before. Then we went to the public bathrooms at

Winterfeldt Placz[33] to shoot up. The doors on all the toilet stalls had been broken off, and the sinks were all broken and dry. I cleaned my syringe with the water from the toilet (which was in a pretty bad way). It was gross, but I used that tactic from time to time because a lot of the bathrooms were too busy for us to risk cleaning the syringe in plain view by the sink.

I don't know what was in it, but the new dope from the new dealer totally knocked me out. I fell flat on my face right outside the bathrooms. And even though I picked myself up right after that, I was still really groggy. For the first time in a long time, we decided to go to The Sound.

Detlef was looking for a party, so he went straight to the dance floor while I positioned myself (strategically) next to this unattended tank of orange juice. It had a hole at the top, so I leaned against the vending machine, pushed two straws together, stuck them into the top, and drank my fill. Without paying a cent, I was able to drink until I had to go to the bathroom to throw up.

When I got back, one of the managers got up in my face. He called me a junkie whore and told me to come with him. He grabbed me by the arm and dragged me across the room. He opened a door that led to the storage area where they stacked the beverage crates. I also noticed that there was just one bar stool inside. Now I was scared.

I knew immediately what was going on. Or at least I thought I did—since I'd heard so much about this room. In here, the management would make the junkies—along with anyone else they

---

33 Berlin's Winterfeldtplatz, named after the Prussian General Hans Karl von Winterfeldt, is a pleasant, leafy square in the borough of Schöneberg. The majority of the square was destroyed in the war, but it still possesses a curious architectural mix, from the '60s-style social housing that runs along one side to distinctive landmarks like the red-brick St. Matthias church, one of the few free-standing Catholic churches in Berlin, and the residential house (and associated buildings) constructed by renowned "green" architect *Hinrich Baller*.

happened to despise—strip down to nothing, and then tie them up to the bar stool. After the person was rendered totally helpless, they'd beat him up with whips and whatever else was on hand. I'd heard about guys who'd ended up in the hospital with cracked skulls or other broken bones after just one session in The Sound's storage room. They were so traumatized and intimidated that they couldn't even go to the police afterward.

I'm sure the management at The Sound justified what they did by saying that it helped to keep junkies and drug addicts away, which in turn kept the authorities from being able to shut the club down—but clearly they also did it because they were natural sadists, and they just wanted to.

There was one thing that the girl junkies could do to save themselves a beating, though, because if you agreed to have sex with the manager then he would leave you alone. The Sound was just an absolutely brutal environment. If parents knew what really went on at "Europe's hottest club," they would never have let their kids go there. Every day more kids started using heroin in and around the club, and every day another young girl was reeled in by one of the pimps or hustlers who lurked around the place, and still the management did nothing. They just didn't care.

So there I was, standing at the door to the storage space and just absolutely consumed with panic and fear. With a strength that was surprising even to me, I ripped myself away from that guy and ran like crazy for the exit. I made it all the way to the street before he caught up with me. He grabbed onto me, but instead of dragging me back down he just threw me, hard, like a piece of trash, against a nearby car. I didn't even feel the impact though. I was more worried about Detlef at that point. They knew that we were always together. And after he'd run over to the dance floor, high as a kite, I hadn't seen him again.

I ran over to a phone booth and called the police. I told the cops that my boyfriend was being assaulted at The Sound. They seemed thrilled to hear it, and it only took them a couple of minutes to show up—a whole vanload of them. They were clearly hoping to be able to finally shut the club down. But after the dozen or so cops that were there had finished combing the place for Detlef, there was still no sign of him. That's when it occurred to me to call Rolf. Detlef was already there, in bed.

After all the drama, one of the cops came over and said, "So, you were just high, right? Listen: Don't you ever pull anything like this again." As I made my way home, I couldn't help thinking that all the heroin was making me lose my grip on reality.

Because I'd been arrested and taken into custody so many times, I was eventually summoned to pay a visit at the police department's criminal division. My appointment was for 3 p.m. at a building on Gothaer Street, room 314. I'll always remember that room number because it was about to become the destination of many future visits as well.

After school I went straight home to shoot up. I gave myself a healthy dose because I thought that if I was high enough, the cops wouldn't be able to rattle me. But it so happened that I was out of lemon, and that was a problem because the dope I had was far from pure. It was hard to get good stuff. Every time the dope changed hands—going from a big dealer to a middleman to a smaller dealer down the line—it was being cut with something else in order to increase the profit.

So I had to find a way to dissolve this dope that had already been cut with so much else. I decided to use vinegar because, like lemons, it also has a fair amount of acid in it. I poured the vinegar onto the spoon with the dope, but I poured too much. So with that done, I had to shoot this vinegar solution into my vein along with the dope. It was either that, or I'd have to throw everything out—and that wasn't going to happen.

As soon as I'd shot up, I was out cold. It took more than an hour for me to regain consciousness. When I did, I could see that the syringe was still stuck in my arm. My head felt like it was going to explode, and at first I couldn't even stand up. I thought that maybe this was it. That I was finally going to die. I just lay on the floor and cried.

I was so afraid. I didn't want to die—especially not like this, all alone. So I made my way over to the phone on my hands and knees. It must have taken me about ten minutes to dial my mom's office number. When I finally did, all I could do was mumble: "Please . . . please Mom . . . come home . . . I'm dying."

Once my mom got back, I was able to stand up again. I pulled myself together, even though my head still felt like it was going to burst. I told her, "I think I just had just another stupid circulatory collapse."

My mom obviously knew that I'd started using again. She had a desperate look on her face but didn't say anything to me about it. She just kept staring at me, and I could see the sadness in her eyes. I couldn't take it. The look on her face pierced me right through and made my head pound even worse than before.

After a while, my mom asked if there was anything I wanted. "Yes," I said. "Strawberries." So she went out and got me a big basket full of strawberries.

In the course of that afternoon, I got the feeling that I was running out of time. I hadn't shot up a huge amount; it was just too much vinegar. When something went wrong, my body didn't have any ability to resist or fight back anymore. I couldn't keep treating it this way. I couldn't keep abusing it.

I could recognize my downward spiral for what it was because of the fact that I'd already seen it happen before with some of my friends who had already died. The first warning sign was when they started to just pass out after shooting up. It kept going on that way, with things getting worse and worse, and then eventually there would be one time when they passed out and just never woke up again. That was it. Game over.

I was afraid to die, but if you had asked me at the time for a reason why, I wouldn't have been able to offer any good reasons. I just didn't want to be alone when it happened. Junkies tend to die alone—and to add insult to injury, the setting for the big event is usually a stinking toilet stall. But all that aside, I had more or less made my peace with death. I mean after all, what was I waiting for at that point? I couldn't think of any reason why I ought to stick around. Even when I was younger, it was hard to think of any real reason for me to be here. And now that I was a heroin addict, it wasn't like things were getting any better. What was the point? The longer I stuck around, the more lives I would probably ruin, including my own. If I died, I would be doing my mom a favor. Sometimes I myself had trouble telling whether I was alive or already gone.

The next morning I was feeling better though. Now at least I had some hope that I could go on for a little longer. But I had to make it to the police, unless I wanted them to come and get me. There was just no way I could handle going by myself now. No way. I called around looking for Stella and was lucky to get ahold of her at this client's place—he was a customer we shared. I asked if she'd come to the police station with me. She was game to go right away. Her mom had just reported her as missing again, but Stella wasn't afraid of anything; she couldn't care less. She wanted to go with me to the precinct, even though she was officially a missing person at the time.

So Stella and I went and sat like a couple of good girls in the long hallway outside of room 314, waiting for my turn with the police. When my name was called, I walked into the room so meek and obedient that if anyone had asked, I would've even curtsied. Mrs. Schipke—an overly friendly woman—took my hand, held it warmly, and told me right away that she also had a daughter like me—even though she was a year older than me and not using drugs. She acted really maternal with me. She asked how I was doing, and like a good aunt she even brought out some chocolate milk, cake, and apples.

This Mrs. Schipke sounded like she cared about some of the people I knew from the drug scene—asking where they were now and how they were doing. She showed me some photos of junkies and dealers and asked if I knew them. Yes, I kept telling her, sure, I recognize him; I've seen him once or twice. Then she told me that a number of these people had said this or that thing about me, and eventually, after enough of that kind of stuff, she got me to talk. I realized that she was setting me up—and not even doing it very delicately—but I still wound up giving her a lot of information. Afterward I signed a statement, swearing the truth to a whole bunch of shit that she'd been feeding me.

While we were wrapping up, another cop happened to ask me about The Sound more generally. That's when I decided to really open up. I told him about all the people I knew who had been seduced into the H scene there and about the brutal tactics that the management used over there. I also let them bring in Stella, who corroborated everything and said she would swear to it all in court.

Mrs. Schipke kept leafing through her files and quickly figured out who Stella really was. She started to grill her, and Stella immediately returned fire and shut Schipke down. Stella was so insulting that I thought that they'd book her right on the spot. But Mrs. Schipke's shift was over and done with, and she wanted to go home, so she just told Stella to come back the next day. Stella, of course, had no intention of obeying any of this woman's orders or requests.

As she was leaving, Mrs. Schipke said to me, "Well, I'm sure you and I will see each other again soon." The tone she used was exactly the same as it had been the whole afternoon—way too fucking sweet and friendly. That was what really stung. Despite her smiles, it was clear that she thought I was a totally lost cause. There was no hope for me.

Gerhard Ulber,
Chief Detective and Head of the Narcotics Division in the Berlin Police Department's Drug Squad

In our fight against drug abuse, the police department believes that by making every effort to restrict the supply of drugs—especially heroin—in and around Berlin, we provide an essential support to the efforts of other state agencies in offering therapy and rehabilitation to drug users and addicts. In 1976 we impounded 6.4 pounds of heroin, in 1977 it was 10.8 pounds, and in the first eight months of 1978 we've already impounded 18.5 pounds of heroin. This increase in seizures doesn't necessarily mean, however, that we're keeping up with the increased amount of drug availability and consumption in the area. In that respect, I am personally rather pessimistic. The quantities of heroin in circulation have definitely increased. Just one year ago, the arrest of a German middleman with a quarter pound of heroin would have been a small sensation. Today it's a pretty regular occurrence.

The success of our investigations have caused the smugglers and dealers to become more cautious, as was to be expected, and we, in turn, have become even more vigilant. But the more visibly we penetrate the areas where drug addicts and small dealers tend to gather and do business, the deeper into the underworld they go, and the harder they are to find and track.

Whatever we as a police department accomplish, and whatever means we try—whether we use quiet surveillance and undercover cops or conduct obvious patrols and raids—the drug market will always find a way to endure. More and more often, heroin is being sold in private homes, where addicts can evade the eye of the police.

To give just one example, twenty-four of the eighty-four people who died of heroin overdoses in Berlin in 1977 were not known to us as users of the drug—and these people most certainly didn't die after just one shot. Even the most persistent drug user often doesn't come to the attention of the police until he gets admitted to a hospital—usually while unconscious.

Otherwise, a person can abuse heroin for years without coming to our attention. To put it bluntly, the police department can't solve the drug problem by itself. As the United States discovered during Prohibition, wherever there's an intense demand, the suppliers will find a way to meet it.

I could, of course, hire another twenty officers and arrest more of the small-time dealers, but the problem would then just shift over to the prison system, where heroin already has a strong presence. Imprisoned addicts are willing to do anything to get their hands on some dope, and imprisoned dealers will do almost anything to supply them. Everyone is corrupted in situations where the profit margins are as high as they are with heroin right now.

Heroin addicts don't care about anything but their next score. Preventative education is the only thing, in my opinion, that has any chance to stop heroin's rise in our community.

Renate Schipke,
Administrator in the Drug Addiction Department

I first met Christiane while working as an administrator in the drug addiction department. She had been summoned to respond to a normal police filing and came to see me with her girlfriend Stella. This was the first of six or seven visits we would have together.

At the time, I was spending most of my time interrogating addicts who had come to the attention of local police, with the idea that they might give up the names of some of their dealers. The police file an incredible number of reports, and that leaves me with more interviews to do than I really have time for. As a rule, there's not much time to spend thinking about the problem as a whole. But I still try to get to know the people who are summoned, and I try to establish some sort of relationship with them because otherwise it's just not possible to conduct a successful interrogation.

When we first started to talk, Christiane was quite open and very willing to supply the information I was looking for. I was struck by her humility; she gave the impression of being a child who was raised the right way. During the first interrogation, she still seemed like a little girl in many ways. She always spoke well of her mother, and I have to say that her mother was very concerned about her compared to many of the other parents I see. I spent a lot of time on the phone with her.

After a few more interviews, Christiane began to act much more insolent and rude. It was hard to believe she was only fourteen. I gave it to her straight and told her that addiction was a one-way street, even if she was able to get clean occasionally. We had a few blowout fights on that score alone.

But I don't want to say anything negative about Christiane. She wasn't one to carry a grudge.

But it's simply impossible to help these addicts. They always feel tricked and wrongfully accused, as they don't understand why they should be punished. In my opinion, these young people are just plain foolish and much too reckless. They start using heroin out of boredom and curiosity and then are surprised when faced with the consequences. I hope that for her own sake, Christiane gets the most severe sentence possible, as I believe that the shock of being in prison could motivate her to want to become sober. At least that's my hope.

IN THE SUBWAY I WAS SO angry it was hard for me to keep it together. I couldn't believe I had let that policewoman wrap me around her little finger like that—with just some hot chocolate, cake, and her revolting, fake friendliness.

After I serviced two clients at Zoo Station and scored some more dope at Kurfürstendamm, I went home. My cat was lying in the kitchen and could hardly get up. He'd been sick for a few days. Now he looked so emaciated and meowed so pitifully that I thought he would die soon, too.

I was more anxious about my kitty than I was about myself. The vet gave me some medicine for him. But the cat wasn't eating anything. He lay in front of his small bowl and didn't even lift his head.

I was planning on shooting up, so I took out my needle, but then I had an idea. I drew some of the medicine into the syringe and used it to squirt a little into his mouth. He was so worn out that he didn't resist. After that, it took me a long time to clean out the needle again, prepare everything, and finally get my fix.

Heroin didn't give me the kind of high that it used to anymore. My fear of death ruined everything. I didn't want to live anymore, but at the same time I became incredibly anxious when I shot up, about the next shot being my last. Maybe it was also true that my cat's illness underlined how really sad and dark death is—especially if you haven't really lived yet.

I felt completely hopeless. I hadn't had a single meaningful conversation with my mom since she discovered that I was shooting up again. I screamed and fought about every little thing, and she just kept giving me that sad, dejected look of hers. The police were after me for real now. The statement that I'd signed at Schipke's office was enough for them to put me on trial and enforce a juvenile court sentence. I also got the feeling that my mom would've been glad to relinquish some of her responsibility for me. After all, she must have realized by that point that there was nothing she could really do for me. She was always on the phone with drug rehab counseling centers and other government agencies, and at the same time she just kept sliding deeper and deeper into despair. It didn't take long for her to get the picture: Nobody thought they could help me, and nobody wanted to anyway. At that point, she decided that the only other thing she could do was probably just send me off to her relatives—so that's what she threatened to do.

Sometime in May of 1977, even I understood (with what was left of my drug-addled brain) that I had two options left: Either I gave myself the "golden shot"—a fatal overdose—as soon as possible, or else I had to make a serious attempt to get off of heroin for good. I knew that I was all alone in making that decision. I couldn't even count on Detlef. But even more important was the fact that, whatever I decided, it had to be my decision, and not Detlef's.

I went to the Center House back at Gropiusstadt—back to the youth center where my drug career had gotten started. It turned out that the whole place had been shut down since by that time the drug problem in the area was totally out of control. In its place they now had a drug-counseling center. Seriously, a real drug-counseling center, just for Gropiusstadt. That's how many heroin addicts were there now, only two years after heroin first cropped up in that area. When I went in, they told me exactly what I was expecting to hear: that the only way I would ever get clean was by going into genuine, serious therapy. They gave me the addresses for the two rehab clinics, that had had the most success in dealing with addicts.

I was pretty apprehensive about these kinds of therapy programs because the word on the street was that they were really pretty brutal. That's what I'd heard anyway. Some people said they were even worse than jail. In one of these clinics, they even shaved you bald first. I guess that was supposed to be a demonstration of the fact that you were ready to begin a new chapter of your life. I didn't think I could let them shave off all my hair; I didn't want to be turned into some cut-rate Kojak.[34] To me, my hair was, in a way, the thing that was more me than anything else. It protected me. I could even hide behind it. And so I thought, If they cut off my hair, I might as well just kill myself.

But then the drug counselor said that I wasn't very likely to actually get admitted to either of these two programs because they didn't have any open spots right then. The admissions requirements were incredibly tough, she told me: You had to still be in pretty good physical shape and be able to prove to them that you still had the willpower to get off of heroin. The drug counselor said that since I was still so young, not even fifteen, that it would be extremely difficult, if not impossible, for me to meet their demands. And for kids, there really wasn't any drug therapy available yet.

---

34 *Kojak* was an American television series starring Telly Savalas as a bald New York City Police Department detective named Lieutenant Theo Kojak. It aired from October 1973 to March 1978 on CBS and was a popular TV series in Germany.

I said that I actually wanted to go to Narcotics Abusers Anonymous anyway. Narcotics Abusers Anonymous—also known as Narc Anon—was the rehab center for the Church of Scientology. There were a few addicts I'd run into who had already spent some time at Narcotics Abusers Anonymous, and they all said that it was actually not that bad. They didn't have any admissions requirements at all so long as you paid in advance. They let patients wear their own clothes, bring their own music, and even keep their own pets.

The drug counselor responded by saying that I should think more carefully about the organization. She asked me why I thought so many junkies said the program at Narc Anon was so great—was it because it worked or because they could enjoy themselves for a while and then keep shooting up when it was over? She said she couldn't call to mind a single case where Narc Anon had helped a person really get clean.

I asked her if she could think of any other place where I could go if I didn't stand a chance of getting in at the other places we'd talked about. At that point, she gave in and passed me the address for Narcotics Abusers Anonymous.

When I got home, I used that same trick again and dribbled some more of that medicine into my cat's mouth with my old syringe. When my mom came home, I told her that I was going to get clean for good at Narc Anon. "I'll have to stay there for a few months," I told her, "or even a year, and then that will be it. I'll be sober."

My mom acted as if she didn't believe a word I said. But still, she went straight to the phone and tried to find out more about the new program.

I was totally into this rehab trip. I felt like I had a chance to start fresh, to start a whole new life. I decided not to see any clients that afternoon, and I stayed away from dope, too. I wanted to get sober before even showing up. I didn't want to have to start out in the "cold turkey room." I wanted to arrive totally clean and get a head start on the others. I wanted to prove right off the bat that I had ability to quit.

I went to bed early and laid the cat (who was sicker than ever now) on the pillow beside me. I was proud of myself. I was withdrawing all by myself, all alone, and it was all my own decision. How many heroin addicts could do that? When I told my mom that I'd stop using right away, all she did was respond with a dubious smile. She didn't even take any time off from work to help me. All these withdrawal sessions seemed hopeless to her now, and she couldn't muster much excitement for them. So yeah, I had to get through it all by myself.

The next morning I felt the full brunt of the challenge I was up against. It was just as bad as ever—the withdrawal symptoms—and maybe even worse, but at no point did I lose my self-belief. When I felt like the pain was going to kill me, I just told myself, That just means you're getting the poison out. You'll survive, and when you're done that will be it. Once the poison's gone, it will never come back. You won't let it.

The one good thing was that when I passed out, I didn't have any nightmares or start tripping in that old kind of horror landscape. Instead I had these beautiful glimpses of my life after the rehab.

When the pain let up after three days, my imagination went wild, and I started creating these idealized scenes in my mind. As I settled into these visions, they seemed almost real. In one of these fantasy worlds, I had stayed in school and even taken the university entrance exams. I had my own apartment, and a VW Cabriolet was parked in the driveway. When I took it out, I drove with the top down.

The apartment was on the outskirts of the city, surrounded by lots of trees. Maybe it was in Rudow, or maybe in Grunewald. My place was located in an old but still elegant building. It wasn't decadent though. It wasn't like all those gaudy old apartment buildings near the Kurfürstendamm—the ones with high ceilings, decorative stucco, huge entrance halls, marble floors, red carpet runners in the hall and up the stairs—the ones with mirrors everywhere and the tenants' names printed in gold leaf on their doors. My place wasn't like that at all—it wasn't poisoned with the stench of money and power. It was already clear to me that wealth on that scale came from a life spent lying and stealing—a high-stress life spent running back and forth on a high wire. That wasn't for me.

I wanted something simpler: an apartment in an old working-class neighborhood with two or three small rooms, low ceilings, small windows, and time-worn steps in the stairwell; I wanted a place where it always smelled a little of someone else's home cooking and where the neighbors would poke their heads out of their doors and say, "Hey there, Christiane! How are you?" The stairs would be so narrow that you'd inevitably brush up against your neighbors when you went up and down. Everyone in the house would work hard, but everyone would be content with what they had. They wouldn't need money or goods for their own sake, and they wouldn't be jealous; they'd help each other out. The people I would live with—like the people who I saw in my daydream—would be as different from the money-hungry elite as they would be from my dingy old neighbors at Gropiusstadt. In the house that I imagined, it was calm and peaceful.

The most important place in my dream apartment was the bedroom. Against the right-hand wall stood a very wide sleeper sofa covered in dark fabric. On either side of it was a night table. (One was for Detlef, for when he stayed with me.) And then there stood a potted palm on each side of the sofa. The room was full of plants and flowers. The wall behind the bed was covered in wallpaper—better than what you got in stores though. This wallpaper depicted a desert scene with enormous sand dunes, some palm trees in the distance, and, at a nearby oasis, some Bedouins with white turbans sitting in a circle, drinking tea. They looked very relaxed. A scene of total peace.

On the left side of the bedroom, in the alcove where the dormer window was built into the roof, was my sitting corner. It was a sitting area like they have in India or in the Middle East. There were a bunch of pillows gathered around a low, round table. That's where I sat at night, peacefulness personified—unworried, unbothered, and lacking for nothing.

The living room in this fantasy was just like the bedroom. The same plants, the same carpets. But in the middle was a large, round, wooden table with wicker chairs. When my friends came over, we would all sit around that table eating what I'd cooked and drinking tea. Books covered the shelves that had been built into the walls. They were all classic books, written by people who, like me, had found inner peace and who enjoyed nature and animals. I'd made the shelves myself out of boards and thick ropes. Most of the things in my apartment I'd made myself because I didn't like whatever was for sale in the furniture stores. The furniture in the stores looked pretentious and was just a way for people to display their wealth. There were no doors in my apartment, only curtains, because I didn't want my guests to have to endure the sound and stress of doors opening and closing all the time.

I had a dog—a Rottweiler—and two cats. I'd taken out the backseats of my Cabriolet so that the dog would have more space and feel more at ease when I drove around with him.

In the evenings, I'd take my time cooking dinner. I wanted to feel peaceful while cooking and not rush around all stressed out (the way my mom did). Then a key would turn in the front door. It was Detlef coming home from work. The dog jumped up on him, and the cats arched their backs and rubbed against his legs. Then Detlef gave me a kiss and sat down at the dinner table.

That was what I saw when I looked inside myself and dreamed. Except I didn't realize that it even was a dream. For me, it was just what was going to happen the day after tomorrow. That's how things would be after rehab. My whole world would change. I was so sure about this total transformation that I even told my mom after my third day of withdrawal that I'd be moving out when I finished with the program. I was going to get my own apartment.

On the fourth day, I was feeling so good already that I was able to get up and walk around again. I still had twenty marks in my pocket, and my awareness of the extra cash kind of set me on edge because right there, I was already halfway to forty, and with forty I could buy myself one last and final fix before I went to Narc Anon the next day.

I started talking to my sick kitty. I told him that I was going to be gone for a couple hours but that he didn't need to worry. With my syringe, I gave him a little chamomile tea with sugar— the only thing he could still keep down. Then, before I left, I promised him that he was going to make it—just like me.

Since I felt so good about things right then, I wanted to go for one last walk along the Kurfürstendamm. I knew that once you were at Narc Anon, there was no going out—or at least no going out alone. But since I was going to be over there, I'd have to shoot up at least a little bit because otherwise that whole area was just way too depressing. I only needed to get another twenty marks, and if I could find even one customer, that would be easy. But I didn't want to run into Detlef over there and have to tell him, "Hey, I just went through withdrawal, all by myself, and I feel really good about it. But now I need to find a john; I need to make a twenty." There was no way Detlef would've understood.

He would've laughed and told me I was never going to change. "Once a junkie, always a junkie." I didn't want to go through that, not under any circumstances.

But then, while I was in the subway, I had an idea: I'd head over to the boulevard. The reason why it first sprang to mind was because of the amount: twenty marks. For a job on the boulevard, the usual payout just happened to be exactly twenty marks. Babsi and Stella already worked the boulevard at the corner of Kurfürstenstrasse and Genthiner Streets, but I was still really freaked out by it. I didn't like that the customers couldn't walk up to you, like at Zoo Station, which gave you some time to check them out; instead, you had to just walk over to the customer's car when he waved. So you could never tell what kind of guy he was going to be.

The worst thing was when you fell into the hands of a pimp. The pimps pretended to be customers, but once they got you into their car, there was nothing you could do. Most pimps didn't really want junkies working for them because too much of the earnings went toward dope. But they did want to drive the junkies away from the area because junkies got in the way of the professionals' business.

Babsi once got into a pimp's car by accident. He kept her locked up for three days. He tortured and then raped her. He gave access to anyone and everyone—hoboes, drunks, criminals—he didn't care. And of course Babsi had to deal with suffering through withdrawal at the same time. Something snapped in her around that time. But she still went back to work the streets. After all, she was the little queen with the angel face.

The professional hookers were almost as dangerous as the pimps. The corner at Potsdamer Street was where all the nastiest, meanest, most time-tested prostitutes in Berlin all worked, and it was only a couple football fields' distance away from where the "baby prostitutes" hung out on the Kurfürstenstrasse. Sometimes they'd organize their own kind of raids on the girls, and if they caught one, they'd scratch her face to shreds.

I got out at the Kurfürstenstrasse subway stop and was immediately petrified with fear. In my head I went over the advice that I'd always heard Stella and Babsi give about the boulevard: Stay away from younger guys in big American cars—they're most likely pimps. The ones to focus on are the older guys, the ones with a gut, a tie, and, better yet, a hat—they're okay. And best of all were the men who had a baby seat in the back. Obedient family men who just wanted a little variety, a little time away from Mommy, and who were guaranteed to be even more frightened than the girls.

I walked the hundred yards or so from the subway station to Genthiner Street, over by where The Sound used to be. I pretended that I just happened to be passing by. I didn't walk close to the street—instead I veered over toward the house—but somebody still stopped right away. But he looked kind of weird to me. Maybe it was the beard, but for whatever reason I suspected that he was a kind of aggressive guy. So I gave him the finger and kept on walking.

There was no one else in sight. After all, it was still before noon. From Stella's and Babsi's stories I knew that the customers got anxious when they'd taken a half-hour off for this and there were no girls to be had. Sometimes there were more customers than there were girls. So before long, a couple more cars stopped, but I still pretended not to see them.

I looked into the shop window of a furniture store and was immediately transported back to that vision I'd had of my future life. I had to remind myself to get a grip, to pull myself together. All I wanted to do was just get this over with as quickly as possible, earn my twenty marks, and go. It took concentration.

You had to focus on the task at hand or else it was going to take too long.

A white car pulled over next to me. There wasn't a child's seat in the back, but the guy didn't look very dangerous. I got in without thinking a second thought, and we agreed on a fee of thirty-five marks.

We drove to Askanischer Place. There was an old, abandoned train station there that belonged to the DDR's national railway. The whole thing didn't take long. The guy was nice, and right away I had that wonderful feeling again. I even forgot that he was a customer. He said that he'd like to see me again, but that it couldn't be anytime soon since he and his wife and kids were going on a vacation to Norway in a few days.

I asked him if he would do me a favor and drive me to Hardenberg Street, to the technical university over there, and he said it would be no problem. There was a big drug scene over by the university in the mornings.

It was a beautiful warm day, May 16, 1977. I remember the date well because it was two days before my fifteenth birthday. After he let me out, I walked all around the area and talked to a few guys. I stopped to pet a dog. I was happy. It felt amazing not to be in any hurry and to wait for as long as I wanted before shooting up. After all, I didn't even need the stuff anymore, did I?

After a while, though, a guy walked past me and asked if I wanted some dope, and I said yes. He walked ahead to Ernst-Reuter Place, where I bought a quarter off of him for forty marks. After that, I went straight into the ladies' bathroom nearby, which happened to be fairly clean. I only put half of the dope on the spoon because after a withdrawal you're not supposed to start with a full dose right off the bat. I made a little ceremony out of giving myself the shot since I thought that it was going to be the absolute last time ever.

Two hours later, I woke up. My butt had slipped way down into the toilet, and the needle was still stuck in my arm. My things were strewn all over the place in the tiny toilet stall where I had passed out. But it only took a few seconds for me to regain my composure. My decision to quit hadn't come a second too soon. My whole plan about taking a nice little walk through the old neighborhood was off the table now. All the optimism that I'd started out with had evaporated. In the cafeteria nearby, I had some mashed potatoes with leeks for a little under three marks, but I couldn't keep it down. I dragged myself to Zoo station to say good-bye to Detlef, but he wasn't there. I had to get home. My kitty needed me.

Kitty was still right where I'd left him, on my pillow. I cleaned out my syringe and then dribbled some more chamomile tea and sugar into his mouth. This wasn't exactly the way I'd imagined I'd be spending my last few hours as a junkie. I thought that maybe I should postpone my check-in at the clinic so that I could still do that last walk down the Ku'damm. But then my mom came in and asked where I'd been all afternoon. I told her, and she asked, "Didn't you want to stop by Narcotics Abusers Anonymous today, to find out about a few things?"

I immediately went ballistic and started yelling at her. "Leave me alone!" I screamed. "I didn't have any time. Don't you understand?"

"You're going over there tonight!" she yelled back at me. "Go pack your things right now. And you're staying there overnight."

I had just cooked myself a pork chop with mashed potatoes. I took the plate, went to the bathroom, locked myself in, and sat on the toilet. So this was my last night at my mom's. I was yelling at her because she'd figured out that I was back on H again and because I hated myself for having shot up one more time. And I was ready to check myself into Narc Anon.

∗

I PACKED A FEW THINGS INTO my duffel bag and then slid the syringe, a spoon, and the rest of the dope into my underpants. We took a taxi to Zehlendorf, where the Narc Anon house was. The Narc Anon people didn't ask me any questions at first. So they really did seem to admit anyone. (They even had recruiters who went out to the drug-saturated areas of the city and talked to the junkies there, trying to convince them to join the Narc Anon rehab program.) But they did question my mom. They wanted to be paid up front—fifteen hundred marks as a down payment for the first month. No way my mom had that much money. But she promised to drop it off the next morning. She needed to take out a loan. She begged and pleaded with them to let me stay, and they finally agreed.

I asked if I could use the bathroom, and they let me. (So it wasn't like at the other rehab centers I'd heard about, where if they found something on you, you had to go home.) When I came out again, they could see that I was high, but they didn't say anything. I gave them my syringe and spoon. The guy who collected it from me looked surprised: "We really appreciate your giving this up voluntarily."

I had to go to the cold turkey room since now they knew I was doped up. There were two others in that room, but one of them hightailed it out of there the next morning. That worked out well for the Narc Anon people because when someone left right away, they still got to keep the full payment for the month.

They gave me some books about the teachings of the Church of Scientology. Some of the stuff I read was pretty incredible. It all sounded okay to me. At least they had some good stories—stories that you could choose to either believe or not believe. So I looked through their books for something that sounded believable.

After two days, they let me leave the cold turkey room since I didn't have bad withdrawal symptoms after only two shots. I was put into a room with someone named Christa. She was certifiable. From the word go, she was resistant to all of their attempts to help her—laughing at the therapists and mocking the therapy in general. She walked into our room and searched the baseboard trim for pills. She was convinced that someone, sometime, must have hidden some acid or pills in there. She took me up to the attic at one point and started talking about how we should bring some mattresses up there, along with some weed and wine, and have an orgy. This woman really depressed me. Even though I knew she was nuts, she made it hard for me to get my mind off drugs, and she was always talking about how the Narc Anon people had "shit for brains." Meanwhile, I was still trying to take it seriously and get clean.

On day two, my mom called to say that my cat had died. That was my fifteenth birthday. She wished me a happy birthday only after she had given me the news about my cat. She was upset about it, too. After that I spent the rest of my birthday morning sitting on my bed and crying.

When the Narc Anon guys saw that I was crying and couldn't make myself stop, they said that I needed a session. I was locked in a room with a guy who used to be a junkie, and he started right out by giving me a bunch of seemingly useless instructions. I was only allowed to say yes and was supposed to obey every command.

The guy said, "See the wall? Go to the wall. Touch the wall." And then he'd point to a different wall and start all over again. For what seemed like forever, I was forced to run wall to wall in this stupid room. At some point, I'd had enough and said, "Come on, what is this crap? Are you guys nuts? Leave me alone. I can't handle this anymore." But he just stared at me with this dumb smile plastered across his face. That smile of his never changed, never wavered, and after a while he wore me down, and I agreed to keep going. After the wall, he would point to something else, and we would keep going. But finally I couldn't move another step, and I threw myself onto the floor, screaming and crying.

He smiled and I kept going after I'd calmed down. By now I was also smiling that same smile. I was completely unemotional, like a robot. I'd touch the wall even before he'd issued his command. The only thing I kept thinking was that, at some point, it had to end.

After exactly five hours he said, "Okay, that's enough for today." I actually felt kind of awesome. I had to follow him into another room. Inside there was a funny-looking, homemade instrument—a kind of pendulum between two tin cans. He told me to touch the pendulum. "Are you feeling well?" he asked.

"I feel good," I told him. "It seems like I'm way more aware of everything I'm experiencing—way more conscious."

The guy stared at the pendulum and then said, "It didn't move, so you weren't lying. The session seems like it was a success."

I guess that funny little thing was a lie detector. In any case, I was happy that the pendulum hadn't moved. For me it was proof that I was really doing well. I was ready to believe anything in order to get off of H.

They were doing all sorts of weird things there. When Christa came down with a fever that same evening, they made her touch a bottle over and over again, and every time she did they would ask her if it was hot or cold. In her feverish state of mind, she didn't seem to care though. After an hour of that routine, they declared that her fever was gone.

I was so excited by all this that first thing the next morning, I ran into their office and asked for another therapy session. For that whole first week, I was a 100 percent committed to the program and really bought into the Scientologists' outlook on things. The therapy program ran all day. Conversation, chores, kitchen duties, etcetera. All day, every day, until 10 p.m. It didn't leave you any time to think.

The only thing that bugged me was the food. I wasn't spoiled or a picky eater—not by any means—but I could hardly swallow the glop they offered up. Plus, I thought that with all the money they were pulling in, they could give us something a lot better. They had almost no other expenses. The sessions were led by former junkies. They were all supposed to have been clean for at least a couple of months, but even these "employees" weren't really paid anything. They were told that it was part of their treatment to lead these sessions, and all they got for compensation was some occasional pocket money. I also didn't like it that the Narc Anon bosses always ate apart from the rest of us. Once, I happened to walk in on them during lunch, and they were feasting on amazing-looking food.

On Sunday, I finally had some time to just sit and reflect. First I thought about Detlef, which made me pretty sad. Then I took a minute to think long and hard about my options after I was finished with this therapy program. I asked myself if the sessions had actually helped me. I had all these questions but no real answers. I wanted to talk to somebody, but who could I go to? One of the first rules of the house was that making friends was not allowed. And the Narc Anon people immediately slapped you with another session if they heard that you wanted to talk about your problems. I suddenly realized that I'd never really talked to anyone the whole time I'd been at this place.

Monday morning I walked into the office and let loose. I didn't let anyone interrupt me. I started with the food. Then I said that almost all my underwear had been stolen. You could never get into the laundry room because the girl who had the key kept disappearing—probably to go shoot up herself. Speaking of which, there were a few patients who ran off to score heroin and shoot up and came back whenever they wanted to. I told them that all this stuff threw me off and made me feel defeated. And then there were the chores. I was totally exhausted because I never had enough time to sleep and rest up. I said, "Okay, your sessions are pretty effective—I really like them. But the thing is, they're not solving my actual problems. Because everything is just one big drill. You're just drilling us into submission. But I also need someone whom I can sometimes talk to about my problems. And anyway, I need some time alone, too, every once in a while, where I can just relax and think."

They heard me out (smiling the whole time, as always), but they didn't even try to offer a response. When I was finished, they just prescribed an extra all-day session for me. After that, I was completely defeated, totally apathetic. And I thought, Well, maybe they do know what they're doing. When she visited, my mom told me that Social Services was reimbursing her for the cost of the Narc Anon program. So I reasoned that if the government was willing to pay for this, then it must be an okay program.

There were other people in the house who had it way worse than I did. Gabi, for example. She had a crush on some guy in the building and was desperate to sleep with him. Being the naïve moron that she was, she told the Narc Anon bosses about it right away and was promptly prescribed an extra session. And when she did have sex with the guy, it came out, and the two of them were exposed and ridiculed in front of everybody. Gabi ran out on the program that same night, and we never saw her again. The guy, who apparently had been clean for a few years and who worked there as an assistant, bailed on the operation a little later on. It sounded like he'd reverted back to his old ways.

The Narc Anon people weren't actually that concerned about the sex—it was really just relationships that they were afraid of. But that guy'd been there for over a year, and how are you supposed to last that long without any friendships?

During the short amount of free time we had late at night, I hung out with the younger crowd. I was the youngest person in the entire house. But in our little friend group that came together, nobody was seventeen yet. It was around about this time that the first wave of addicts came in who had first starting using when they were literally kids. After one or two years, they'd become just as devastated as I was; the younger you were, the more the poison seemed to affect you. Like me, there was no way they would be accepted by any of the other programs.

Almost all of these new admissions struggled with the methods here just as badly as I had. When two of us—the younger ones, I mean—were together, the whole session dissolved into chaos. How could you stay serious for long, anyway, when you were supposed to yell at a soccer ball or stare into each other's eyes for hours on end? There wasn't any need to worry about the lie detector anymore because we'd readily admit that the session hadn't done anything for us anyway. I guess that wasn't true because it made us laugh, but that was it. The poor session leaders were totally at a loss when they had to work with us.

At the end of the day, there was just one thing we talked about now: H. I started making plans to leave.

After two weeks at Narc Anon, I'd figured out an escape plan, and it worked: Two boys and I disguised ourselves as the "great housecleaning platoon." With a garbage can, a mop, and a bucket, we got through all the doors. The three of us were blissfully happy. We almost peed our pants in our giddy anticipation of shooting up. At the subway station we went our separate ways. I was headed to Zoo Station, to see Detlef.

Detlef wasn't there but Stella was. She almost fainted when she saw me. She said that nobody had seen Detlef lately, and I was afraid that he'd landed in jail. Stella said that Zoo Station was in a real depression, so we went to the boulevard at Kurfürstenstrasse instead. Things were dead there, too. We made our way from the subway stop at Kurfürstenstrasse up to Lützow Place before someone finally pulled over beside us. We recognized the car and the guy inside it. He'd followed us before—and one time he even stuck around when we went to a public bathroom to shoot up. We always thought he was an undercover cop, but apparently he was just a customer who had a thing for young heroin junkies.

He only wanted me, but Stella came along for the ride.

I said, "Thirty-five for a blow job—and I won't do anything more than that."

He said, "I'll give you a hundred marks."

I was blown away. That was totally unprecedented. Even the customers in the biggest, brightest Mercedes had a fit over a mere five marks. And this guy, in a dinged-up rusty old VW, was volunteering to give me a hundred. After a minute, he said that he was an officer in the Federal Intelligence Service—so in other words, he was probably full of shit. But these kinds of cocky, con-man types were also some of my best clients back at Zoo Station because they liked to puff themselves up by throwing money around. He really did give me a hundred marks though.

Right away Stella found us some dope, and the first thing we did was give ourselves a shot, right there in the car. We drove over to the Pension Ameise, a small hotel. Stella waited in the hallway outside. I took my time with this guy because I was super high from my first fix in two weeks, but also because he had paid a pretty decent amount. I was so doped up that I didn't want to get up off the narrow cot in that grubby hotel room.

I talked with the guy for a little bit afterward. He was a funny kind of show-off. At the end, he said that he had half a gram of heroin, and that he would give it to us if we would come back to the Kurfürstenstrasse in three hours. And then, after that, I managed to squeeze even more out of him—another thirty marks.

I said we needed the money to get some good food for a change. I told him that I had never been fooled by his VW. I knew it was a cover-up, and that he was rich since he was working in intelligence. So he couldn't very well say no then. He had to hand over the cash.

Stella and I went back to Zoo Station because I was still hoping I'd be able to find Detlef. Suddenly this small, shaggy, spotted dog ran over and jumped up on me. I must have reminded the dog of someone. I thought the dog was unbelievably cute. It looked like a sled dog that had shrunk a few sizes in the wash. A couple seconds later, this ratty, disheveled old guy came after the dog and actually asked me if I wanted to buy it. I did. He wanted seventy marks, but I talked him down to forty. I was high—both on dope and due to the fact that I finally had a dog again. Stella thought I should call it Lady Jane. I decided to go with Janie.

We ate pork chops with vegetables and potatoes at a restaurant in the Kurfürstenstrasse, and Janie got the leftovers. The intelligence officer really did come by, right on time, and he gave me a real half of a gram. I couldn't believe it. This half-gram was worth a hundred marks.

Stella and I then went and paid one last visit to Zoo Station in the hopes of finding Detlef. We ran into Babsi instead, and I was so, so happy to see her because despite all of our fights, I liked her a lot—even better than Stella. The three of us went into the station café and sat down. Babsi looked terrible. Her legs were like matchsticks, and her chest had completely flattened out. She said she weighed sixty-six pounds. Only her face was as beautiful as always.

I told them about Narc Anon and how cool it had been over there. Stella didn't want to hear anything about it. She said she was born to be a junkie and that's the way it was always going to be. Babsi, however, was totally into the idea of the two of us going to Narc Anon together and quitting H for good. Her parents and grandma had also unsuccessfully tried to find a place in a rehab program for her. Babsi was couch surfing again, but she really wanted to quit. She was in a horrible state.

Once we'd all caught up, I took Janie into Metro, an expensive but still pretty underwhelming store in the station that stayed open at night for a while. I bought two bags of dog food and a whole bunch of instant pudding for myself. Then I called Narc Anon to ask if I could come back. They said yes. I said that I'd be bringing along a girlfriend but didn't let on that the friend was Janie.

Although I'd never actually spent time thinking about it, I'd basically always known that I'd be heading back to Narc Anon. Where else could I have gone? My mom would have freaked out if I showed up on her doorstep. Also, my sister had moved out of my dad's place and was now living at my mom's, taking up my old room and my bed. Couch surfing wasn't for me. And the last thing I wanted to do was be completely dependent on a john who took me in for the night. I'd never stayed overnight with a customer because that automatically meant we'd have to have sex. But most importantly, I still wanted to get clean for good. And I still believed that I could do it at Narc Anon because for me there were no other choices left.

In the house—we always called it just "the house"—they were cold, but they didn't say anything. Not about my escape, and not about Janie. There were already about twenty cats in the house, so how much of a difference would a dog make?

I brought some old blankets down from the attic and made up a dog bed for Janie, right next to me. The next morning, the dog had covered the entire room in shit and piss. Janie had never been house-trained. She was a total nutcase. But then again, so was I. I loved Janie, so I didn't mind having to clean up after her again and again.

I was immediately given an extra session. It didn't bother me. I just went through the motions automatically. The only thing that got on my nerves was the fact that, so long as I was in here, I couldn't be with my dog. Other people were taking care of her while I was in sessions, and that made me sick. She was my dog. Everyone played with her, and she played with everyone; she was kind of a slut like that. Everybody fed her, and she just got fatter and fatter. But I only talked to her when we were alone. It was nice to have someone I could talk to.

I ran away two more times. The last time I was gone for four days. That was my first experience with couch surfing. I could stay with Stella because at that time her mom was in a psychiatric clinic with the DTs.[35] All the old shit started up again. Customers, shooting up, customers, shooting up.

Then I found out that Detlef had gone to Paris with Bernd, and I had a fit.

The idea that Detlef, who was basically like my husband, would just up and leave Berlin without even letting me know—that was the last straw. We'd always dreamed about going to Paris together. We were going to rent a small room in Montmartre or some neighborhood like that and go cold turkey together because neither of us had ever heard of there being a heroin scene in Paris. We believed that there were no drugs in Paris, only a lot of cool artists who drank a lot of coffee and maybe sometimes had some wine.

So now Detlef was in Paris with Bernd. I'd lost my boyfriend. I was all alone. All the old fights and irritations had risen up again with Babsi and Stella. The only one I had left was Janie.

I called in to Narc Anon at one point while I was away, and they told me that my mom had already picked up my stuff. So my

---

35 DT is short for delirium tremens, a psychiatric disorder, usually caused by withdrawal from alcohol addiction.

mom had given up on me, too. Somehow that made me furious. Now I wanted to show them all. I wanted to show them that I could do it all on my own.

I went to Narc Anon and they took me in again. I participated in their therapies like I was possessed. I did everything I was told to do. I became a real model student and was allowed to use the lie-detector apparatus, and its pendulum never moved when I said that a session had been good for me. I thought, Now you'll make it. I didn't call my mom because, what did she care? She'd already checked me out. I just borrowed the stuff I needed, like boys' underpants. I didn't care one bit. I just didn't want to ask my mom to bring back my stuff.

One day my dad called: "Hi, Christiane," he said. "So tell me, where the hell's this place you're living now? I just happened to find out about it."

I just said, "It's great that sometimes you remember that you actually have a daughter. Awesome job, Dad."

He: "So, do you really want to stay at that place, with all those wackos?"

Me: "Definitely, for sure."

I could hear my dad taking a long, deep breath before he asked if I would like to come out to eat with him and a friend. "Yeah," I said. "Sure. I can do that."

Half an hour later, I had to go down to the office to meet him. There he was, my dad, live and in the flesh. He came up to see my room, where I was housed with four other patients. "Look at this friggin' mess," he mumbled. After all, he'd been a neat freak all his life. And it really did look like a bomb had gone off in there. Every room was like that, a total mess, with clothes everywhere.

Because we were heading outside, one of the bosses said to my dad, "You're required to sign a statement that you'll be bringing Christiane back."

My dad went ballistic. He shouted that he was my father, and that he alone could determine where his daughter was allowed to go, and when. He was going to take me with him, and they wouldn't need to wait up.

I started moving backward, toward the therapy room, and said, "I want to stay. I don't want to die, Daddy. Please let me stay."

The Narc Anon people, who'd been attracted by the yelling, all came running and backed me up. My dad ran outside and shouted, "I'm coming back with the police!"

I knew that he wasn't bluffing. I ran up to the attic and climbed onto the roof. There was a kind of platform for the chimney sweep. I crouched down on that and shivered with cold.

Then two patrol cars arrived. The cops searched the house with my dad from top to bottom. Meanwhile, the Narc Anon bosses started getting scared and also started calling for me. But nobody found me on the roof. Eventually the cops drove off, and my dad left with them.

The next morning I called my mom at work. I started crying right away. "What's going on?" I asked her. "What's happening?"

My mom responded with a voice that was as cold as ice: "I couldn't care less about what happens to you."

I said, "I don't want Dad to take me away from here. You are the custodial parent. You can't just give up on me and leave me to fend for myself. I'm staying here and I'll never leave again, I swear. Please, do something so that Dad can't just take me out of here. I really truly need to stay here. Otherwise I'll die, Mom. Seriously, you have to believe me!"

When she spoke she sounded impatient: "No. I can't. I won't." Then she hung up.

At first I felt like I was now a completely lost cause. But then my rage returned. They can all kiss my ass, I thought. Your whole life they didn't care one iota about what was happening to you.

And now they feel like they can do whatever they want with you, when they've never done anything right. Those assholes totally let you get sucked down the drain. Kessi's mom made sure that Kessi didn't end up totally fucked up. And now that you're really struggling, they're trying to tell you what to do? They're fucking crazy.

I asked for an extra session and totally immersed myself in it. I wanted to stay at Narcotics Abusers Anonymous and maybe even become a member of the Church of Scientology. In any case, I wouldn't let anyone take me away from here. I didn't want my parents to damage me any further. That's what I was thinking to myself while my anger burned itself out anyway.

Three days later my dad came back, and I was forced to come down to the office. He was really calm. He said that I had to go with him to the Social Services Department since they were reimbursing my mom for her payments to Narc Anon.

I said, "No, I'm not coming along. I know you, Dad. If I come with you, I'll never see this house again. And I don't want to die."

My dad showed an authorization document to the Narc Anon managers, that stated that he was permitted to take me out of here. My mom had given him the authority. The head of Narc Anon said that there was nothing he could do, and that I had to go with my dad. They couldn't keep me here against his will.

When we said good-bye, the head of Narc Anon said that I shouldn't forget to do my exercises. "Always confront!"

Confronting was one of their magic words. We were supposed to confront everything. What a bunch of idiots, I thought. There's nothing for me to confront. I'll have to die. I just can't take it anymore. After two weeks I'll get doped up again. I can't do it. I'll never make it on my own. This was one of the rare moments when I saw my situation as clear as day. In my despair I really believed that Narcotics Abusers Anonymous was my only lifeline. I was sobbing with rage and despair, on and on and on; it seemed I would never stop.

I cried so hard that I could barely breathe.

Christiane's Mom

After that fiasco at Narc Anon, I didn't think it was a very good idea for my ex-husband to take Christiane in and help "bring her to her senses," as he put it. Aside from the fact that he couldn't supervise her around the clock, thinking about Christiane in the care of her dad caused me emotional indigestion. Mainly because of the memories of my relationship with him, but also because her sister had just moved back in with me as a result of his overbearing tactics.

But I didn't know what else to do and hoped that maybe he'd succeed where I had failed. But I also don't want to exclude the possibility that I was eager to find any reason—however implausible—that would give me a break from Christiane and her issues. Since her first withdrawal, I'd been swinging back and forth between hope and despair. When I asked her dad to intervene, I was physically and emotionally drained; I was at the end of my rope.

Just three weeks after her first withdrawal (which Christiane bravely endured, along with Detlef, back at my place), the police called me at work and informed me that they'd picked up Christiane at Zoo Station. I was asked to come and get her.

That first relapse hit me like a ton of bricks. I sat at my desk, shaking. Every two minutes I glanced at the clock to see if it was 4 p.m. yet. I didn't dare leave before the end of the workday. I didn't want to entrust my family's pain and trouble to anyone else. My boss's two daughters would have basically condemned me. I suddenly gained some understanding of what Detlef's dad had tried to express. You really are very ashamed, especially at first.

Christiane's eyes were almost swollen shut when I got to the police station. That's how hard she must have cried. The police officer showed me the fresh needle track on her arm and told me she had been arrested at Zoo Station in an "unambiguous position."

At first I couldn't imagine what "unambiguous position" meant, but maybe I really didn't want to know anyway. Christiane was intensely unhappy about her relapse. I helped her withdraw again. Without Detlef. She stayed at home and seemed determined to make it work. I got up my courage and let her school advisor know about what was going on. He was shocked, but he thanked me for my openness. He wasn't used to that from other parents. He suspected that there were more heroin addicts at the school, and he would've liked to help Christiane. The only problem was that he didn't know how.

It was always the same. It didn't matter who I talked to— either people were as helpless as I was, or they had already completely given up on people like Christiane. I saw this same thing over and over again.

Slowly I began to realize how easily teenagers came into contact with heroin. The dealers were already waiting for them on their way to school. I couldn't believe my ears when Christiane was once approached by one of these guys, in my presence, while we were out shopping. She told me how she knew these people: That guy deals with this guy; and this guy sells that; and that one over there does this or that.

It all seemed so crazy. What's going on here, anyway? What kind of a place to live is this? I wanted to transfer Christiane to a different school, so that she could at least avoid that particular route to school and its inherent dangers.

It was right before spring break, so right before I wanted her to start at the new school. I hoped that this was a way I could pull her out of the environment she was used to and away from the dangers at the subway stations. Of course, that was a naïve idea and my plan didn't even come to fruition anyway. The principal of the other school told us right off the bat that they didn't like to take students from a comprehensive school like Christiane's. And Christiane's grades were far too poor for him to make an exception. Out of curiosity, he asked why Christiane wanted to switch schools. When Christiane said that there was no sense of community or camaraderie there, the principal smirked. "Camaraderie? Of course there's no camaraderie at a school like yours." He said that since the students were always being shuffled and resorted in their classes, there was just no chance for any kind of community spirit to develop.

I don't know who was more disappointed, Christiane or I. She just said, "This is so pointless. Rehab is the only thing that can help me." But how would I ever get her a spot in a rehab program? I called each and every regional office and state office, every department, every authority. The best thing they could come up with were the drug-counseling centers. And the drug-counseling centers insisted that Christiane approach them voluntarily. As much as they all fought with each other and berated the other centers for their methods, they all agreed on that one point: Voluntary participation was the only way to start. Otherwise, a recovery would be impossible.

When I begged Christiane to go to a counseling center, she became obstinate and combative: "What good would that do?" she said. "And anyway, they don't have any openings for me. No way I'm going to hang around their place for weeks on end, doing absolutely nothing."

What was I supposed to do? If I'd dragged her against her will, I would've been betraying their primary requirement. That being said, today I can at least understand their position. At the time, Christiane probably wasn't emotionally mature enough to undergo a serious therapy program. On the other hand, it still seems wrong to deny assistance to addicts who are still so young. We should do whatever we can to help them.

Later, at the various points when Christiane felt run-down, depressed, and helpless—when she felt so bad that she would have happily checked herself into a strict rehab program, it was always the same: There were no spots open, and she'd have to spend six to eight weeks on a waiting list. It left me speechless. The only thing I could respond with was, "What if she's dead by then?"

"Well, in the meantime, she should come to us for some advisory interviews, so that we can figure out if she's serious about quitting." Looking back, I have a hard time finding fault with the drug counselors. With the few spots that they had available for addicts in rehab programs, they invariably had to make some tough choices.

So I never managed to get her a place in a rehab program. But when Christiane returned from spring vacation, I had the impression that she didn't need one anymore. She looked really refreshed and healthy. I thought that she had finally quit for good.

She also made a lot of disparaging remarks about her friend Babsi. She said that Babsi was selling herself to old men for heroin. Christiane insisted that she would never be able to do something like that. She talked a lot about how glad she was to be away from all that crap. She seemed dedicated to staying sober. I could've sworn that she really meant it.

However, after just a few days she slid right back into the same old behavior. I could tell by her tiny pupils. I didn't want to hear her lame excuses anymore. When I confronted her, she would say things like, "What? I just smoked a little weed, that's all. Relax!" This was the start of a very bad time. She told me bald-faced lies and stuck with them even when I knew she was lying and told her so. I grounded her, but she didn't care; she left the house anyway. I considered locking her up inside, but then she would've jumped out of the window. We were in a second-floor apartment, and I didn't want to risk her injuring herself.

I was at the end of my rope; my nerves were completely frayed. I couldn't stand looking into her distant eyes anymore. Three months had gone by since I'd caught her in the bathroom. Every couple of days the newspapers reported on yet another heroin-related death. Most of the time they only dedicated a couple of lines to each incident. They reported on heroin overdoses as routinely and dispassionately as they covered traffic accidents.

I was a wreck—just so insanely worried all the time. Especially now that Christiane had stopped opening up. She wouldn't admit to anything, and the constant lies and deception were really unnerving to me. When she felt like I'd figured her out or if I caught her in a lie, she'd become obscene and aggressive. Slowly but surely, her personality began to change.

I worried about her survival. I stopped automatically providing her with her allowance of twenty marks. There was this constant fear living inside me: If I give her an allowance, then she'll buy herself a shot, and that could be the one that kills her. I could almost live with the fact that she was addicted. But it was the fear that the next shot could be her last that destroyed me. I was at least a little reassured by the fact that she was at home now; otherwise I'd be like Babsi's mom, who had to call me all the time, in tears, asking if I knew where her daughter was.

I was constantly on edge. When the phone rang, I feared that it was the police or the morgue or some other horrible place. To this day, I still sit bolt upright in bed when the phone rings at night.

There was absolutely no reasoning with Christiane anymore. When I'd address her addiction, she would just scream, "Leave me alone!" I got the impression that Christiane had given up on herself.

Even though she kept insisting that she was only doing pot now, and not heroin, I was able to see through those kinds of lines. I'd stopped deceiving myself.

I searched her room regularly and would often come across her drug paraphernalia. Two or three times I even found a syringe. I'd throw them at her feet, which only made her yell at me, totally offended. She said they were Detlef's, and that she'd taken them away from him.

One day when I came home from work, they were both sitting on her bed and had just heated up a spoon. I was dumbfounded by their audacity. All I could do was scream at them. "Get out!" I yelled. "Just leave! Now!"

After they'd left I broke down and cried. I felt an incredible rage toward the police and toward the government. I felt completely abandoned. One of the Berlin papers reported another death from heroin overdose. There had already been more than thirty victims in that year alone. And it was only May. I couldn't grasp any of it. You could see on TV what huge sums the government was spending on the fight against terrorism. But in Berlin the dealers were running around unencumbered, selling heroin like ice cream cones openly in the streets.

I was really getting myself worked up. Who knows what else was running through my mind at that moment? I sat there in my living room, looking at my furniture, piece by piece. I think I was in the right frame of mind to smash it all to bits. This furniture was all I had. This was the reward for all my hard work. I started to cry again.

That night, when Christiane returned, I had decided to give her some measure of real punishment. While I was waiting for her to come home, sitting alone on my bed, my thoughts ran wild with a mixture of fear, guilt, and regret. I felt like I'd failed, not only because my marriage had broken down, and because I had so little time to for my kids, but also because I'd been too ashamed—too cowardly—to face up to the reality of Christiane's situation.

That evening I lost my last illusion.

Christiane didn't come home until after midnight. From my window I could see her get out of a Mercedes. She was dropped off right at the front door. My God, I thought, that's it. That's the end. She's given up all self-respect. The catastrophe was complete. I was shattered. I grabbed her and spanked her so hard and long that my hands hurt. In the end, we both sat on the carpet and cried. Christiane was in pieces. I looked her dead in the eyes and told her that I knew she was prostituting herself. She shook her head and sobbed: "But not in the way you think, Mom."

I didn't want to hear about the details. I sent her off to take a bath and then get in bed. Nobody can imagine how I felt. The thought of her selling her body was killing me. It was even worse than the news about her heroin addiction.

I didn't get any sleep that night. What other options did we have? What could we still do? In my desperate state of mind, I even thought of putting her in an institution, but that would've only made things worse. Initially, they would've placed Christiane in the central home on Ollenhauer Street. And I'd already heard some negative things about that place. Apparently the girls there have a tendency to recruit each other into prostitution.

There was only one thing to do: I had to send Christiane away from Berlin immediately. Forever. Whether she wanted to go or not. She had to get away from this place, from this morass that sucked her down over and over again. She needed to go someplace far away from all this heroin.

My own mother, who lived in the state of Hessia, was willing to take Christiane in, as was my sister-in-law in Schleswig-Holstein. But when I told Christiane about my decision, she was

272

dejected, almost distraught. Still, I'd already begun making plans and preparations, and I would have followed through with them, but eventually Christiane came to me, meek and full of regret, and declared she was ready to begin with a rehab program. She'd already found a place that had an opening. A place called Narcotics Abusers Anonymous.

That was a weight off my shoulders. I wasn't sure if she could make it without any professional assistance, and I was also afraid that she might run away from my relatives.

I didn't know much about this Narcotics Abusers Anonymous program, but I had heard that it involved a substantial fee for services rendered. So two days before Christiane's fifteenth birthday, I called for a taxi and went with her to Narc Anon. A young man did the intake interview with us. He congratulated us on our decision and reassured me that from now on I didn't have to worry anymore. He said that the therapy at Narc Anon was usually successful. He seemed really confident, and, to be honest, I couldn't remember the last time I felt so relieved.

Then he put the contract in front of me and went over all the details of the program, including my own financial responsibility. It cost fifty-two marks a day, and the payment had to be made four weeks in advance. That was more than I made at work in that same amount of time. But what did that matter when you considered what was at stake? Besides, the representative indicated that I could probably get the costs for the program reimbursed by Social Services.

The next day I scraped together five hundred marks and brought them to the Narc Anon offices. Then I took out a loan for a thousand marks and made the payment at the next parents' evening. A group of reformed addicts ran these evenings. You couldn't tell that the one I saw used to be a junkie—at least I couldn't. He looked pretty normal. That was thanks to Narc

Anon, he said. After getting clean, he'd become a new person. That certainly impressed all the parents. And he assured me, in particular, that Christiane was making good progress.

It turned out that they were just putting on an act. Like everyone else, they just wanted our money. Later I found out, in a newspaper article, that Narc Anon belonged to a dubious American religious organization, and that it was profiting from parents' fears about their children.

But as usual, I didn't realize what was going on before much too late. Initially, I thought that Christiane was in the best of hands. I wanted to leave her there for as long as possible. But in order to do that, I needed money.

I ran from one government office to the next, from one department to the next. But nobody wanted to take any responsibility for Christiane. And at the same time, nobody told me what was really going on at Narc Anon. I felt discouraged. I felt conned. Everyone acted like I was just wasting their time. Then finally, somebody told me that I first needed to get a statement from a government-approved doctor certifying that Christiane was indeed a drug addict before I could even begin to apply for reimbursement of her therapy fees. I thought that was a joke. Anyone who knew even a little bit about this topic could plainly recognize the misery in Christiane's face. But those were the rules. The thing was, when I finally managed to get an appointment with the officially approved doctor (an appointment that took two weeks for me to get), Christiane had run away from Narc Anon again. It was already the third time.

I broke down and cried. I thought, Now it'll start all over again. We're back at square one. Every time that she returned, I was convinced that this was the time that she would finally make it, and every time, I was disappointed. My boyfriend and I went out to look for her. In the afternoons we'd check out the park *that young people often hung out at called Hasenheide[36]; at night we'd go downtown and to the clubs, and in between we'd go scouring the subway stations. We went wherever the drugs were. With each new day, we'd renew the hunt. We even checked the public bathrooms all over the city, just in case. We'd reported her as missing, but they only said that they'd add Christiane to their missing-persons list. She'd show up again, they said.*

All I wanted to do was crawl into a hole and disappear. I was consumed by fear. Fear of that phone call: Your daughter is dead. I was just a bundle of nerves. I wasn't interested in anything anymore, and I didn't want to do anything, I had to force myself to go to work. I started getting heart palpitations, and I could hardly move my left arm. At night it would tingle and go numb. My stomach was constantly upset. My kidneys hurt and my head felt like it was going to explode. I was physically and mentally spent.

I went to my doctor, who told me it was all nerves and prescribed me some Valium. When I told him why I was such a mess, he said that a couple of days ago another such young girl had come to him, confessed her drug addiction, and asked him for advice on what she should do. "And what did you tell her?" I asked.

"I told her to go and hang herself." That was his answer. Just like that. It was hopeless.

When Christiane showed up again at Narc Anon a week later, I couldn't even bring myself to feel relief. It was like a part of me had died. I was of the opinion that I had done everything humanly possible, but nothing had helped. Whatever I did, things always got worse.

---

36 A public park in the borough of Neukölln. Hasenheide literally means "rabbits' heath" or "rabbits' field."

It was like a snowball tumbling downhill. Narc Anon had done more harm than good. Christiane had changed during her time there. She made a bad impression now—she was vulgar, almost to the point of repulsiveness—and had lost whatever girlish innocence she still had left.

I was suspicious even during my first visit to Narc Anon. Christiane had become a stranger to me already. Something had been destroyed. Up until then, despite everything, she'd still had a connection to me—but now that was gone. It was like she'd been brainwashed.

It was at this point that I asked my ex-husband to take Christiane out of Berlin, to Western Germany. But he preferred to take her in himself. He'd be able to deal with her, he said. And if she didn't cooperate, then maybe a little corporal punishment would help.

I didn't object. I'd reached the end of my rope. I'd already made so many mistakes and miscalculations that suddenly I was afraid to take any further actions of my own.

BEFORE WE WENT HOME TO MY DAD'S, he dragged me with him to his favorite bar, the Hungry Woodpecker, at the Wutzkyallee subway station. He wanted to order me a drink,[37] but I just wanted some juice. He said I had to put a stop to taking drugs if I didn't want to die, and I said, "Well, yeah, that's exactly why I wanted to stay at Narc Anon."

The jukebox kept playing the same song over and over again. A few teens were playing pinball and pool. My dad said that they were all just good, normal teens. If I hung out here more often, I'd

---

37 In Germany, after the age of fourteen, minors are allowed drink alcoholic beverages, such as beer and wine, as long as they are in the company of their parents.

make some new friends and realize how crazy and stupid it was to mess around with junkies and other dope fiends all the time.

I was barely listening. I was angry and exhausted and just wanted to be left alone. I hated everyone, and just when I felt like I might have found a kind of escape, a route to a better life, my dad had slammed the door right in my face. I took Janie into bed with me that night and asked her, "Janie, do you understand us humans?" I answered for her: "No, of course you don't. You run up to everyone, wagging your tail. You think people are good."

I didn't like that about her. I would've preferred it if she would have growled at people first. She shouldn't be so trusting.

When I woke up, I saw that Janie hadn't yet peed on the floor, so I was eager to take her out right away. My dad had already left for work. When I went to open the front door, it was locked. I yanked at the door handle; I threw myself against the door. It stayed shut. I forced myself to stay calm and not to freak out. How could my own dad lock me up like a wild animal? Especially when he knew I had a dog.

I tore through the apartment, looking for a key. I thought he must have put a key somewhere. What if there was a fire? I looked under the bed, on the windowsills, even in the fridge. No key. I didn't have time to really freak out because I had to do something with Janie before she ruined the carpet. I took her out on the balcony, and she understood what to do.

Then I went to take a tour of my little prison. A lot had changed since I'd last been here. The bedroom was empty since my mom had taken the beds with her. There was a new couch in the living room, where my dad now slept, and a brand-new color TV. The rubber plant was gone and so was the bamboo rod that my dad used to beat me with and store in that pot. Now there was a jade tree plant instead.

The old wardrobe was still in the kids' room, and you could still only open one of its doors; otherwise the whole thing would collapse. The bed made creaking and cracking noises whenever you moved. It's pretty sad when your own dad can't even provide you with a decently furnished holding cell.

I went back out to the balcony with Janie. She put her front paws on the railing and looked down from our eleventh-floor apartment. All we could see were the desolate high-rises and barren landscapes of Gropiusstadt.

I had to talk to someone, so I called up Narc Anon. They had a surprise for me. Babsi had shown up. So I guess she'd actually been serious about quitting. She told me that they'd given her my bed. I was so sad that I wasn't there with her. We talked for a long time.

When my dad came back, I gave him the silent treatment, but that just had the effect of making him talk even more. He'd planned my whole future out for me. Gave me an actual schedule for every day, including housework, grocery shopping, and feeding his homing pigeons and cleaning up their roost.

He had a shelter for his pigeons out in Rudow, too. Every time he went out, he wanted to be able to check up on me by phone. To fill up all my free time, he'd found an old friend of mine, Katharina, who was willing to come and hang out with me. She was a real teenybopper, still in love with top 40 radio and other crap like that.

A reward was in it for me, too. He wanted to take me to Thailand with him sometime. He flew to Thailand at least once a year now. He loved it there because of the girls, but also because he was able to get some really cheap clothes. He saved up all of his money for these trips of his. In a way, that was his drug of choice.

So I listened to my dad's plans and thought I'd just play along for a while. I didn't really have a choice, anyway. At least that way I wouldn't be locked up.

The next day I had a packed schedule. First I had to clean the apartment and then go shopping. Then Katharina came over to take me for a walk. We went all over the place, and then when I told her that I still had to go to Rudow to feed the pigeons, she lost interest and gave up.

So I had the rest of the afternoon to myself. I was miserable, and one way or another I just wanted to get high. I didn't really know what to do though. I thought that maybe I could go to the Hasenheide for an hour. That's a public park in Neukölln and a good place to go if you want to smoke some weed. A joint sounded pretty good right then.

I didn't have any cash, but I knew where I could find some. My dad collected silver coins in an oversized brandy bottle. There were more than a hundred marks in that bottle, stored up for his next trip to Thailand. I shook fifty marks out of the bottle. I wanted to have a little extra with me, just in case. Whatever was left over I could put back, and then I thought I could probably replace what I'd spent with money I saved while shopping. That was my plan anyway.

In Hasenheide park, I ran into Piet. (He was the kid from Center House who was with me when I'd smoked pot for the first time in my life.) He'd become a heroin addict, too. So I asked him if they had anything besides weed at this park of his.

He asked, "Do you have cash?" I told him I did.

"Come with me then." He took me to a couple of dealers, and I bought a quarter. I had ten marks left now. We went to the public bathrooms at the entrance to the park, and Piet let me borrow his syringe. He'd become a really slick old junkie in the time since I'd last seen him, and I had to give him half of my dope to use his syringe. We both gave ourselves a little fix.

I felt amazing. The atmosphere at Hasenheide park was way better, way less fucked up than at places like Kurfürstendamm or Zoo Station. The fact that it was mainly just a place to smoke some weed made all the difference in the world. But there were still some junkies, if you poked around a little bit. It didn't cause problems, though, as the junkies and the potheads were generally able to chill out together, side by side. At the Ku'damm, pot was disdained—it was "for lightweights"—and potheads were generally snubbed. The two groups never mixed at Kurfürstendamm.

At Hasenheide, it didn't matter what drug you were on. You could even be sober. It wasn't an issue. You just needed to be cool. That was it. Whether you were high or not, if you were cool, then everyone else was cool with you. It was like everyone was part of a big, peaceful community—making music, banging on drums, and just hanging out. The whole atmosphere reminded me of Woodstock.

I was home again before my dad got back from work around six. He didn't notice that I was high. I was feeling a little guilty because I hadn't been able to feed the pigeons. I decided to give them a double portion the next day. I thought that the next time I went to the park I wouldn't shoot up because even if I just smoked a little pot I would feel all right, and I would still be accepted, too. I never wanted to return to the nasty heroin scene at Kurfürstendamm. I truly believed I could manage to get off of H at Hasenheide.

I started going to the park with Janie every afternoon, even if it was just for a minute. The dog loved it there because there were lots of other dogs running around. And even the dogs were totally friendly. Everyone liked Janie, and she got a lot of attention.

I only fed the pigeons every second or third day. That was more than enough as long as I stuffed them and left some extra on the floor for them.

I would smoke weed whenever someone asked me—and someone always did. That's also one of the major differences between the people who smoke pot and the people who shoot heroin: Potheads are always willing to share. I also got to know the foreign guy who had dealt to Piet and me on that first day. When I saw him again, he was lying down on a blanket with a couple of other friends of his—also foreigners. He invited me over, and I lay down in the grass next to their blanket. The dealer's name was Mustafa and he was Turkish. The others were Arabs, and they were all under twenty years old. They were just having a picnic of flatbread with cheese and melon, and they shared some of their lunch with me and Janie.

Mustafa was kind of cool, I thought. He was a dealer, but he was cool about it. He wasn't crazy or cocky or unpredictable like all the big-shot dealers were. While we talked, Mustafa pulled up clumps of grass and buried his bags of dope inside the cavities. So even if the cops raided the whole area, they'd never find his dope. If someone wanted to buy from him, Mustafa would then calmly poke around in the grass with his pocketknife until he found the supply.

He didn't weigh out his baggies like all the other dealers did. He just gave you what he took out with his knife. The portions were good though. Whatever stuck to the knife, he'd wipe off with two fingers and let you snort.

Mustafa said right off the bat that shooting up was fucked up. The only way to keep from getting addicted was to snort it. So that's what he and all his friends were doing. They only snorted once in a while, if they felt like it. None of them appeared to be addicted.

Mustafa didn't want me to become addicted again, so he was careful about how much he gave to me. These guys really knew how to handle heroin. I started seeing Mustafa and the other foreigners in a different light. They weren't like the predatory customers that had always offended Stella, Babsi, and me. They were very proud and easy to offend. They accepted me because

I seemed very self-confident and maybe because I was a pretty quick study and realized quickly how things worked with them. To give just one example, you weren't ever allowed to ask for anything. Hospitality was extremely important to them. If you wanted something, you just helped yourself—whether it was sunflower seeds or heroin that you wanted. But you had to be careful not to give them the impression that you were taking advantage of their hospitality. So it would've never crossed my mind to ask them if I could take some H with me when I left. Whatever I took from them, I snorted immediately. Because I was able to assimilate so quickly, they kind of took me in—despite the fact that they didn't generally think very highly of German girls. And they had a point: In a lot of ways, they really were better than us.

I loved everything about this world and even started to think that I'd kicked the habit for good—until, that is, I took a look in the mirror and saw that, once more, I was physically dependent on the drug.

In the evenings, I played the role of the rehabilitated daughter for my dad. I'd go to the Hungry Woodpecker with him and would sometimes drink a small glass of beer, just to please him. To some extent I hated this bar, but at the same time I couldn't help wanting to be accepted here as well. I wanted to have a place here and be able to assert myself in this world where drugs didn't really have a role.

I practiced on the pinball machines and practiced intensely at the pool table. I also wanted to eventually learn how to play skat.[38] I wanted to master all the masculine games. I wanted to be better than the men. If I had to spend time in this sorry environment, then at least I wanted to be able to make a reputation for myself. I didn't want to feel like people were looking down on me. I wanted to be treated like a star. I wanted to be strong and

---

38 A popular card game in Germany at the time—especially among men.

independent. Like Mustafa and his friends. I didn't want to have to ask for anything.

However, my first goal—to learn to play skat—was already falling apart. I now had other things to worry about: I was going into withdrawal again. I absolutely had to get over to the park every afternoon, and I needed to be able to spend some time there, as I couldn't just snort some of Mustafa's dope and go. I had to sit there and, in an unspoken way, negotiate with him, calmly chewing on sunflower seeds. Meanwhile, my dad's pigeons were now on their third day of going without. Every afternoon I had to lose Katharina, my chaperone, all over again, and then there was all the housework and grocery shopping to be done—and I had to always be careful to stay near the phone, in case my dad started calling. I was already running out of explanations for why I hadn't answered earlier. I wasn't feeling very good about things anymore.

Then, one day, someone came up behind me and clasped his hands over my eyes. I turned around, and there was Detlef. We hugged and kissed each other like our lives depended on it, and Janie jumped excitedly beside us. Detlef looked good. He said he was clean. I looked him in the eyes and said, "Yeah right, clean as a hog in mud. Your pupils are almost invisible already." Detlef had quit while he was in Paris, but back at Zoo Station he'd had a shot.

We went home to my dad's. We still had some time before he got back from work. My bed was too rickety, so I laid the comforter on the floor and we had sex. It was great.

When it was over, we talked about getting clean again. Not right away, of course, but we planned to start the following week. Detlef told the story of how he and his friend had ripped off a customer to get the cash they needed for the trip to Paris. They'd simply locked the guy into his kitchen, calmly swiped his packet of Eurochecks,[39] and sold the checks for a thousand marks to someone at Zoo Station. Bernd was already in jail for it, but Detlef didn't think that the cops would be able to find him since the customer didn't know his name.

We started meeting at the park every day, and most of the time we also managed to spend some time at my dad's as well, after we'd shot up. We didn't talk much about our plans for getting clean because we were just so happy to be together again. But it was getting more and more difficult for me to keep all the balls up in the air. My dad was checking up on me more often now and kept finding new chores for me to do. I needed even more time with Mustafa to get enough dope for Detlef, too. And I wanted to be able to spend some time alone with Detlef as well. All the old stresses had returned.

Also, at around this time I realized that in order to get all the money we needed, I would have to start working at Zoo Station again. I kept that fact secret from Detlef. But my feelings of optimism and hope were being gradually eroded as I was drawn into the junkie's routine all over again. The honeymoon period after withdrawal—the time when you can just relax and not worry about the pressure of scoring—was decreasing with every successive withdrawal.

About a week after Detlef came back, Rolf turned up at Hasenheide park. He was distraught and told me that the police had caught Detlef. They'd picked him up during a drug raid, and while they were at it, they also slapped him with the burglary charge. The guy who bought the checks from them had ratted him out.

---

39 The Eurocheck was a type of check used in Europe that was accepted across national borders and that could be written in a variety of currencies. Eurochecks were particularly popular in German-speaking countries, where they were often issued as standard domestic checks.

I went to the bathrooms at the Hermannplatz, locked myself in, and cried until I felt totally drained. We'd flushed everything down the drain again. I was back in the real world, where I felt more hopeless than ever. I was scared about how much I was craving my next fix already. I just couldn't bear the thought of having to sit next to the Arab guys, calmly spitting out sunflower seeds and just waiting for them to offer me a snort. So instead, I took the subway to Zoo Station, sat on a ledge, and waited for customers. It was dead at the station, however, because apparently there was some big soccer game on TV.

But eventually someone showed up, and it turned out to be someone I knew. It was Heinz, who'd been Stella's and Babsi's regular. He was the guy who always paid in heroin and would add syringes as a bonus—but the thing was, he wanted to have sex. I didn't care anymore though. I knew that Detlef would be in jail for a long time. I walked over to him. He didn't recognize me at first, so I introduced myself again. "I'm Christiane," I told him. "Babsi's and Stella's friend." That got his attention. He asked me if I wanted to go with him and offered me two quarters.

We used the same currency, and that was nice. In fact, it was his best quality. Two quarters was good pay—about eighty marks when converted into cash. I negotiated some extra change for cigarettes, soda, and stuff, and off we went.

Heinz stopped at a corner on the way to buy some dope because I guess his reserves had run dry. It was kind of funny to see this accountant-type guy skulking in the shadows with the dealers. But he knew what he was doing. He had a reliable dealer here who always got him really good shit.

I had the itch pretty bad and could feel the withdrawal symptoms coming on. I would have preferred to shoot up right then and there in the car. But Heinz wasn't offering.

On the way to his apartment, he insisted on taking me to the stationery store that he owned, at street level. When we got there, he pulled open a desk drawer and showed me some photos he had taken. Just some trashy nude pictures of at least a dozen girls or so. Sometimes their whole body was in the photo; other times it was just a close-up. It was like being in a gynecologist's office. And all I could think was, You sad, pathetic asshole. In the meantime, I was still fixated on the dope in his pockets. I only started paying attention to the photos again when I recognized Stella and Babsi.

"Great photos," I said. "But now let's get down to business. I need a shot." We went upstairs to his apartment. He gave me my dope and also brought a tablespoon out for cooking it up. He apologized that he was out of teaspoons. (They'd all been taken by the other girls who had been over.) I banged in the shot, and then he brought me a bottle of nonalcoholic beer. After that, he left me alone for fifteen minutes. He had enough experience with junkies to know that they needed fifteen minutes of quiet afterward.

His apartment didn't look like it belonged to a business-man. And that's what Babsi and Stella had always said he was. In the old living room hutch I found some of his ties along with cheesy porcelain trinkets and a bunch of empty Chianti bottles. The curtains (which were yellow with dirt) were drawn, so that nobody could look into his shabby surroundings. There were two old sofas pushed together against the wall, and that's where we hooked up—on top of an old checkered wool blanket that had fringes at the end. There weren't any linens around here.

This Heinz guy wasn't that rude or mean or anything, but he definitely got on your nerves. That was his main talent. He was so persistent and so annoying that in the end I agreed to sleep with him so that he would finally leave me in peace and let me go home. He also insisted that I enjoy it myself, and so I pretended that I did. At least he paid well.

After that, I became Heinz's regular girl—just like Stella and Babsi had been. At first, I thought that the arrangement was really practical and convenient because he saved me a lot of time. I didn't have to hang around the park for hours just for one tiny snort, I didn't have to wait around at Zoo Station for johns, and I didn't even have to go to the corner to score my dope. So now I was able to take care of the house again, tend to the pigeons, and get all my shopping done without all the old stress.

I spent almost every afternoon with Heinz, and to tell the truth, I didn't really mind him anymore. He loved me, in his strange way. He constantly told me that he loved me, and I had to tell him that I loved him back because he would get mad if I didn't reciprocate. He was super jealous and was always afraid that I was still working Zoo Station. But all in all, he was pretty nice.

He was the only person left that I could still talk to. Detlef was in jail. Bernd was in jail. Babsi was in rehab. Stella had somehow fallen off the face of the earth. My mom didn't want to have anything to do with me. And as for my dad, I had to constantly lie to him. Every sentence that I told him was a lie of one kind or another. Heinz was the only one I could be honest with, the only one who I didn't have to hide things from. The one exception to that rule, of course, was the fact that we couldn't ever talk honestly about our own relationship.

Sometimes, when Heinz held me, it just felt so good. I got the feeling that he respected me and that I meant something to him. Who else respected me? When we weren't on his grungy couch, I felt more like his daughter than his lover. But he really did have a talent for annoying people, and that problem only got worse the more time you spent with him. He wanted me to be with him constantly. I had to help him in his store and was supposed to be there when he wanted to show me off to his so-called friends. In truth, he didn't have any friends.

The amount of time that Heinz required of me was making my dad suspicious again. It was putting me under pressure.

My dad was constantly snooping around in my stuff, so I was careful not to bring anything that would be at all suspicious into the apartment. I encoded all the phone numbers and addresses that were connected to drugs or prostitution. For example, Heinz lived on Forest Street. So I drew some trees in my notebook. House number and phone number I converted to currency figures. The phone number 395-4773 I wrote out as: 3.95 marks plus 47 pfennigs plus 73 pfennigs. And then I also worked out the answer like a good girl. So I hadn't totally abandoned math in the end.

One day, Heinz solved the mystery of where Stella had gone: She was in jail. I hadn't heard anything about it before he told me since I didn't spend any time at Zoo Station anymore. Heinz was pretty shocked by the news. Not because of Stella—but because of the cops. He was terrified of them. He was afraid that Stella would turn him in. In the course of this conversation, I learned that a while back the police had begun to put together a case against Heinz, on suspicion of seducing minors and some other stuff. Up to that point, he hadn't let it bother him, even though he had in fact been previously convicted. He said he had the best lawyer in Berlin. But now he was scared to death by the thought that Stella would tell the police about how he paid the girls in dope.

I was shocked, too. And like Heinz, it wasn't Stella that I was worried about, but me. If they put Stella in jail at fourteen, then they certainly wouldn't hesitate to do the same to me. That was not my idea of a good time.

I called Narc Anon to give Babsi the bad news. We usually talked on the phone about once a day. Up to that point, she'd agreed that the withdrawal therapy at Narc Anon was okay— although it should be noted that she had already slipped out twice to get a quick fix. But when I called in, they told me that Babsi was in the West End hospital with jaundice.

It seemed like Babsi and I tended to stumble over a lot of the same obstacles. She was just as fragile as I was. As soon as we started withdrawing, we both got jaundice. Babsi had tried to get clean countless times before. The last time she'd even gone all the way to Tübingen[40] with a drug counselor to begin a therapy program there. But she'd chickened out at the last second because of how strict the program was supposed to be. We always kept a close eye on each other. We could always tell how run-down the other one was because we were usually dealing with the same issues, the same illnesses.

The first thing the next morning, I left to visit her at the West End hospital. I took the subway with Janie to Theodor-Heuss Place, and then we ran through the district of West End. It's a really cool area. Beautiful villas and lots and lots of trees. I had no idea that a place like this existed in Berlin. It made me realize that when it really came down to it, I didn't know the city that well after all. I knew how to get around in Gropiusstadt and the surrounding areas, and I'd spent a lot of time in the little quarter of Kreuzberg where my mom's apartment was, and I knew my way around the four main drug markets, but that was it.

It was pouring. Janie and I were soaked. But we were both in a great mood. We were happy about having all these trees around us, and I was especially happy that I would get a chance to see Babsi soon.

After we got to the hospital, we ran into a little problem that I hadn't quite anticipated: Janie wasn't allowed inside. But one of the doormen was great. He offered to take Janie into his little kiosk and look after her. I asked him the way to the ward where

---

40 Tübingen is a university town in southwestern Germany, in the state of Baden-Württemberg, about twenty miles south of the state capitol of Stuttgart.

Babsi was, and when I got there, I asked the first doctor I saw where she was. He said, "Well, that's what we'd like to know, too." Babsi had taken off the day before. He said that if she did any drugs right now it could be fatal because she hadn't yet recovered from the jaundice, and her liver wouldn't be able to take much more.

Janie and I walked back to the subway. I considered the fact that my own liver was probably just as poor off as Babsi's. Our lives already had so many parallels. I missed Babsi and I longed to see her. I'd forgotten all about our fights. We both needed each other—now more than ever. I wanted to let her talk about whatever she wanted to talk about and for as long as she wanted to talk. And I wanted to convince her to check herself back into the hospital.

But then I sobered up again. I knew that Babsi wouldn't go back to the hospital after she'd been on H again for two days. I knew what I would do myself. I wouldn't have gone back either. she and I were so damn similar. But I didn't know where I should be looking for her. She was either flitting around on one of the drug scenes or working the streets, or she was with one of her regulars. I didn't have time to look for her everywhere because my dad was due to make his checkup calls home. So I did what any self-respecting addict would do: I looked after myself. I went home. I still had dope from Heinz, so I didn't have any reason to head out to the streets or to the station.

The next morning, I went downstairs to get the paper, the B.Z.[41] Ever since my mom had stopped confronting me with all the death notices, I'd started buying the paper myself—and without even thinking about it, I still searched the paper for news about heroin victims before I read anything else. As the heroin-related deaths increased, the write-ups got smaller and smaller.

41 One of the Berlin dailies.

But the more I read, the more people I was able to recognize. A lot of them had been found with a needle still stuck in their arm.

So on that particular morning, I was making myself toast with jam while flipping through the paper. On the first page was a headline in giant print: "She Was Only 14." I didn't even need to read the rest of the article. I knew right away. I'd had a feeling it was coming. Babsi was gone. I don't know what I was feeling. It felt like nothing. It felt like I was dead—like I was reading my own obituary.

I went into the bathroom and shot up. That helped me to cry a little. I wasn't sure if I was crying about Babsi or myself. I sat on my bed and lit a cigarette, and then I read the rest of the article. It was written up like a sensational entertainment piece:

When they found her, the syringe was still stuck in the vein of her left hand. The name of this young girl: Babette D. (14), a student from Schöneberg. Dead. The youngest victim yet in Berlin's heroin epidemic. Nadjy R. (30), the acquaintance who found her, explained to the police that he'd picked the girl up at "The Sound," a club on Genthiner Street. Since she didn't have a place to stay, he took her to his apartment. Babette is the 46th drug victim in Berlin this year.

And so on. Pleasantly callous, and so simplistic. In the papers, every junkie was the same. Even the magazines got in on the story because up to that point she was still the youngest victim of a heroin overdose in all of Germany.

Around noon I'd recovered enough to experience a feeling of intense, wild rage. I was convinced that some slimy dealer had tried to make a few extra marks by selling Babsi a bag of dope that was laced with some cheap poison, maybe even strychnine. Every month, more and more strychnine found its way into the dope that was sold on the streets. I took the subway and went to the police. I ran straight into Mrs. Schipke's office without knocking and started to just vent. I told her everything I knew about corrupt dealers and about pimps who were in the heroin business and about The Sound. Most of it didn't seem to interest her very much. At the end of it all, she just repeated her standard goodbye: "Well then, until next time, Christiane."

I thought the cops didn't give a shit if someone sold dirty dope. They were just glad when they could cross another addict off their lists. I swore to myself to find Babsi's murderer on my own.

The guy who lived in the apartment where Babsi was found seemed innocent enough. He was an okay guy. I knew him pretty well from before. He was a little weird—but kind of funny—and he had a lot of cash. He liked to surround himself with very young girls. He'd once given me a ride through the city in his sports car, invited me to dinner, and then given me some money. But he would only sleep with a girl if she was actually interested in him. So it never went any further with me. I wasn't interested.

Even though the guy was a businessman, he never seemed to realize that all the young girls he chased after were also running their own kind of business.

I decided to go to Kurfürstenstrasse, where there was never any shortage of girls or clients. My plan was to make as much money as I could so that I could buy dope from all kinds of sleazy dealers and then test it to figure out who was selling the deadly shit that was killing all these girls. But then I just flitted around the drug scene, scored dope from a couple of guys, and succeeded only in getting super high. It wouldn't have made a difference anyway: Nobody seemed to know who had sold Babsi her last shot.

Obviously, my plan to find Babsi's "killer" was just an excuse to get as high as I could. It was a way of taking my foot off the brakes. I was telling myself, "You've got to find that scumbag, even if it kills you."

That's the point when I stopped worrying about how anything would look to anyone else. I just wanted to get high.

I didn't bother putting on an act for my dad anymore. He'd known something was up for a long time already. I think he was just waiting for proof. And he wouldn't have to wait long to get it.

One night when I'd used up my morning's supply of H prematurely and couldn't get away (because my dad was home), I called Heinz and told him to meet me in Gropiusstadt. My dad surprised Heinz and me in front of the Hungry Woodpecker. Heinz barely managed to clear out in time. But after a determined search, my dad found the dope that Heinz had given me.

I confessed everything right away—including the developments with Heinz. I didn't have it in me to lie anymore. My dad forced me to make a date with Heinz for the next day. We set up a meeting at the park, where he was supposed to give me dope again. Then my dad called the cops, told them everything, and demanded that they arrest Heinz during his meeting with me. The cops told him that they'd have to conduct a real raid at the park, and that sort of thing was impossible to organize on such short notice. They weren't that interested in going after this kind of "cradle-robber"—as my dad referred to Heinz—because it just created too much trouble for them. But of course I was hugely relieved that I didn't have to play the role of a police informant.

I always thought that my dad would beat me half to death if he found out how much I was getting away with. But it wasn't like that at all. He seemed desperate. Almost like my mom. He spoke to me very gently. He'd finally figured out that you can't quit H just like that, even if you seriously want to. However, he was still hopeful that somehow he'd be able to help me work through it.

The next day, he locked me into the apartment again and took my dog, Janie, with him. I never saw Janie again after that. I started going into withdrawal in a very bad way. By the middle of the day, I already felt like I was dying. That's when Heinz called. I begged him to bring me some dope. Since he couldn't even get into the building without a key, I came up with the idea of letting down a rope out the window. I finally convinced Heinz to do it, but in exchange he wanted me to write him a love letter and lower the letter down to him along with a pair of my panties. He never gave out dope without getting something in return. After all, he was a businessman.

So I looked through the apartment for anything that resembled a rope. Kitchen string, plastic laundry line, a belt from a bathrobe, etcetera. I had to tie dozens of knots and keep testing the length, until the makeshift knotted rope could reach down to the ground from the eleventh floor. Then I scribbled out the letter as best I could without the aid of any dope.

Heinz announced himself with the signature doorbell ring that we'd agreed upon. I grabbed a pair of panties (a pair that I'd embroidered myself) out of the wardrobe, stuffed it, along with the letter, into the plastic cover for my hair dryer, and sent the mail down through the window. It worked. At the bottom, Heinz put in the dope. Meanwhile, a bunch of people had started paying attention to this strange little game of ours. But it didn't seem to faze Heinz, and I definitely didn't care what other people thought. I just wanted to get high. But when a little boy leaned out of a window on the ninth floor and tried to grab the string, I lost it. I screamed at him and swung the rope away. I was terrified about losing my heroin.

After an eternity, I finally managed to haul it all inside, and I was just about to cook up the dope when the phone rang. It was Heinz. There'd been a misunderstanding. He wanted a pair of panties that hadn't been washed yet. I had the dope and, in a way, I didn't care about anything else. But I knew that he would keep at it if I didn't give in, so I reached down to the bottom of the hamper and threw the oldest pair of panties I could find out of the window. It landed in a shrub. At first Heinz ran away, but then he snuck back to fish his prize out of the bushes.

Heinz was a total perv. As I found out later, while I was lowering my panties down to him with a rope, he already had an arrest warrant out on him. The cops just hadn't had the time to come and pick him up yet. And his lawyer had already told him how bad things looked. But when it came to girls, Heinz didn't care. He would risk everything.

I had to appear as a witness at his trial, and I told the truth. Honestly, Heinz didn't matter to me anymore than any other customer. But despite that, it wasn't easy for me to testify against him; I felt sorry for him. He wasn't any worse than my other customers. I just felt bad for him because he was literally addicted to girls. If anything, he should've been put in a psychiatric ward rather than in a jail.[42]

Heinz's dope just about lasted for the couple of days that my dad kept me locked up. Then, when he left the front door unlocked one day, I took off. I managed to bum around on people's couches for an entire week before my dad found me and took me home again. I was sure that he was going to give me a serious beating. But instead, he just seemed to sink deeper into his own brand of despair.

I told him that I couldn't do this by myself. There was no way anyone could if she was completely alone all day. Babsi was dead. Detlef was in jail. Stella was in jail.

I told him about how Stella was already rotting away in jail, at only fourteen. I'd heard all about it from a girl who used to share a cell with her and had since been set free. Stella

---

42 On February 10, 1978, Heinz G. was sentenced to three-and-a-half years imprisonment by Berlin's state court for passing heroin to Christiane and Babsi, as well as for the sexual abuse of another child.

was consumed with suicidal thoughts. The only support she was getting was from some female terrorists who were being held in the same jail. Stella had talked to Monika Berberich from the RAF[43] a couple of times and had become a fan of hers. A lot of the addicts thought the terrorists were awesome. Some of them had even attempted to join a terrorist group themselves before they washed out on H. When the Schleyer[44] kidnapping happened, even I thought it seemed pretty cool. That being said, I was still opposed to any kind of violence; I could never have hurt anyone myself. But all the people in the RAF seemed like they knew what was going on behind the scenes. And maybe they were right. Maybe you needed to resort to violence if you wanted to make a difference in a society like this that was already so totally fucked up.

Stella's story had a profound effect on my dad. He wanted to get her out of jail and adopt her. I had convinced him that together with Stella I could make it. I could quit heroin and stay clean. That's what he was hoping for, too. It was idiotic, but how could he have known any better? My dad didn't always do the right thing during the time that I lived with him, I'm sure. But still, he did what he could. Just like my mom.

So my dad barged through the doors of the youth welfare office like a bull chasing red. He finally wore them down and managed to pry Stella out of jail. She was a complete and utter wreck—both physically and emotionally. She was even worse off now than she was before she went to jail. I was still using when she came to live with us—even though I'd planned on getting

<hr>

43 RAF is short for Royal Air Force, the British national air force.
44 Hanns Martin Schleyer was one of several people who had been kidnapped and/or murdered by the West German terrorist group RAF in the 1970s and early 1980s. He was the president of the West German federal employers' union and was targeted partly because of his past as an SS officer in the Nazi regime. He was kidnapped and murdered in the fall of 1977.

clean—and I got her to shoot up again with me on the very first day. She would've started using again anyway. We only talked seriously about withdrawing during the first few days. Between the two of us, we figured out a way to get around my dad's rules. We divided up all the chores and then went out and worked the streets in shifts—sticking to the Kurfürstenstrasse, waiting for cars to pull over.

I didn't care about anything anymore, so getting into strange cars with strange men no longer horrified me. There were four of us at the corner of Kurfürstenstrasse and Genthiner Streets. Besides Stella and me, there were the two Tinas. Apart from their names, they had little else in common. One of them was still a year younger than me, so only just fourteen.

We always worked in pairs—never less than that at least. When one of us drove off with a customer, the other would write down the license plate number, and we made sure that the driver saw us do it to stop him from getting any funny ideas. That was also a protection against pimps. We weren't scared of cops. The cop cars would drive by, and some of them would even wave. One of them was even a regular customer of mine. He was a strange guy with a lot of funny ideas. He wanted to feel like he was loved. And it was always a chore to explain to him that prostitution was work; love had nothing to do with it.

He wasn't the only one who was like that either. A lot of them wanted someone to talk to. It was always the same script. How did such a pretty girl like me end up on the street? I really didn't need to do that, and so on. Those were the comments that really got on my nerves. I hated it when people talked like they also wanted to save me. I got real marriage proposals. And all the while they knew full well that they were only taking advantage of our misery, the misery of the addicts, to satisfy their own desires. They were a bunch of fucking liars. They said they could help us, when they already had more than enough problems of their own.

As a general rule, these were mostly guys who couldn't even manage to deal with professional hookers. These guys had difficulties with women in general, and as a result they preferred young girls. They talked about how frustrated they were with their wives and their families and their whole lives; they complained about how nothing ever changed. Sometimes they even seemed to be a bit jealous of us—of the fact that we were still so young. They wanted to know what we thought was cool, what we were into, what kind of music we liked, what clothes we wore, and what kind of slang we used.

One guy, almost fifty, was dead set on smoking some weed because he was convinced that that's what all the young people were doing now. So in return for some extra cash, I hiked with him over half of Berlin to find a dealer who had some pot. I'd never noticed it before, and it seemed crazy, but it was true: You could get heroin everywhere, at every corner, but it was almost impossible to find any marijuana. It took us almost three hours to find a dealer who had some. After this customer of mine had smoked his joint, he was ecstatic. It was like his dreams had come true just because he'd managed to smoke some pot.

Our customers—who were all pretty bizarre in one way or another—broke up into two distinct sets: Some were just weird, but the others were malicious. One of them always insisted that I knock on the steel rod in his leg, which he'd had since a motorcycle accident. And another guy arrived with an official document of some kind or other. It had a stamp on it, and it said that he was infertile. (So obviously he didn't want to use any condoms.) The worst of them was the guy who pretended to be from a modeling agency and wanted to take some sample pictures. In the car, he pulled out a gun and demanded service without pay.

The ones I liked best were the college students who came trudging over to us on foot. They were pretty inhibited, as a rule.

But at least you could talk to them. They were mostly interested in talking about how fucked up our society was. Those were
the only ones whose apartments I would go to. With the others,
I'd do it in the car or in a hotel room. The room would cost the
customer an extra ten marks minimum. And they'd put up an
extra cot for us, as we weren't allowed to use the freshly made-up
double bed. The hotels were the most depressing places ever.

Stella and I communicated through coded messages on the
advertising pillars (the iconic Berliner Litfa säule[45]) or empty
poster walls. This way we always knew when we were changing
shifts, what the other one was up to, and what my dad had in
store for us when we got home: what new system he was going to
implement to keep us under control.

When I felt run-down and depressed, I sometimes walked
into a store that called itself Teen Challenge. They'd set up
shop suspiciously close by The Sound—not to mention the
Kurfürstenstrasse, the street where all the teen prostitutes hung
out—and they were hoping to convert kids just like us. Once you
were in their shop, they handed you brochures and books about
little, young prostitutes and child addicts in the United States.
These were all kids who'd been saved by Teen Challenge and
turned on to the righteous path of God. I'd unload my troubles
there while drinking tea and eating sandwiches. Then, when they
started talking about our dear Lord, I just took off.

It's funny, because when you stop to think about it, the Teen
Challenge people were just as interested in taking advantage of
us as everybody else was. They tried to reel us in, because that's
when we were the most vulnerable.

---

45 These advertising pillars were invented by the Berlin-born printer Ernst Litfass
in 1854. They are cylindrical outdoor sidewalk structures with a characteristic
style that are used for advertising, public announcements, and other purposes.
They are common in Berlin, where the first hundred columns were installed in
1855, but can be found all over Germany, and also in Paris, where they are called
colonne Morris (Morris columns).

Right next to their basement shop there was a communist group that had managed to set up a storefront. Sometimes I'd stop and read their posters in their shop window. They wanted to completely change society. I liked the idea. But their slogans didn't do anything for me in my situation either.

Then I'd stroll by the shop windows of the big furniture stores located nearby on the Kurfürstenstrasse. But after a while, I couldn't stop myself from thinking about all of my old hopes and dreams with Detlef. And that just made me feel worse.

At that point, I was pretty much at the bottom of the heap—even for a longtime addict. If nothing was happening on the street and I wasn't getting any customers, I turned to crime. Just small stuff because I wasn't a born criminal and didn't have the nerves for it. When some junkie pals invited me to come along on a robbery, I chickened out. My most impressive deed to date—which required almost an entire bottle of vermouth beforehand—was when I smashed in a car window with some brass knuckles and stole a boom box. Other than that, I mostly just helped people transport or hide stolen goods. I also worked as a mule, transporting stolen merchandise for lifetime criminals. I put the stolen stuff into lockers at Zoo Station and picked it up again for them, too. For that I got twenty marks, at most. And when it came down to it, that was even more dangerous than stealing. But I'd totally lost all perspective at that point anyway.

At home, I lied to my dad and fought with Stella. I'd made an agreement with Stella that we'd split everything fifty-fifty: the jobs and the dope. That's what caused most of our fights. Because each of us believed that the other was ripping her off. It doesn't get much sadder than that, I don't think.

My dad had figured out, of course, what was going on with me. But by that point, he was at a complete loss as to what to do. And so was I. I knew, however, that my parents couldn't do anything to help me anymore.

I couldn't handle school any longer, even if I just sat there doing nothing. I also couldn't stand sitting around. I couldn't stand anything anymore. I couldn't fool around with customers, I couldn't relax on the scene with my friends, and I couldn't stand being around my dad.

So it had come to this: end-of-the-world doom and gloom. Thoughts of suicide. I recognized this situation, and I knew that it absolutely couldn't go on this way. But I was still too chicken to give myself the golden shot, the overdose. I was still looking for some way out.

That's when it occurred to me that I could voluntarily check myself into the asylum. That would be the Bonhoeffer Asylum, or Bonnie's Ranch, as it was called. This was pretty much the last option for a heroin addict. Bonnie's Ranch represented complete and utter horror to every junkie. On the streets, there was a saying: "Better four years in jail than four weeks at Bonnie's Ranch." Some addicts who were forcibly admitted to Bonnie's after a breakdown would usually come back with horrific stories of their time there.

But, naïve as I was, I thought that someone would start paying attention to me there, especially if I checked myself in voluntarily and freely submitted myself to this horror. Then the youth welfare office, or whoever, would have to finally notice that I was a teenager who desperately needed help. And that her parents were completely incapable of helping her. The decision to go to Bonnie's Ranch was like a suicide attempt from which I was secretly hoping to wake up again so that everyone would say afterward: That poor girl. If only we'd taken better care of her. From now on, we'll do better.

Once I'd made that decision, I went to see my mom. At first she acted pretty distant. I mean, after all, she'd already written me off. But I couldn't help it: Right away I started crying, really crying. Then I tried to tell her my story, sticking to the truth as best as I could. Then she also started crying, and took me into her arms and didn't let me go. We both cried so long, we cried ourselves happy. My sister was also really happy that I was back. We spent the night together in my old bed. And then, after that, I went into withdrawal again. Another, new withdrawal.

I'd lost count of how many withdrawals I'd been through at that point. If withdrawing was an Olympic sport, I probably would have medaled in it. I didn't know anyone else who'd voluntarily gotten clean as many times as I had. And on top of that, I'd done it even though I knew that it wasn't going to make any difference. My mom took time off from work again and brought me what I needed: Valium, wine, pudding, and fruit. On the fourth day, she took me to Bonnie's Ranch. I really truly wanted to go there since I'd realized in the meantime that I would have just started shooting up again right away.

As soon as we got there, I was forced to strip naked, and then I was pushed into a bathroom. They treated me like I was a leper. Two bathtubs were already occupied by two clearly insane old women. I was put into the third tub and was told to scrub myself. I had to do it under supervision. I didn't get my own clothes back afterward. Instead, they gave me a pair of underpants that stretched from my rib cage all the way to my knees and that I had to hold onto if I didn't want them to slide off me. And a pretty old granny nightgown. I was taken to the observation ward, where I was the only one under sixty. The ladies there were all very far gone—just totally crazy. There was only one exception. Everyone called her Dolly.

Dolly was busy all day with one job or another. All on behalf of the ward. She really made herself useful and relieved the nurses of all sorts of work. I talked to her, and she didn't seem insane; she was just a bit slow. I mean her thought process. She'd been there for fifteen years. Fifteen years ago, her brothers and sisters had committed her to Bonnie's Ranch. Apparently, she'd never had any kind of therapy. She'd just always stayed in the observation ward. Maybe because she'd been making herself so useful there. I thought that something was very wrong if someone could be kept on the observation ward for fifteen years just because they happened to be a little bit slow.

On the first day, wasting no time, a whole team of doctors came in to inspect me. I guess most of the white coats were probably students, who brazenly gave me a once-over as I was standing there in my thin little nightie. The lead physician asked me a few questions, and I answered, very naïvely, that in a few days I wanted to do a therapy program and then go to a boarding school in Western Germany so that I could eventually take the college entrance exams. He kept just saying, "Yes, mm-hm, yes," the way you would when talking to a lunatic.

When I was back in bed, I remembered a few jokes about lunatics. I wondered if I'd said or done something wrong that gave them the idea that I was yet another frothing maniac who thought he was Napoléon. I was suddenly scared that I'd never be able to leave the observation ward, just like old Dolly, and would have to doze away the rest of my days in my depressing hospital uniform.

After two days, I was transferred to B ward since I didn't have any withdrawal symptoms anymore. I got my clothes back and was even allowed to eat with a knife and fork again, instead of just with a baby spoon like in the observation ward. In B ward, there were three more addicts whom I recognized from the outside world. The four of us sat at one table, which one old nut immediately dubbed the "terrorists' table."

One of the girls, Liane, had already done a lot of jail time. She said that Bonnie's Ranch was much worse than jail because in jail you could easily get some dope, whereas at Bonnie's Ranch it was almost impossible.

So far, it was kind of fun on Bonnie's Ranch because there were four of us. Still, I was starting to get a little panicky. The doctors wouldn't give me a straight answer as to when I could leave to start a drug therapy program. All they said was, "We'll see," and whatever other platitudes they dispensed to the lunatics on a daily basis.

The agreement with my mom and the youth welfare office was that I'd be at Bonnie's Ranch for four days, to make sure that I was clean. And then I was supposed to get a spot in a therapy program. But I'd already done the withdrawal by myself and had arrived there almost clean. Nonetheless, nobody was talking about my spot in a therapy program anymore.

The big blow came after a couple of days. They brought me a document, which I was supposed to sign, stating I was voluntarily staying in the asylum for three months. Of course, I refused to sign and said that I wanted to leave immediately. I'd come here of my own free will and could leave whenever I wanted. Then the supervising doctor came and said that if I didn't sign off on staying for three months, he'd commit me to involuntary hospitalization for six months.

I felt totally conned. I got chills; I was so horrified. The truth hit me like a bolt of lightning: I was completely dependent on these idiotic doctors. I had no idea what kind of diagnosis they were manufacturing for me. They could say I had a severe neurosis or schizophrenia or who knew what. As a patient in an asylum, you didn't have any rights at all. I thought that I was going to become Dolly's heir.

The worst thing was that I myself wasn't convinced of my own sanity. I already knew that I was neurotic. I had learned through conversation with my drug counselors that an addiction is a neurosis, a compulsive action you can't control. I thought about all the things that I'd done. All those withdrawals I'd gone through, only to start shooting up again as soon as they were over, even though I knew full well that it was the path to my own destruction, and that someday it would lead to my death. I'd fucked up every single thing in my life. I caused other people pain, including my mom. That wasn't normal. So I was kind of a maniac when you thought about it. Now it was just a matter of figuring out how I could hide my craziness from the doctors and nurses.

The nurses all treated me like an idiot—the same way they treated all the other patients in the ward. I pulled myself together—to an extent that I could hardly believe—and restrained my own impulses so that I stopped reacting in my usual aggressive way when they provoked me. When the doctors came and asked questions, I tried to give them the answers that they wanted to hear (despite the fact that it went completely against my nature to do so). I tried desperately to hide my real self and appear to be someone who was completely and totally "normal." And once the doctors were gone, I was always convinced that I'd made a mistake and said the wrong thing. I was afraid that they'd seen through me and thought I was crazy for sure.

The only thing they offered me in terms of rehabilitation was knitting. I couldn't have cared less about knitting, and I didn't think it would help.

In front of the windows were iron bars, of course. But these weren't the normal kind of bars like you'd see in jail; no, these were nice, ornately curved bars—because this was no jail (obviously). But after a while, I realized that, if you twisted yourself just so, you could get your head through the curves in the bars and get a good look at the outside world. Sometimes I stood there for hours, the iron bars around my neck, just looking around. The season was changing to autumn, the leaves were turning yellow and red, the sun was low in the sky, and, for an hour each afternoon, it shone directly through two trees right in front of the window.

Sometimes I would tie one of the tin cups to a length of wool thread, let it dangle out of the window, and bang against the house wall. Or I'd try all afternoon to pull a branch close to the window using the wool thread, in order to get at a leaf. At night I thought, If you weren't crazy before, you've certainly gone crazy now. This was the place for it.

I wasn't even allowed to go into the little garden to walk in circles with the grandmas. Even a terrorist has a right to go outside once a day. Not me though. I was considered a flight risk. And I was. Damn right.

In an old cupboard, I found a soccer ball. I kept kicking it again and again against a locked glass door, hoping that it would break the glass. But then they took the soccer ball away. Then I rammed the glass with my head. But of course it was made of reinforced glass. I felt like a wild animal in a tiny cage. Like a tiger, I prowled along the walls for hours. Once, I thought I couldn't stand it anymore. I just had to run. And so I just started running. Always up and down the hallway. Until I couldn't take another step and literally collapsed.

I got hold of a knife, and at night Liane and I scratched and scraped at the putty of a window that was locked but not barred. The glass pane didn't move an inch though. The next night, we took a bed apart and tried to break the bars of an open window. Before we started on this plan, we intimidated the old ladies in the room to such a degree that they didn't dare make a peep. Some of them actually thought we were terrorists. The plan didn't work though since the bars were so strong. And anyway, we made so much noise that the night watch caught on pretty soon.

The way I was acting pretty much eliminated any chance that I would ever get free of this insane asylum. I kept sliding further and further downhill. The only thing that seemed to be doing okay without drugs was my body. In other words, I got chubby. But my skin was pasty, and my face looked at once sunken and puffy. In the mirror, I looked like someone who'd been at Bonnie's Ranch for fifteen years already. I hardly slept. That was no surprise. Almost every night there was some huge commotion on the ward. And I also didn't want to miss a chance to escape. Although it all seemed so hopeless, I still made myself look nice every morning—like I was ready to go out. I brushed my hair with incredible patience, put on makeup, and slipped on my nicest jacket.

At one point, someone finally came by from the youth welfare office. Like everyone else, he just said, "Okay, well, let's see." But he was at least able to tell me where Detlef was being held and his case number. As soon as he left, I sat down and wrote just page after page after page. And as soon as I handed in my first letter, I started to write another one. Finally, I was able to talk to someone again. But still, I had to watch what I said since all the letters were reviewed. Probably at Bonnie's, but definitely at the jail. So I had to diligently continue constructing my string of lies in the letters. I had no interest in drugs. I felt no cravings. And so on.

I got a whole pile of letters from Detlef, too, all at once. He wrote that he'd fucked up royally when he stole those Eurochecks from that customer. But that he'd only done it so that he could go to Paris to quit. He'd wanted to surprise me with it because the two of us could've never done it together. Detlef wrote that he'd be released soon, and then he'd go into a therapy program. I wrote that I'd also be going into therapy soon, too. And we both wrote that after our therapy programs we'd get an apartment together. So once again, we were busy cooking up our imaginary paradise where we'd live together after all of our problems had been solved. But when I wasn't writing to Detlef, I was convinced that I'd spend the rest of my life right here at Bonnie's Ranch.

But eventually, a real chance opened up for me. An old infection started giving me some problems again, and I told the

doctor repeatedly that I needed to go to a hospital for an operation because the pain was getting to be more than I could stand.
Then one morning I was taken to the Rudolf-Virchow Hospital,
escorted by guards who were instructed to keep a close eye on
me. After the medical exam, they decided to keep me in the hospital because it was really quite bad. I'd already gotten some solid
information about how to escape from there. I finagled a park
pass for myself—which wasn't easy; trust me. Not if you're an
addict. But I had a trick up my sleve. I walked up to a really sweet
nurse and told her that I wanted to take one of the old ladies
for a walk. She was stuck in her chair, so I would help to push
her around in a wheelchair. The nurse didn't suspect a thing and
thought it was incredibly sweet of me.

I grabbed one of the old ladies, who thought I couldn't be
sweeter. I pushed her out into the park and said, "Wait a sec,
grandma. I'll be right back." And a few seconds later, I was over
the fence.

I ran to the Amrumer Street subway station and then made my
way over toward the Zoo. I'd never felt so free in my entire life. I
dove immediately back into the scene at the University cafeteria.
I flitted around a bit, getting a sense of what was happening and
then sat down next to three young dudes on a bench. I told them
that I'd just escaped from Bonnie's. That impressed them.

I was dying for a shot. One of the boys was a dealer. I asked if
I could barter with him or have some on credit. He said I could if
I'd help him negotiate some deals. I agreed. So he gave me some,
and right away I gave myself a shot in the cafeteria bathroom.

It was less than an eighth, and the dope wasn't that good,
but it still improved my mood. I still had a good grasp on things
and had my head on pretty straight. Which was a good thing
because I was still supposed to negotiate for this guy. He was still
kind of young, and I knew him a little from the pot scene at the
park. He was still in school, about sixteen. It was obvious to me

308

that he didn't have much experience with dealing; otherwise, he wouldn't have given me the shot before I had paid him back with some work.

Suddenly, I sensed undercover cops all over the place, just outside the cafeteria. The guy didn't notice a thing. I had to go right up to him and whisper, "Cops!" before he finally caught on. I started walking slowly in the direction of the Zoo, and he padded after me. When a junkie came toward me from the station, I said, "Better stop right here. There's a raid going on at the cafeteria. But I can get you some first-class stuff." The boy dealer came up at once and actually took all of his dope out of his pocket and said that the guy was welcome to try some. I couldn't fucking believe my eyes. There's a raid going on a block behind us, and this moron pulls his whole supply of dope right out of his pocket.

Right away, two cops (who'd obviously been lying in wait) trotted up to us. Running made no sense. This rookie of a dealer was just throwing his little baggies all around him. Purple foil fluttered everywhere. Apparently, he thought that he could pin it on me or the other guy and kept blabbing about how he had nothing to do with it.

We had to lean up against a VW, arms up in the air, and were searched for weapons, even though none of us was older than sixteen. The asshole cop felt me up while he was at it. But I stayed totally cool. After all, I'd had my fix, and after Bonnie's, nothing could rattle me. I immediately adopted the persona of the polite and well-brought-up child. That prompted them to be very friendly when taking down my personal information. One of them said to me, "Listen girl, you're barely fifteen; what the heck are you doing here?" I said, "Window-shopping," and lit up a cigarette. That got him angry: "Hey, throw that butt away. That's poison at your age." So I had to throw away the cigarette.

We were taken to the police station at Ernst-Reuter Place and put in a cell. The wannabe dealer immediately came unglued and shouted, "Let me out! Let me out!" I took off my jacket, rolled it into a pillow, lay down on the cot, and dozed off. An arrest like this wasn't about to faze me. I wasn't worried about the cops finding out where I'd come from, about how I'd escaped from Bonnie's. I was confident that I hadn't been reported missing yet.

After two hours, they let me go again, and I went back to the university cafeteria. On the way there, my emotions caught up with me. I started to bawl. So once again, I'd shot up some smack as soon as I could after a withdrawal. And I didn't know where to go next. I couldn't possibly show up at my mom's place with pupils the size of pinpoints and say, "Hey Mom, I'm back. I ran away. Could you make me some dinner?"

I went to the drug counseling office in the old cafeteria of the technical university. There were some cool guys there, and they made me feel a lot better and gave me the confidence I needed to call my mom. My mom was reassured to know that I had called from the university. On the way home, I noticed that I had a fever. By the time I got into bed, it was over 104°F. My mom called the emergency hotline because I was becoming delirious. The doctor, when he came over, wanted to give me an injection, but that idea terrified me because I was supposed to get the shot in my butt. I could stick a needle into my arm two or three times a day, but when the doctor stuck the needle into my butt, I freaked out.

The fever started to subside immediately, but I was completely drained. Bonnie's Ranch did me in, physically and mentally. When I was able to get up again after three days, I went back right away to the drug counseling office at the university. On the way there, I had to pass through the heroin scene outside the dining hall. But I ran right past it without looking left or right.

For a whole week, I went to that drug advice place every day. When I was there, I could finally talk about what was on my mind. It was the first time that I'd come to a place where I was allowed to unload absolutely everything. Up until now, I'd always been talked at. My mom had always talked at me, my dad, the Narc Anon people, everyone. But here at the university, I was supposed to do the talking and figure out myself what was going on with me. I was still spending all my time with the advisors when my face began to turn yellow again. When I ran into some people I knew in front of the university, they literally ran away from me. "Get the fuck out of here," they yelled at me. "And take your jaundice with you!"

I couldn't believe it. I guess I'd been trying to ignore reality, but here it was: jaundice again. This was crazy. Every time I'd stayed clean for a while and dared to regain some hope, I wound up suffering from some typical addict's disease. When the abdominal pains became unbearable, my mom took me to the clinic at Steglitz. I wanted to go to Steglitz because they had a really good kitchen there. So I sat in the waiting room for two hours, doubled over with pain. Any nurse who walked by could tell by my yellow face what was wrong with me. But none of them did anything. The waiting room was full of people, including kids. I could have infected all of them if I were contagious.

After two hours, I started to walk. I had to stick to the wall because I was so weak and in so much pain. I wanted to ask the way to the isolation ward, and when a doctor passed me, I told him, "I need a bed. I don't want to infect all these people here. I have jaundice, obviously." He said that he couldn't help me with that, and that I first had to go through the intake process. So back I went.

When I finally had a chance to speak, I told my doctor that I had contracted the jaundice from shooting heroin. She looked back at me, cold as ice, and said, "Sorry, but we're not responsible for cases like yours."

The thing is, nobody wants to be responsible for the addicts. So back into a taxi we go. My mom was furious with the doctors as a result of their refusal to help. The next morning, she took me to Rudolf-Virchow Hospital. I wasn't happy about that at all since I'd escaped from there once already.

A young resident physician came to take a blood sample. Right away I showed him the state of my arms. He wouldn't ever be able to get a needle in my veins. "This is where I have a thrombosis. That vein is totally knotted up anyway. You'll have to take one that's below it. Not straight down with the needle but from a side angle; otherwise you won't get through."

The poor guy, now totally unsure of himself, of course, stuck the needle into a completely knotted-up vein. He pulled and pulled, but no blood came, and due to the vacuum in the syringe, the needle literally exploded right back out of my arm. The next few times, he asked me where to stick the needle first.

I slept for two days straight. The jaundice wasn't contagious. On the fourth day, the liver tests came back okay, there wasn't any more urine in my blood (or not much), and my face was slowly coming back to its natural color.

I had to call the people at the university's drug advice office every day, and I did. I hoped to get a spot in a therapy program there very soon. And then I got a huge surprise: Detlef had been released from jail. My mom brought him along on the next visiting day, a Sunday.

Well, as you can imagine, it was a whirlwind: love, hugs, kisses, bliss. We wanted to have some time alone so we went outside into the hospital park. It was as if we'd never been apart. No sooner had we walked out than we were riding in the subway again, bound for Zoo Station. A small coincidence played a part in that decision. While outside, we ran straight into an old acquaintance of ours, Wilhelm, who'd recently struck gold. He was living with a very prominent doctor and author who not only gave him plenty of cash but also paid for him to go to a private school.

So right away, Wilhelm bought us a couple of shots. I came back to the hospital for dinner. The next afternoon, Detlef returned. This time we had some real difficulties scoring dope, so I wasn't back at the hospital until ten thirty that night. Meanwhile, my dad had also tried visiting me since he was flying to Thailand the next day.

My mom had that desperate look on her face again when she came by. I felt like a piece of shit. And then my drug counselor also stopped in and said that I was a helpless case. I swore to myself and everyone else that I was serious about quitting. Detlef cried also and said it was all his fault. Then he also went to the drug counselors. And when he returned on Sunday, he had a spot in a therapy program for the next day.

I said, "I'm so happy for you that you got that spot. Now everything will turn out okay. I'll get a spot, too. We'll do it together; I'll make it. We won't fuck things up again."

We went into the hospital park again, and I said, "Let's just go to the Zoo real quick. I need to get a book from over there—the third part of a trilogy. I've already read the first two parts, and my mom couldn't find the last installment anywhere."

Detlef said, "Yeah, right. Why do you need to go to the Zoo to buy a stupid book? Why don't you just come right out and say it? You want a fix."

I was super annoyed that Detlef was suddenly pretending to be all high and mighty and on the pious path to clean living. I wasn't even thinking about the dope. I just wanted to get part three of the Death's Head Moon series. So I said, "Stop being so self-righteous. You don't know what I'm thinking. And you don't even have to come along, you know, if you don't want to."

But of course Detlef came with me. In the subway, we fell back into our old routine. Right away I started in on some old ladies, getting them all upset and annoyed. This was, as always, very embarrassing to Detlef, so he moved to the back of the subway car. So then, just like always, I yelled back at him from the other end of the train: "Hey dipshit, don't pretend you don't know me! You're not any better than I am. Get back here!" But then I got a nosebleed again. I'd been getting nosebleeds for a couple of weeks, every time I went underground to take a train. I was already feeling pissy, and now I had to keep wiping that damn blood off my face, too.

Luckily, I was able to find the book I was looking for at the Zoo. I was feeling better and said to Detlef, "Let's just walk around a bit before we go back. This is your last day of freedom." The heroin scene at Zoo Station acted like a magnet on us. Stella was there and both of the Tinas. Stella flipped out when she saw me again. She was so happy. But the two Tinas were both in withdrawal and doing really badly. They'd been on Kurfürstenstrasse with Stella but forgot that it was Sunday. And on Sundays, Kurfürstenstrasse is dead. That's when the customers spend time with wives and kids instead of creeping along Kurfürstenstrasse in their cars.

I was kind of glad to have escaped all that shit. Not to live with the constant anxiety of going into withdrawal, and not having to deal with customers. I hadn't had any contact with any johns for weeks. I was feeling superior to the others; I was really happy, even cocky. I realized that this was probably the first time I'd been able to hang around Zoo Station without craving a shot.

We were standing at the bus stop near the subway station. Next to us were two Turkish guys who kept winking at me. Despite the jaundice, I probably looked the freshest of all four of us since I'd been relatively clean for a while. Also, I wasn't wearing any of the usual street clothes. I'd borrowed some clothes from my sister and was dressed in the normal teenage style. I didn't want to look like an addict anymore. I'd even had my hair cut while I was in the hospital.

The two guys didn't stop winking. So I asked the two Tinas if they wanted me to set something up for them. "Even if you just get forty marks out of it," I told them, "you can at least share a quarter." The two Tinas didn't care about any of the details. They just wanted to score. Feeling on top of the world, I walked up to the two guys and said, "You want the girls? I can ask for you. Fifty marks. Capito?" I pointed to the Tinas.

They grinned stupidly and said, "No. You. We fuck you, at hotel."

I was completely in control. Without being at all aggressive, I told them bluntly, "Nope, that's not happening. But you'll like these girls. They're young and cheap. Only fifty marks." The younger of the Tinas had just recently turned fourteen.

The men were stubborn though. And when I looked at the two Tinas, I could understand their thinking. The Tinas didn't look very appetizing now that they were in full withdrawal. I went back to the girls and told them that the deal was off. But then the devil got inside of me. I took Stella off to the side and said to her, "The two Tinas won't be able to manage any customers in the state that they're in. Especially not these guys. Let's go with them. We'll get them going, and then the Tinas can come and finish them off. They're used to fucking customers anyway. We'll ask for a hundred marks and buy half a gram."

Stella was on board right away—despite the fact that we'd always said that we'd never sink so low as to sleep with these foreign types.

So I went back over to the two Turks and suggested our plan, to which they immediately agreed. Only Detlef resisted. He was pissed and demanded to know why I was hell-bent on prostituting myself. I replied, "Oh, stop it, will you. I'm not doing anything. There's four of us." I was telling myself that I was doing it all out of pity for the Tinas, and pity may have played a role. But I'm sure I was also interested at the time in getting my hands on some more dope.

I told the others that we'd have to go to the Hotel Norma in Nürnberger Street because they had the largest rooms. In the other hotels, they wouldn't let the six of us go up to a room together. Then off we went. And suddenly, there was a third guy following us. The other two explained, "He friend. Also to hotel."

We let that slide for the moment and collected the hundred marks. Stella went off with one of the men to score some dope. She knew a dealer who sold the biggest half-gram packets on the scene. When she got back, all eight of us went strolling down Tauentzien Street together. All of us girls walked in front, arm in arm with Detlef, and behind us were the Turkish guys.

But there was some tension in the air. The two Tinas wanted the dope right away, and Stella wouldn't hand it over. She was afraid that once they had it, the Tinas would just take off. Besides, we wanted to shake off the new guy, who wasn't part of the original deal.

After a minute, Stella turned around, pointed to the third guy, and started in on all three of them together: "If that asshole keeps following along, then the whole deal's off. Got it!?" She had balls anyway, that Stella.

The three foreigners, however—who had their arms around each other's shoulders in a very collegial fashion—were unimpressed. Stella then suggested we just cut and run. At first, I was all for it because it would be easy in my flat-soled shoes. (It was the first time in at least three years that I had worn flats, incidentally. I'd borrowed the pair from my sister.) But then I had second thoughts. I said, "We'll probably run into them again sometime, and then we'll be in for it." I'd forgotten that this was supposed to be my last afternoon out here.

Stella was pissed. She stopped and waited for the foreigners to catch up, and then she tried once again to get them to stick to the original deal. We were just passing under the stairs of the

Europacenter, and after a pause I noticed that it'd gotten very quiet behind us. I turned around and Stella was gone. It was as if she'd been swallowed up by the earth. And the dope had gone with her. The three customers noticed this as well, and they looked pissed.

This was typical Stella. I was fuming. Suspecting that she had to have disappeared into the Europacenter, I sprinted up the stairs of the pedestrian bridge toward the center with Detlef right behind me. The two Tinas didn't get away though. The foreigners had grabbed them. When we got inside the complex, I went to the left and Detlef went to the right, running like lunatics. Not a trace of Stella. And now Detlef was gone, too, and on top of that, I felt guilty because of the Tinas. In the distance I could see them being dragged into a hotel by the Turks, and I had to wait for hours outside, all alone, until they finally came back. At that point, they at the very least deserved to get their share of the dope.

I had an idea where to find Stella. The Tinas and I took the subway to the Kurfürstendamm station. There wasn't much happening there because around this time of day the action moved to the club down the street. But we knew where to look and made a beeline for the station's bathrooms. As soon as we were through the door, I heard her. She was yapping at someone. This bathroom had a lot of stalls, but it was easy to find her. I banged against the stall door with my fists and yelled, "Stella, open this door right now, or else."

The door flew open immediately and out she came. Little Tina slapped her across the face. But Stella, flying high, just said, "Here, here's your dope. I don't want any of it." And with that, she was gone.

That was bullshit, of course. Stella had shot up a good quarter gram right away, just so that we couldn't get at it. But the two Tinas and I threw the remaining quarter in with the dope that we'd just bought and divided it all fairly amongst ourselves.

For me, it was more than enough. In fact, I had trouble getting up again from the toilet. We went to Treibhaus—the club down the street. There was Stella, doing her thing. She was negotiating with a dealer. We got right in her face and told her to give us the half-gram that she had taken. She coughed it up without a fuss. So she did feel a little guilty after all.

But I still let her know my mind. "You're a piece of shit, Stella. I never want to see you or have anything to do with you ever again."

In the club, I shot up my share of Stella's dope and got myself a Coke. I sat alone in a corner. It was the first time since the beginning of this afternoon that I'd had some quiet time. For a moment, I was hoping that Detlef would turn up again. But at that point, it was too late: I'd started to do some thinking.

It all started harmlessly enough. I thought to myself, This is all so fucked. First your boyfriend ditches you, and then your best girlfriend rips you off. Friendships just can't exist among addicts. You're completely alone. You're always alone. Everything else is in your imagination. That whole terror this afternoon over just one shot. And what good did that shot do you. It wasn't anything special. Every day there's some new kind of terror. And for what?

It was a moment of real lucidity. I did have lucid moments sometimes—but only when I was on H. When I was sober, I was completely unreliable and irresponsible (as this day, among others, proved so clearly).

I sat there and continued to reflect on my existence. It wasn't at all dramatic. I was very calm about it—in fact, I couldn't have gotten animated even if I wanted to, with all that heroin in my system. I decided that there was no way I would be going back to the hospital. I mean, it was already after eleven o'clock.

I would've been kicked out anyway, and no other hospital would've taken me in. The doctor had told my mom that my liver was about to go into cirrhosis.[46] If I kept on going like this, he estimated that I had two years left to live—at most. As for the drug counseling center at the university, they were done with me. There was no point in even trying to call them since they would have heard all the news about me from the hospital. They were right not to take in someone like me. After all, there were plenty of addicts in Berlin who sincerely wanted therapy, and not everyone could get a spot. It made sense that they would only work with the people who wanted to help themselves out of their condition and who had enough willpower to really do it. I obviously was not such a person. I had probably started shooting up a bit too early to ever get clean again.

I was thinking very clearly. I looked soberly at the facts of my life and sipped on my Coke. Where should I go tonight? My mom would've slammed the door in my face. Or she would've called the police the next morning to pick me up and put me into a home. That's what I would've done if I was in her shoes. My dad was in Thailand. Stella and I were over. And Detlef—I didn't even know where he was sleeping that night, or with whom. If he was serious about getting clean, then he'd be at his dad's. And if that was the case, then he'd be gone again soon anyway. So I didn't even have a bed. Not for that night, and not for the next night either.

The last time I'd done some sober thinking, I'd come to the conclusion that I had two options: I had to either quit H for good and all, or I had to give myself the golden shot. The first option seemed like it was out. Five or six relapses were all the evidence I needed anyway. I was no better and no worse than any of the other addicts. Why should I of all people belong to the

---

46 Cirrhosis is a chronic liver disease most commonly caused by alcoholism, hepatitis B and C, and fatty liver disease. Cirrhosis is generally irreversible, and in advanced stages of cirrhosis the only option is a liver transplant.

lucky subset of people who were able to get away from heroin? I was nobody special. I went onto the Ku'damm and took the subway to the Kurfürstenstrasse. I'd never done any whoring on the Kurfürstenstrasse at night. Girls avoided it at night because that's when the pros took over. I wasn't afraid though. I quickly did two customers and took the subway back to Treibhaus. With a hundred marks in my hand, I bought myself half a gram.

I didn't want to use the bathroom in Treibhaus for my shot or the one at Kurfürstendamm. There was too much activity over there at night. I got myself another Coke and thought about where I could go. The toilets at the Bundesplatz came to mind. There wasn't a soul there at night. Even in the mornings it was usually pretty quiet.

So I made my way over there. I wasn't panicking. I was totally calm. There's something really creepy about empty public bathrooms at night. But somehow I felt sheltered and safe when I got there. It was clean and bright. I had the whole place to myself. The bathrooms at the Bundesplatz are the best ones in Berlin. The toilet stalls are huge. There was one time when we crammed six of us into one stall. There's no space between the bottom of the doors and the floor, and there are no holes drilled into any of the walls. Because it was so nice and private, quite a few addicts had already killed themselves over here.

No old ladies, no peeping toms, and no cops. So there wasn't any rush. I took my time. I washed my face and brushed my hair before I cleaned the syringe that I'd borrowed from Tina. I was sure that half a gram would be enough. After the last few withdrawals of mine, a quarter of a gram had been sufficient to knock me out. And I already had more than a quarter in my system. My body was also pretty worn down from the jaundice. I would've rather had a whole gram though. Atze had done it with a full gram. But I couldn't face doing another two customers.

So with peace in my heart, I picked out the cleanest stall. I felt really calm. I wasn't scared. I'd never thought that committing suicide would be so prosaic. I didn't think about my past life. I didn't think about my mom. I didn't think about Detlef. I only thought about the shot.

I spread my stuff out around me in the stall like I always did. I put the dope on the spoon (another thing I'd borrowed from Tina), and suddenly realized that I, too, had ripped off Tina. She was sitting at Treibhaus right now, waiting for me to come back with her syringe and spoon. But there was nothing I could do about it now.

I'd forgotten to bring some lemon, but the dope was good and dissolved without it. I looked for a vein in my left arm. It was just like with every other shot I'd ever done, with the sole difference being that this was supposed to be my last one. On the second try, I hit the vein. I could see blood. Then I banged the whole half-gram into my arm. I didn't get a chance to pull back the plunger and shoot in the remainder. What I felt was how it first tore through my heart and then absolutely exploded through the roof of my brain.

When I woke up, it was light outside. The cars were making a huge amount of noise. I was lying next to the toilet. I pulled the plunger and the needle out of my arm. When I wanted to stand up, I realized that my right leg was somehow paralyzed. I could move it a little, but it made the joints hurt like hell. Especially my hip joint. Somehow I managed to open the stall door. I crawled at first, but then I pulled myself up. I could hop along the wall on my one good leg.

When I came out of the bathrooms, there were two boys out in front, both about fifteen or so. Satin jackets and skintight jeans. Two young gay boys. I was glad that they were gay. They literally caught me as I came hopping out of the bathrooms, looking like a ghost. They immediately figured it out and one of them said, "Jeez, what the hell were you thinking?" I didn't know them, but they'd seen me at Zoo Station a couple of times. The boys brought me over to a bench. It was a freezing cold October morning. One of them gave me a Marlboro. I thought, Funny that these gay hipster-types are always smoking Marlboros or Camels. Must be because of all the attractive guys in the ads. Somewhere inside me, I was kind of glad that it hadn't worked with the half gram.

I told the boys the story of how Stella had ripped me off and explained that afterward I'd shot up a full half gram. They were very sweet and asked if they could take me anywhere. The question bugged me because I didn't want to have to think. I said that they should just let me sit on the bench. But I was shivering with cold, and they thought I should go see a doctor since I couldn't even walk.

I didn't want to go to any doctor. They said that they knew a really cool doctor, a gay guy, who could help me out. It reassured me that the guy was gay because in a situation like this I trusted them more. The boys hailed a cab and took me over to see this guy. It was just like they said: He was really cool. He let me lie down on his bed and examined me. He wanted to talk to me about heroin abuse and other stuff like that, but I didn't feel like talking to anyone. I asked him for some sleeping pills. He gave me one sleeping pill and some other medication as well.

Almost immediately afterward, my nose started to bleed again, and I started to run a fever. I slept for the next two days. When my brain started working again on the third day, I couldn't stand it anymore. I didn't want to think. I had to really pull myself together and work at it just to keep from going crazy. I was obsessed with just two thoughts: (1) God wasn't ready for me to quit yet. And (2), the next time you try something like that, be sure to take a full gram.

I wanted to get outside, out onto the heroin scene. I wanted to shoot up, wander around from person to person and group to group, and not think about anything again, until it was time to end things for real. I still couldn't walk normally. The doctor was really worried about me. When he realized that he couldn't hold me back anymore, he got me some crutches. I hobbled off on the crutches and then threw them into the bushes somewhere along the way when I got close. I didn't want people to see me with crutches. If I pulled myself together, I could still move around.

I struggled over to Zoo station and made arrangements with a few johns pretty quickly. One of the sessions was with a foreigner, but I didn't care anymore about the taboo of not doing foreigners. I didn't care what Stella and Babsi would have thought. I didn't care about anything.

Maybe I was still hoping against hope that my mom would come looking for me. If she'd been looking for me, she would have come here. That's why I probably didn't go to Kurfürstenstrasse. But I knew in my heart of hearts that no one was looking for me anymore. And for a moment, I remembered how wonderful it was when my mom was still concerned about me.

I bought dope, shot up, and went back to the station. I needed money in case I couldn't find a customer who would invite me to spend the night with him.

At the station, I met Rolf, Detlef's regular from before. In those days, I spent lots of weekend nights at his place. As it turned out, Detlef had been staying with Rolf again over the last few weeks, but Rolf wasn't a customer anymore. He'd been shooting dope for a while now, too, and was at the station looking for customers. He didn't have an easy time finding johns since he was already twenty-six.

When I asked Rolf about Detlef, Rolf started crying. Detlef was in a therapy program, and now that he was gone, Rolf was absolutely distraught. He felt like life was meaningless; he wanted to withdraw, too, and he kept talking about how much he loved Detlef. He wanted to kill himself.

All in all, it was the usual junkie soap opera. All this talk about Detlef kind of pissed me off. I didn't get why this run-down, sorry excuse for a man thought he had any claim to Detlef. He actually, in all seriousness, wanted Detlef to quit and come back to join him. He'd even given Detlef a key to his apartment. When I heard that, I lost it: "God you're such a dick," I told him. "Giving Detlef a key to your place and encouraging him to abandon his plan to get clean? That's so selfish. If you really cared about him, then you'd do everything you could to support him right now. You're unbelievable."

Rolf was already in withdrawal, so it was easy for me to humiliate him. But then I realized that I could probably stay at his place if I played my cards right, so I forced myself to be more pleasant. I told him that if he'd let me crash at his place, I'd go off with a john myself and buy some dope. Rolf could not have been happier as it turned out—and I guess that sort of makes sense since Detlef and I were the only people that he knew in Berlin.

That's how I came to share his big French bed with him. We actually got along great when Detlef wasn't there. He grossed me out, but in the end he was just kind of a sad, pathetic character.

So there we were, Detlef's two lovers, lying together in a big French bed. It was the same thing every night: Rolf would start blabbering about how much he loved Detlef, and then he would cry his eyes out before he went to sleep. That whole act got on my nerves, but I didn't say anything. I needed that spot in Rolf's bed. I didn't even say anything when he bragged about how he wanted to furnish a nice apartment for Detlef once they were both clean and sober. I didn't give a shit, but I guess I was paying the price, in a way, for my previous crimes because what had happened to Rolf was really our fault. If he hadn't met us, he would've stayed a poor, lonely crane operator, who occasionally drowned his sorrows in alcohol.

Things went on like this for a week. Whoring, shooting up, whoring, shooting up, and at night, Rolf's lovesick chatter. Then one morning I woke up earlier than usual, just as someone was unlocking the front door and banging stuff around in the hall. I thought it was Rolf, so I yelled at him to shut up and let me sleep. But then I saw Detlef.

We grabbed a hold of each other and didn't let go—until it suddenly dawned on me why he was here: "Oh no," I said. "Did they kick you out?" He nodded and then explained why.

Like all the other people who had been newly admitted, Detlef had been given three weeks of early morning wake-up duty as his first chore. It's almost impossible for any heroin addict to show up anywhere on time. To wake up every morning at the same time and immediately jump into action is just about the most difficult thing for an addict to do. That's exactly why they demanded this of the new arrivals, to make sure that the few available spots were given to those who really had the strength and willpower to make it. Detlef, in any case, couldn't do it. He overslept three times and was sent packing.

Detlef told me that he'd actually liked it in the program. It was tough, but he would be able to make it the next time. Now his goal was to stay clean as best as he could, and then try once again for a spot in a therapy program. He said there'd been a few people there that we knew pretty well, like Frank, for example. Frank was there because his friend Ingo had recently died. He'd been fourteen, just like Babsi.

I asked Detlef what he wanted to do, and he said, "First thing, score some dope." I asked him to bring me back some. Two hours later, Detlef returned. He'd brought a former customer with him, a guy named Piko. Piko reached into his pocket, pulled out a plastic bag, and set it on the table. I thought I was seeing things. It was full of dope. Ten grams. Never in my whole life had I seen that much heroin. After I was done gaping at it in disbelief, I asked Detlef, "Did you lose your mind? Ten grams, here in the apartment?"

He said, "Definitely not. I'm a dealer now."

I asked, "Did you think about the cops? If they catch you, you'll go straight back to jail. You'd wind up doing serious time. It could be a few years."

Detlef said, "I don't have time to worry about cops right now. First I need to make sure that I can make a living. So just let it go. Stop badgering me."

He started to measure off small quantities with his pocket-knife and gathered little piles of the stuff on bits of foil paper. I could see that the pieces of foil were way too small. I said, "Listen to me. People are just begging to be ripped off. You have to take larger pieces of foil, put the same amount of dope in it, and then roll it out so it looks bigger. People trust what they see, and they don't look too carefully either. Think of the candy at movie theaters. Gigantic boxes, but they're always never more than two-thirds full."

"Will you please get off my back?" he whined. "I'm putting extra dope into each packet. People will notice it. And then word will get around that I'm the man they need to see."

"Whose dope is this, anyway?" I finally asked. It belonged to Piko of course, that slimy little crook. He used to survive on office burglaries. He'd recently gotten out of jail, on probation, and now he wanted to make a quick buck off of Detlef. Detlef, who was always too sweet for his own good. Piko had gotten the dope from some pimps on Potsdamer Street. They were his friends from jail. He got the stuff at dealer rates, but he didn't want to have to deal himself; instead, he wanted Detlef to take care of it. Piko didn't know the first thing about the heroin scene. He was a drinker.

When Detlef was finished up with his packets, we counted and added up the quarters, halves, and full grams for him. Math was never my strong suit, but I realized before Detlef did that we only had eight grams to sell, all told. He'd put too much in each of the packets, and if he'd sold them like this, he would've had to pay for two grams out of his own pocket.

So we had to go back and redistribute the dope. (I made sure to pocket any scraps that stuck to the papers for my own use later on.) Detlef made bigger foil packets and rolled out the dope with a beer bottle to make it look like a bigger supply. He only packaged halves and actually ended up with twenty-five packets. Not bad.

We shot up two packets to test the supply. It was good shit.

That same night, we took to the entire supply to Treibhaus, but for the moment, we decided to stash most of it. We buried it next to the dumpsters in the back. We never had more than three packets on us at any time. If there'd been a raid, they couldn't have nailed us as dealers. And in the end, it went pretty well. We sold five grams that first night. Word got around that the dope was good and that our portions were decent. Stella was the only one who complained about us. But in the end, even she got on board and asked if she could broker some deals for us. Like an idiot, I let her. For five halves that she sold for us, she got a quarter. But for us, there was nothing left. We didn't get one single penny from Piko for our dealing. If we sold ten grams, we could keep one and a half. And out of that, we still had to pay our own agents. That meant our earnings from dealing only amounted to our own daily requirement of H.

Piko came by every morning to collect his take. On most nights, we managed to bring in about two thousand marks. That was one thousand marks net profit for Piko because the profit margin from the middleman to the dealer is 100 percent. What we got was our one-and-a-half grams. In the meantime, Piko also didn't have to run hardly any of the risk, unless we ratted him out.

But that had already occurred to Piko, so he'd planned ahead. He threatened that if we ever got arrested and even so much as breathed one word to the police, we might as well go ahead and pick out a coffin that we liked. His buddies from Potsdamer Street would take care of us. And he said that he wouldn't even have to wait until we were out of jail. He had friends everywhere. He also threatened to set his pimps on us if we tried to cheat him of any of his money. We believed every word he said. The pimps had me legitimately terrified. I knew all about what they'd done to Babsi.

But Detlef refused to acknowledge that Piko was ripping us off. He said, "What do you want? The main thing is that you don't have to work as a prostitute anymore. I don't want you to do that ever again. And I don't want to do it either! And what other options do we have?"

Most of the small street dealers didn't fare any better than we did. They could never even get enough cash together to buy ten grams and start their own careers as middlemen. Besides, they didn't have the connections. How could we have gotten access to the pimps and other big-time dealers on Potsdamer Street? The small street dealers—who were all addicts themselves—needed a middleman who could pay them in dope. And the small-timers were always the ones who wound up in jail. Guys like Piko hardly ever got tangled up with the cops. They had an almost endless supply of street dealers to do their dirty work. Almost any junkie was willing to risk some prison time for two shots a day.

After a couple of days spent dealing at Treibhaus, things were already getting too hot for us. There were always undercover cops lurking around. I was having a hard time dealing with the stress. So we reorganized the whole thing: I kept negotiating at Treibhaus, and Detlef hung around Steglitz Station. Then, when I found a buyer, I'd send him over to Detlef at Steglitz Station.

The next week, when Detlef was back at Treibhaus and had some dope on him, a guy pulled over next to him and asked how to get to Zoo Station. Detlef freaked out and just started running. He threw the dope into the bushes somewhere.

When we met up again later that night, Detlef said he was sure the guy was a cop because nobody in Berlin would have to ask where Zoo Station was.

It was bad. It was like everywhere we turned, we saw a cop—in every car and around every corner at the Ku'damm. We didn't even dare look for the dope that Detlef had thrown away. We thought that the cops would be waiting for us.

We went into the Athener Grill to discuss our next move. We couldn't settle up with Piko the next morning because the dope was gone. And he would never believe our story. Then I got the idea to tell him that we'd been ripped off by some foreigners. We would say that a bunch of them had mugged us and taken all the dope and all our money. I said, "Weird shit's gonna happen with Piko anyway. So we should just spend the rest of the money. It's crazy that we haven't made a single cent while Piko is able to pull in a thousand marks every day. At the very least, I need to buy myself some clothes. I don't have anything for the winter right now. I can't run around all winter in the same clothes that I wore when I escaped from the hospital."

We weren't born to be dealers. And although Detlef wasn't ready to admit that yet, he did finally agree that it didn't matter whether we gave Piko two hundred marks or nothing at all.

Very early the next morning we went to the flea market. If I liked something, Detlef would try it on first, and then me. We only wanted to buy what we could both wear, so that we could swap clothes occasionally. I ended up buying a used fur coat that looked really cute on Detlef. Then we bought some perfume, a music box, and other junk. But we just couldn't manage to spend all the cash because we couldn't bring ourselves to buy stuff that was expensive and useless. So we just stashed the rest of the money.

As soon as we walked through the door of Rolf's apartment, Piko showed up. Detlef said that he hadn't had his fix yet and needed to shoot up before cashing out. That wasn't true, of course, since as usual we'd had our fix as soon as we gotten up. But Detlef just wasn't ready to deal with this shit with Piko.

Piko said, "Okay," and sat down to read a thriller that I had on me. Detlef rammed another quarter into his veins and then passed out without even pulling out the spike first.

It wasn't too surprising that he'd passed out like that because he already had another quarter in his system. I pulled the syringe out of his arm for him because if you just left it in then the blood would clot in the needle, and it would be hard to flush it out again. And this was our last syringe and needle, so that was pretty thoughtless of him, I thought. As I was dabbing the puncture in his arm with a cotton ball, I noticed that he wasn't really resisting me at all. I lifted his arm, and when I let go it just flopped back down, completely limp. I shook him and tried to wake him up, but he just slid out of the armchair. His face was ashen and his lips were blue. I tore open his shirt and tried to find a heartbeat. I couldn't.

I ran out of the apartment and into the hallway, still in just my underwear, but Piko was right behind me: "Don't do anything stupid!" he yelled. I rang the doorbell of a neighbor who had a phone, and told her I had to call the police immediately. I called 911 and said, "My boyfriend's not breathing. He's overdosing." I had just given the cop the address when Piko came running back and yelled, "Stop, stop, he's conscious again!"

So I told the cop, "Sorry, never mind. It was a false alarm. You don't need to come after all." Then I hung up.

Detlef lay on his back with his eyes wide open. Piko asked if I'd said something about drugs on the phone, and if I'd given them the address. I said, "No, not directly. I don't think they could really take everything in that fast."

Piko called me a hysterical bitch. He was frantic, slapping Detlef in the face and forcing him to stand up immediately. I told him he should leave Detlef alone for a while. Then he screamed, "Shut up and get me some water, you stupid fucking cow!" When I came back, Detlef was upright and Piko was berating him. I was so relieved to see Detlef conscious again that all I wanted to do was go and hug him, but Detlef literally shoved me away. Piko splashed some water in his face and said, "Come on, boy, we've got to go."

Detlef still looked pale as a ghost, and he could barely stay upright. I told him he should lie down again. "Shut up!" Piko screamed at me. Detlef agreed that he didn't have time. And then they left the apartment together, with Piko acting as Detlef's support.

I was having a hard time coming to grips with what had happened. I was shaking like crazy. After all, for a second I was convinced that Detlef had died. I lay down on the bed and tried to concentrate on my thriller. Then the doorbell rang. I peered through the peephole. It was the cops.

I don't know what I was thinking, but instead of hightailing it out the window, I just went and opened the door. I admitted that yes, it was me who had called. I told them that the apartment belonged to a gay guy who was on vacation. And this morning two young guys came by and injected something into their arms. One of them had keeled over afterward and that's when I'd called the police.

The cops wanted me to give them names and descriptions, and I managed to come up with something for them. They took down my personal information and called it in. It didn't take long for a reply to come back. One of the cops said, "Well, why don't you come along then? You've been reported as missing."

The cops were pretty nice though. They waited for me to put two of my books into a bag, and then they gave me time to write a note to Detlef. "Dear Detlef," I wrote, "you can probably guess that I've been picked up. More news soon. Lots of love, Christiane." I taped the note to the front door with some Scotch tape.

First they took me to the Friedrichstrasse police station and then to a holding cell. It was like something straight out of an American Western. Seriously, it even had iron bars instead of walls. When they locked me up, the iron door clanged into the lock with the same sound that I recognized from movies about Dodge City and Deadwood. And when they turned the key, it even made that famous creaky, grinding noise. There I stood, hands wrapped around the bars, utterly defeated. I couldn't even bear to take stock of how depressing it all was, so instead I just lay down on the cot and fell asleep. (At that point I was also still pretty doped up.) Later on, they brought me a little plastic container for my urine sample and a backup bucket to put below, so that I wouldn't pee on the floor. Anyone walking by would have been able to watch me pee. I got nothing to eat or drink for the entire day.

My mom came by around nightfall. She walked right past my cell without really looking at me. I guess she had to clear something up with the cops first. When they did finally unlock the door for her to get me, my mom just said, "Good evening," as if I was a stranger. Then she grabbed me firmly by the arm and pulled me away with her. Klaus was outside, waiting for us in the car. My mom shoved me into the middle seat and sat down beside me. Nobody said anything. Klaus got lost on the way back, and we wound up driving all over Berlin. It seemed like we would never get home.

When we stopped at a gas station, I told my mom that I was hungry and asked I if she could buy me three Bounty chocolate bars.[47] She said okay, and got out to buy them.

After the second Bounty, I got sick. Klaus had to stop the car so that I could throw up. We started heading northbound on the autobahn, and that's when I realized that we weren't going home at all. Maybe it was going to be another institution or maybe a home, but either way I would break out soon enough. But then I started paying attention to the highway signs, and I realized where they were taking me: the airport. That's just fucking perfect, I thought. Now they want to ship me out of Berlin entirely.

As soon as we got out at the airport, my mom grabbed hold of me again, tightly. Then I spoke for just the second time since our reunion. Very slowly, emphasizing each and every word, I said, "Would you please let go of me?" But she held tight and stayed close by my side. Klaus was trailing behind us, ready to chase me down if need be. At that point, I just kind of resigned myself to whatever they were going to do. In the end, it didn't matter what they tried. There was nothing anyone could do for me. That's how I felt at the time anyway. I did survey my options for escape when I saw the signs for Hamburg, but in the end I was too weak-willed to really do anything.

Hamburg. Jesus. I had a grandmother, an aunt, an uncle, and a cousin who all lived in a small town about thirty miles outside of Hamburg. They were all incredibly dull, sad little people. Very bourgeois. Their house was so neat and tidy, it made me want to barf. You couldn't find a speck of dust, even if you tried. I once

---

47 Bounty is the German version of the American candy bar Mounds.

walked around that house in bare feet for an entire afternoon, and at night my feet were still so clean that I didn't have to wash them.

On the plane, I pretended to read my book. I got through a few pages. My mom was still playing deaf and dumb. She hadn't even told me where we were going yet.

As the flight attendant rattled off her little speech and got to the part where she said she hoped we'd had a pleasant flight, I noticed that my mom was crying. Then the words poured out of her. Without hardly stopping to take a breath, she told me how she just wanted to do what was best for me. She'd had a dream recently, where I was lying dead in a bathroom stall with blood all over the place and my legs all twisted up. A dealer had killed me, and she had to come identify me.

I'd always believed that my mom had psychic powers. Whenever she had a bad feeling about how the day was going to go, she would tell me to stay home, and when I didn't, then presto!—I'd get tangled up in a raid or get ripped off, or some other disaster would happen. It made me think of Piko, about how, when everything fell apart, Detlef and I had just ripped him off. Maybe my mom was saving my life with this intervention of hers. I didn't think any further than that. I didn't want to. Since my failed suicide attempt, I didn't want to think about much of anything.

After we landed in Hamburg, I went with my mom and my aunt to the airport restaurant. My mom had to take the next flight back. I ordered an orange soda—Florida Boy, my favorite brand—but they didn't have it. I guess they thought they were too good for orange soda here. So I didn't drink anything, although I was dying of thirst.

Together, my mom and my aunt started in on me. In a half hour, they laid out my whole future. I would have to go back to school, I would have to behave well and find new friends, and then later on I could do some kind of an apprenticeship. And then, once I was done training for a career, I could return to Berlin.

For them, it was simple. My mom was bawling again when we said good-bye. And I had to fight to keep from crying myself. That was on November 13, 1977.

Christiane's Mom

That whole day, I had to make an incredible effort to control myself and pull myself together. On the return flight to Berlin, I broke down and cried until all of the accumulated stress and anxiety had drained out of my system. I was sad and relieved at the same time. Sad because I had to give Christiane away. Relieved because I'd finally gotten her away from heroin.

I was convinced that I'd finally done the right thing. After the failure of the Narc Anon therapy, I realized that Christiane's only chance for survival depended on me taking her to a place where there simply was no heroin. When Christiane was living with her dad, and I had some distance from the whole thing, and some peace and quiet, it became clear as day to me that she'd die if she stayed in Berlin. Although my ex-husband assured me that Christiane had been off heroin since she'd been with him, I didn't put any stock in that. I would've never thought that my fear for Christiane's life could get even worse. But after the death of her friend Babsi, I didn't have even one single minute of peace.

When Babsi died, I wanted to take Christiane to stay with her relatives in Western Germany immediately. But her dad refused to agree to that. Since Christiane had moved in with him, he had obtained a court order for temporary custody. Anything I said was useless. He just didn't understand. Maybe because he hadn't yet experienced what I'd experienced. Maybe because he couldn't admit defeat.

While Christiane was living with her dad, I received the indictment against her. She was supposed to stand trial on account of her offenses against the narcotics law. Mrs. Schipke from the Narcotics Department had already called to give me a heads-up. To comfort me, she said that I shouldn't blame myself for what Christiane was doing. "Anyone who wants to do drugs will do drugs," she said. "It's ultimately up to them." She knew lots of addicts who came from good, upstanding families. And they also had to appear in court to deal with charges like these. I shouldn't torture myself about it.

I thought it was really cynical of them to use a little packet of heroin that I had once found in Christiane's room as evidence against her. Mrs. Schipke had innocently asked me to send her that packet for inspection. She had told me not to put my return address on the letter because that way nothing could be proven.

I don't think it's right that young people like Christiane are condemned for their drug use. Christiane never hurt anyone. She only destroyed herself. Who should sit as judge on that? And everyone knows how useless prisons are in curing addiction. The indictment was one more reason for me to send Christiane to West Germany.[48] I was determined to get her to safety. I went to the guardianship office and explained the whole situation to them, everything, down to the last detail. For the first time, I felt like someone in some government agency or department was actually listening to me. Mr. Tillmann, the social worker responsible for our case, also thought that Christiane would be better off in Western Germany. He wanted to try to secure a spot for her in a rehab program since it was impossible to predict how soon he could restore custody of Christiane to me. In the mean

---

48 West Berlin was an "island" within East Germany, so to get to West Germany from West Berlin, residents had to make two border crossings: once in going from West Berlin to East Germany and then again when moving into West Germany.

time, it would be easier to get my ex-husband to agree to enroll Christiane in a rehab program than it would be to get him to agree simply to send her to her relatives in Western Germany. I could sense that Mr. Tillmann was really engaged and interested in helping Christiane and wasn't just making empty promises.

One afternoon shortly after my discussion with Tillmann, Christiane suddenly appeared on my doorstep. She'd just returned from the drug advice center again. She was a complete wreck, pumped full of heroin and talking about suicide and giving herself the "golden shot." I calmed her down first, then put her to bed. Then I immediately called up Mr. Tillmann. He came by right away. When Christiane awoke, the three of us drew up a solid plan: First, Christiane should do her physical withdrawal in the state's psychiatric hospital. After that, she should get a spot in a therapeutic community home called Bonnie's Ranch. Both the drug counseling center and Mr. Tillmann were in contact with this therapy program on behalf of Christiane.

Christiane was very willing and allowed all of this to be done for her. Mr. Tillmann immediately jumped on making the most urgent necessary arrangements. We got an appointment with the child psychiatrist and the chief doctor at Bonnie's Ranch, who issued the admission papers for Christiane. After that, Mr. Tillmann drove to Christiane's dad's with the admission papers and put the pressure on him until he agreed to let me take Christiane to the hospital.

Two weeks after Christiane was admitted to Bonnie's Ranch, she was transferred to the Rudolf-Virchow Hospital for an operation to treat her infection. I assumed, of course, that a child who was a heroin addict being transferred from Bonnie's Ranch to Rudolf-Virchow Hospital for an operation would be closely supervised and continue to receive appropriate care. But all they did was unload Christiane at the hospital. Whatever happened *after that wasn't their concern. Christiane walked right out of the hospital and made her way back to the streets.*

I was incredibly bitter about the sloppy coordination between the therapy program and the hospital, which threatened to undo everything we'd accomplished up to that point.

After that experience, I lost all faith in institutions. I told myself that it was up to me to help my child. Mr. Tillmann tried to give me renewed courage. He was the only one I felt like I could trust.

Luckily, Christiane didn't stay away for long. She came back the next evening to cry her eyes out on my shoulder. She had shot up again, but I didn't get mad at her. I'd lost all aggressive feelings toward her. How many times in the past had I vented all my rage on Christiane out of sheer frustration over not being able to help her? Now that she had come back to me, I just took her into my arms and we had a calm, quiet talk with each other.

Christiane was determined to keep following the plan that we'd set up together with Mr. Tillmann. And I said, "Good, that's what we'll do." But I also made it absolutely clear to her that if she messed up one more time, she'd have to leave Berlin and go to Western Germany. She really took this to heart and gave me her word that she would stay clean.

During those next few days, she regularly went to the drug counseling center. She really hung on to the hope of a future spot in a drug therapy program. Sometimes she waited for hours for her turn with a drug advisor. At home she sat down and wrote out her résumé because that was one of the admission requirements.

Everything was looking good. Her spot in the drug therapy program seemed as good as certain. The community home, that would take her in was all set. We were planning how to celebrate Christmas when she was in the community home, since it was already the beginning of November.

Her dad had, in the meantime, admitted to the fruitlessness of his attempts to help Christiane and agreed to the plan we had decided on. Finally, there seemed to be light at the end of the tunnel. But then Christiane came down with her second case of jaundice, which threw a wrench in the works. Her temperature climbed to almost 105°F overnight. The next morning, I took her to Steglitz Hospital. Christiane was completely yellow. She couldn't stand up and had to crawl to get down the hallway. After the exam, the doctor said that Christiane was suffering from congestion of the liver due to her drug abuse. Unfortunately, they couldn't keep her there because they didn't have an isolation ward at Steglitz Hospital. (I later found out that this wasn't true. Steglitz Hospital had an isolation ward with twenty-five beds. The truth was that they just didn't want to take in a heroin addict.) The doctor there still made an intake appointment for us at the Rudolf-Virchow Hospital for the next morning.

Within a couple of days, Christiane's yellow coloring began to disappear. Soon she was feeling much better and was looking forward to the therapy program. Her counselor from the drug advice center even came by to visit. I was as hopeful for her recovery as I'd been in a long time.

Then I let my guard down and made the unforgivable mistake of allowing Detlef to visit Christiane in the hospital. Christiane had really wanted to see him. Detlef had been released from jail, where he'd gotten clean, and he was out on parole. He'd also managed to secure a spot in a drug therapy program for himself. I didn't want to deny them a reunion. After all, I knew they loved each other. And I thought that maybe it would strengthen their resolve, and they would mutually encourage each other, knowing that the other was also going into rehab. How could I have been so impossibly naïve?

Soon after Detlef's visit, Christiane slipped out for an afternoon. When I stopped by to visit her after work, she had just *returned, and I could tell that she'd gotten high while she was away. That alone wouldn't have knocked me over. Not anymore. But when she tried to tell me that she'd just gone to the Gedächtniskirche[49] to eat spaghetti—when she lied to me—that almost made my knees buckle.*

I asked the nurse on duty if I could stay with Christiane to keep her out of trouble. I would pay for the bed of course. She said that that wasn't possible. She would keep an eye on Christiane in the future. Three days later, when I came by after work again, the nurse walked up to me and said, "Your daughter's gone."

"Well, could you tell me where she is?" I asked.

"We don't know. She got permission to go for a walk in the park and then she didn't return."

I can't even describe how I felt. At home I lay down in the living room right next to the phone. At 11:20 p.m. at night, the hospital called to say that Christiane had returned. The indifference of the nurse was disturbing. Their attitude was, "If she escapes, then she escapes. That's her business. We've had enough addicts here to know that they all bolt eventually."

The doctor seemed pretty cold about it, too. All she did was explain to me that she didn't have any influence over Christiane's behavior. If Christiane violated hospital regulations one more time, she'd have to be released due to lack of self-discipline. The results of the liver tests showed that if she continued on her current trajectory, she'd only reach the age of twenty, at most. The doctor promised to have a serious talk with Christiane. Unfortunately that was all she could say and do in Christiane's case.

---

49 The Gedächtniskirche is one of the most well-known landmarks in Berlin. The Kaiser Wilhelm Memorial Church (in German, Kaiser-Wilhelm-Gedächtniskirche, but mostly its' just known as Gedächtniskirche) is located on the Kurfürstendamm not far from the Zoo. The original church on the site was built in the 1890s. During World War II, on the night of November 23, 1943, the church was irreparably damaged in an air raid. The damaged spire of the old church was retained, and its ground floor was made into a memorial hall.

The next evening, the hospital called to say that Christiane was gone again. Once again, I spent the whole night on the sofa next to the phone. This time, Christiane didn't come back at all. She was gone for two weeks. I didn't know if she was alive or dead.

The first two or three days, my boyfriend and I continued to go out looking for her. We did the usual search through the clubs and subway stations. Then I was asked to pick up her things from the hospital. When I brought her bag home and unpacked her books and toiletries and personal items that I'd brought her while she was in the hospital, I finally sank down to the point where I told myself, There, now you just have to let her fall flat on her face.

I told myself, Okay, if this is what she wants, then she's got to deal with it herself. I stopped looking for her. I was too hurt for words. I wanted her to feel that my patience with her was over and that I would really stick to my guns this time. How long I could've kept that up is anyone's guess.

I reported her as missing at the next police station and left a photo of her for the cops. I was sure they'd pick her up during one of their next drug raids. And then I'd get on the next plane with her and take her to Western Germany.

After fourteen days, on a Monday morning, I got the call from the police station. The officer at the other end of the line was unusually nice, considering how loudly Christiane was shouting and screaming at them in the station. I asked the officer to hold her there. I said I'd pick her up in the early afternoon.

Next, I ordered the tickets: a round-trip ticket for me and a one-way ticket for Christiane. As I ordered her one-way ticket, I felt a stab of sadness and pain. But I pushed through it and called my relatives with our flight information.

By that afternoon, everything was taken care of. On the way to the police station, I stopped to pick up my boyfriend. I thought, if she sits between the two of us, she can't jump out of the car.

Christiane didn't say a word when I picked her up from the station. I didn't either. I just couldn't.

At the airport, my knees were shaking, and my heart was in my throat. Christiane still didn't say anything. She completely ignored me. Right up until departure time, she sat in her seat, chewing her fingernails and reading a novel that she'd brought with her. But at least she hadn't make any attempts to run away.

Only when we were on the plane did I breathe a sigh of relief. During takeoff, she looked out the window. It was dark already. I said to her, "Well, now that's over. This chapter of our lives has come to an end. You're going to stay with Aunt Evelyn. I hope that you'll finally be able to start a new life out there."

●

I **SPENT THE FIRST FOUR DAYS** at my aunt and grandma's just going absolutely cold turkey. Then, once that was over and I was able to stand up again, I put back on my old uniform. It was the outfit of a junkie bride: From the rabbit fur coat to the high-heeled boots, I definitely managed to stand out from the pack. I put on my makeup and took my aunt's dog for a walk in the woods every morning, and every morning I'd get dressed up as if I was about to hit Berlin's heroin scene. My high heels got stuck in the sand, and I tripped a lot and got my knees covered in bruises, but when my grandma suggested that she could take me shopping to buy me some more sensible walking shoes, I could feel my entire body constricting. Just those two words alone—walking shoes—made me shudder in horror.

It turned out that my aunt, who had just turned thirty, was pretty fun to talk to—not about any of the real problems that I had, but I didn't want to talk about that stuff anyway. My real problems all boiled down to one thing, of course: H. Dope and everything that was connected to dope. Detlef, the scene, Ku'damm, the peace of a good shot, calmness, freedom. I tried not to think too much, even now that I was clean. When I did think, it was mainly about how I'd eventually be able to clear out of this place. But unlike before, I never really made a plan to escape. I kept putting it off, pushing it away. I just thought, Someday you'll run away. I was probably afraid to leave because freedom, over the last two years, had turned out to be a pretty terrifying thing.

My aunt's rules were oppressive. At fifteen years of age, I had to be back in the house exactly at 9:30 p.m. on the nights that I was allowed out at all. I hadn't had a curfew like that since I was twelve. Her rules really got on my nerves. But it was funny how I followed them.

During the holidays, we went to Hamburg to do our Christmas shopping. We got up early and tried to get to the department stores before they got too crowded, but that didn't work. It was a nightmare. Hours and hours of squeezing our way through these desperate packs of wild-eyed shoppers. Everywhere we went, they were snatching at boxes and packages, and digging around in their fat purses.

My grandma and my aunt and my uncle and my cousin kept trying on clothes and taking them off again. But it seemed like they could never find the exact right gift for Aunt Hedwig or Aunt Ida, for Jochen and for whoever else they had on their list. And my uncle still needed to find a pair of insoles for his shoes and something else for the car, which he thought he could get for cheaper at these department stores than he could back at home.

My grandma's tiny, and she's still able to slip through crowds like a weasel—so we were always losing her in the crowds. Then we'd have to launch another "find grandma" expedition. In the course of those recovery missions, I'd sometimes think about running away.

I already knew that there was a heroin scene in Hamburg, on Mönckeberg Street. All I would've had to do was run out of the department store and talk to a few junkies—the rest would've been easy. But I couldn't bring myself to do it. I don't think I really knew what I wanted in the end. All I knew was that I'd rather die in a toilet stall somewhere than spend the rest of my life at a department store with these people. So yeah, I think if a junkie had walked up to me that day and talked to me, I would've been gone.

I realized that my mood was kind of dangerous, so I told my aunts a few times that I needed to go. "I can't take this anymore," I said. "You can come back later and keep shopping without me; I won't mind." But they looked at me like I'd just dropped in from outer space. For them, going Christmas shopping was probably the highlight of their year.

When we'd finally finished up for the day, no one could remember where we'd parked the car. We ran from one garage level to the next and still nothing. I thought that it was a kind of fun situation since all of a sudden we were being forced to work together as a team. We talked over one another; everyone had different suggestions, but at least we had a common goal: We wanted to find that damn car. The only difference between the others and me was that I thought the whole thing was hilarious, and I couldn't stop laughing, while the others were already in a full-blown panic. In the meantime, it had gotten really cold, and everyone's teeth were chattering. I was still doing okay. I'd been through a lot worse.

Then my aunt found a hot air vent in the entrance to Karstadt,[50] and she decided to settle there. She stood right under the blower and refused to take another step. My uncle had to forcibly remove her.

When we finally did find the car, we couldn't help but laugh. On the drive home, I felt really good. I felt like I was part of a real family.

I adapted a little to my new family life. At least I tried to. It was hard. I had to keep a constant watch on my language—on every sentence, every word. When "shit" slipped out, my grandma would say, "Christiane. That's a very ugly word for such a pretty girl." Then a little fight would break out because those kinds of comments always pissed me off, and I couldn't keep myself from sulking. It led to a lot of outbursts from me.

Christmas came. It was the first time in two years that I celebrated Christmas next to a Christmas tree. I'd spent the last two Christmas Eves out on the streets. I wasn't sure how I should feel about this Christmas tree. However, I decided to put on a smile and at least show some gratitude for the presents they'd bought for me. I really was happy about my presents. I'd never gotten this much for Christmas. But at some point, I caught myself adding up the cash value of my gifts and converting that amount into quarters.

My dad visited over Christmas. As usual, he couldn't stay for long. On both Christmas nights[51] he took me to a club for the eighteen-and-over crowd. My dad bought me all the rum and Cokes I wanted, so I had like six or seven each night and then dozed off at the bar. My dad was really pleased to see me drinking with him instead of shooting up. I was almost able to convince myself that I could eventually get used to these kinds of clubs and the people who went to them.

---

50 One of Germany's large department stores, a chain, which still exists to this day.
51 In Germany, Christmas is celebrated over two days, December 25 and 26.

My dad flew back to Berlin the next day. Apparently he'd become a hockey fan at some point, and there was some hockey game that he wanted to see.

After Christmas vacation was over, I had to go back to school. I was set to begin ninth grade in the Realschule. At first, I was scared about starting up at school again. After all, I'd basically been AWOL for the past three years. The year before, I only showed up for a couple of months because the rest of the time I was either sick or in withdrawal again or just cutting class. But as it turned out, I kind of liked it at this school. On the first day, the class was busy painting a picture onto one of the boring white walls of the classroom. So I was able to join in immediately. We painted these beautiful houses—exactly the kinds of houses that I'd imagined I would live in. Out in front were happy, cheerful people. On the street out in front there was a palm tree with a camel tied to it. I loved it. Above the painting, we wrote the words, "There's a beach under every sidewalk."

But before long I could see that the kids out here weren't all that different from the young people in Berlin. There was a lot of dissatisfaction and anger out here, too. At the same time, things were more concealed in the country. The kids weren't as rowdy in school, and there were nowhere nearly as many pranks. Most of the teachers could still assert themselves. And most of the teens still dressed pretty conventionally.

I wanted to do well in school, even though I'd already missed so much. I really wanted to graduate at least. For the first time since elementary school, I was doing homework. After three weeks, I'd adjusted myself pretty well and had settled into class. I got the feeling that I could really do this.

We had just started in cooking class when I was called to the principal's office. When I got there, the principal was fiddling around with some document behind his desk. He looked nervous. It didn't take me more than a second to realize what was going on: He'd just received my file from Berlin. It explained everything about me. The youth welfare office had at some point sent a complete report to my school in Berlin, and after that they had sent it here.

The principal spent some time clearing his throat before he said that, much to his regret, he couldn't allow me to continue at this school. I was, apparently, unable to cope with the demands of the program here.

My file must have made me seem so hardened and intimidating that he couldn't even come get me himself. He had to send someone else. And it was so urgent that he couldn't even wait until the end of the school day to kick me out.

I didn't say anything. I was speechless. The principal wanted me to leave right that instant. During the next break between classes, I was supposed to check in with the principal of the lower-track secondary school, the Hauptschule. I was devastated. I went over to the other school in a complete daze. And once I was sitting in the office of my new principal, I just broke down and cried. He said that things really weren't as bad as I made them out to be. I should just take a seat, get to work, and set my sights on graduating with good grades.

When I got outside, I took another good look at my situation. I didn't feel sorry for myself at all. I told myself, It goes without saying that now you're paying the price for all your old mistakes. All at once, I understood that all those dreams of a brand-new life without dope were a total pile of crap. When other people looked at me now, they didn't see my "new self"—they just saw me. What's worse, they saw me through the lenses of my past actions and judged me by my past. Everybody did that: my mom, my aunt, and of course the principal, too.

It was obvious that I couldn't change into a new person from one day to the next. My body and my mind kept handing me new bills. My liver reminded me constantly of what I'd done in the past. And it wasn't like I was perfectly well adjusted to life at my aunt's house either. The smallest thing would make me go totally crazy. There were constant fights. I couldn't bear the least bit of noise or stress around me. And when I was really depressed, I couldn't help remembering how effective drugs could be at banishing those kinds of feelings.

After I got kicked out of the Realschule, I lost all my confidence in myself. I became really apathetic again. I couldn't defend myself against the expulsion, even though after only three weeks, there was no way this principal could have any informed opinion about whether or not I could actually make it in his school. I had no plans for the future. I could've gone back to a comprehensive school. There was one that I could get to by bus. In the comprehensive school, I'd have a chance to prove that I had brains. But I was way too afraid that I might fail there, too.

It took a while for me to fully grasp what it meant to be downgraded to the Hauptschule program. We had two rec centers in our area, kind of like youth clubs. One was the hangout for students from the Gymnasium and the Realschule, and the other one was the place where the Hauptschule students, along with some of the trade school kids, hung out. When I first arrived, I spent my time at the former. But once I was booted out of the Realschule, I got the feeling that the teens there were shunning me and shooting me disapproving looks. That's when I switched to the other club.

That was a brand-new experience for me. This sort of segregation didn't exist in Berlin—not in school, and not on the streets. The distinction was evident even when we gathered in the common ground outside. Right across the yard, they'd painted a white line. On one side were the students from the Realschule, and on the other side were the students from the Hauptschule. You weren't allowed to cross the white line.

So now I could only talk to my former classmates from across this stupid line. I thought this was such bullshit. We had been separated into two groups: Young people in the Realschule still had a chance to achieve some success in life, while the young people in the Hauptschule were already being thought of as a lost cause.

And so this was the new society in which I was supposed to adapt. Adapt was my grandma's favorite word. But at the same time, she told me that I shouldn't associate with kids from the Hauptschule when we weren't in class. Instead, she told me to try and make friends with the kids in the other programs. So I told her, "Why can't you just get used to the idea that your granddaughter is a student in the Hauptschule. That's where they stuck me, and that's where I'll have to adapt. So deal with it." That, of course, provoked a huge fight.

At first, I wanted to just zone out at school. But then I realized that my new head teacher was actually okay. He was an older guy. Really old-fashioned. Really conservative, to put it bluntly. Sometimes I got the impression that he thought the Nazis might have had some good ideas. But he was able to maintain his authority without having to yell at us. He was the only teacher for whom everyone stood, on their own, when he came into the classroom. He was always calm, and he paid attention to each individual, giving us the time we all deserved. Even me.

Some of the younger teachers were, I'm sure, hugely idealistic. But for the most part, that didn't get them very far: They couldn't handle the job. They were just about as clueless as their own students. They didn't know where to turn. Sometimes they just let it all go, and when the chaos was complete, they'd start screaming at us, totally unhinged. But the biggest problem was that none of these idealists had any good answers to the problems and questions that actually preoccupied us. They always came out with their "ifs" and "buts" because they were so unsure of everything. Their lack of self-confidence made them easily intimidated.

Our head teacher, however, didn't sugarcoat anything; he didn't want to give us any false expectations about what it meant to be a student in the Hauptschule. He told us that it was going to be incredibly difficult for us at each and every turn. But with some hard work and discipline, we could even do better in some areas than students in the Gymnasium. For example, in spelling and grammar. These days, no one taking the university entrance exams could spell, write grammatically, or punctuate properly. As a result, we stood a better chance if we wrote our job applications in completely perfect German.

He tried to teach us how to handle people who spoke down to us. And he knew some great sayings and quotes, which he never hesitated to use if a situation called for it. Mostly they were snippets of wisdom from the not-too-distant past. He let us laugh at them if we wanted and most students did, but I also found that there was always a kernel of truth in them. I disagreed with him a lot, but what I liked about him was that he still seemed to know the difference between north and south. In other words, he knew where he was going and what he was about.

Most of my classmates didn't like him as much as I did. They probably thought he was too tough, and his sermonizing got on their nerves. But most of them didn't care about school anyway. A few of them saw to it that they'd get a good report card and a diploma, hoping that maybe they could manage to snatch up an apprenticeship somewhere. Those types would do all their homework like good boys and girls, following the instructions to the letter. But reading a book or taking an interest in something that wasn't assigned as homework—that never would've occurred to them.

When our head teacher or one of the younger teachers tried to get a discussion going, then they all just sat and stared, looking stupid. Their plans for their future were just like mine—basically nonexistent. What sorts of plans can a student in a Hauptschule have, anyway? If he were lucky, he'd get a spot as some kind of an apprentice. He couldn't just choose an apprenticeship according to what he thought would be fun or interesting, but he'd have to go with whatever was offered.

Many didn't care anyway what they'd do after school. Maybe an apprenticeship or working as an unskilled laborer or collecting unemployment. The prevailing opinion was that nobody died of hunger in Germany. As a graduate from a Hauptschule, you didn't have much of a chance of doing something cool, so why bother wasting your energy? Why try hard? With some guys, you could already tell that they had criminal tendencies, and a few were already alcoholics. The girls didn't think too much about anything anyway. They'd preset their minds that some guy would take care of them someday, and until then they could work as a salesperson in a store or take a factory job in an assembly line or just hang around at their parents' house.

Not everyone was like that but that was definitely the general mood at school. Totally bleak, with no illusions and certainly no goals or ideals. When I thought about things that way, it hurt. I had imagined my life very differently.

I'd often tried to figure out why the young people here were so miserable. They couldn't find any joy in anything. A moped at sixteen, a car at eighteen—that was somehow expected and taken for granted. And when that didn't happen, then it was a letdown, and you were considered inferior. In all my fantasies about my future, it always went without saying that when I set out on my own, I'd have an apartment to sleep in and a car to drive. To break your back working for an apartment or a new sofa like my mom did, that wasn't part of my plan. Those were the old-fashioned ideals of our parents: to live in order to just accumulate some stuff. For me, and I believe for many others also, those few material things were considered the minimum requirements for life. But then something else had to follow—that elusive thing that makes life meaningful. And that was nowhere in sight. But a few of us, at least, were still searching for it. I know I was.

●

WHEN WE WERE TALKING about German history and the Nazis in school, I had very conflicting feelings. On the one hand, it turned my stomach when I thought about the horrendous, gruesome brutality that these human beings were capable of. On the other hand, I liked it that the possibility existed for people to believe in something. I said as much in class, "In some ways I think I would've liked to have been a teenager during the time of the Nazis. At least the young people back then had some ideals and could believe in something." I wasn't really serious about that. But there was some truth in it.

Even out here in the country, the teens were into all kinds of crazy shit because they wanted a little more out of life than their parents could give them back at home. Hooliganism had even found a place in our small village. The youth were into giving punches instead of taking them. Two years prior, in Berlin, there were a couple of kids who were really into the punk movement. It always gave me the chills when I realized that some people, who were otherwise okay people, would think that being a punk was cool. When it comes down to it, it's really just sheer brutality—at least what I've seen of it. The music reflects that: just a driving, brutal rhythm without any imagination.

I knew a punk in our area pretty well. You could actually talk to him as long as he didn't stick a safety pin through his cheek or start pulling his brass knuckles out of his pocket. Later, he got beat up in our local pub. His attackers broke two chairs over his head and then rammed a broken bottle into his stomach. He just barely pulled through in the hospital.

Violence always really upset me—especially when it happened in the course of a relationship. Everybody talks about women's liberation now. But it seems to me that, without a doubt, boys have never treated girls as brutally as they do now. That's where all the guys' frustration comes out. They want to have power and success, and when they feel disappointment, they wind up taking it out on women and mistreating women.

I developed a real revulsion toward most of the guys at the local clubs. Maybe it was because I looked a little different from the other girls, but for whatever reason I was a constant target for these guys. I heard a lot of whistles and come-ons, and I heard the word *bitch* a lot—and honestly, it bothered me even more now than it did when the customers driving by on the Kurfürstenstrasse would make a gesture toward me. When a customer in Berlin waves you to his car, then at least he's smiling. But the guys here—who all thought they were God's gift to women—didn't think they needed to make the slightest effort. I think that most johns were friendlier and more affectionate than these assholes out here. These guys wanted to fuck you without knowing the first thing about you, without showing the least bit of kindness or affection, and, of course, without having the decency to pay for the privilege either.

My revulsion against guys went so far that I wouldn't let anyone touch me. Their "rules" were disgusting. According to them, a boy had the right to start kissing and feeling up a girl after their second date. And the girls went along with it, even if they didn't have the slightest interest in the guy who had asked them out. They went along with it because those were the rules. And because if they didn't, they were afraid that the guy would dump them, and then the guys would all talk about what a frigid bitch she was.

I just couldn't do that. I didn't want to. Even if I really liked a boy and started going on some dates with him, I made it very clear right from the start, "Don't ever try any funny stuff with me. Don't touch me. If something's going to happen between us, then I will be the one to start it."

In the six months since I'd first left Berlin, I hadn't had one serious boyfriend. Up to that point, every friendship had ended abruptly—as soon as the boy tried to sleep with me. As soon as I said no.

Even though I'd gotten away from drugs and my old life, my past was still with me. Even though I imagined that the business of prostitution didn't have any real connection to me anymore, that it was only an unavoidable side effect of my heroin addiction, it still played a major role in the way I dealt with boys. The way they usually behaved just reinforced my impression that men just wanted to use me and take advantage of me.

I tried to communicate something of my past experiences to the girls in my class without being too explicit. But I never got my message through to them. The only thing that changed was that now I became a sort of "Dear Abby" type in my class and had to listen to all kinds of problems and offer my advice because they did pick up on the fact that I was, somehow, a little more experienced than they were. But still, they never understood what I was really trying to tell them.

Most of the girls were obsessed with boys. They didn't think there was anything wrong with all the cruelty and even violence that was part and parcel of their relationships. When a guy stood up his girlfriend to go out with a different girl, she didn't get pissed at the guy; instead, they developed a grudge against the new girlfriend. That new girl was immediately transformed into a cow, a bitch, a fucking whore, and God knows what else. And the darker and more distant a guy was, the more the girls wanted him.

I only really understood this when our class went on a trip to the German state of Rhineland-Palatinate. Not far from where we were staying was a dance club. Most of the girls were obsessed with going over there on the first night. When they got back, they raved about all the awesome guys that were there. They told me all about their motorcycles, too.

I took a walk over to the club, and it didn't take me long to figure out what was going on there. Guys from all over the neighborhood came there on their mopeds, motorcycles, and cars in order to seduce schoolgirls who were there visiting on their class trips. I tried to explain that to the girls in my class—that in a place like this, the guys were literally only interested in sex—but they didn't have much interest in my warnings or experience. An hour before the club opened, these chicks were all in front of the mirrors, putting on makeup and fussing with their hair. Then they refused to move because they didn't want to mess up their hairdos.

It seemed like they were losing an essential part of themselves when they stood in front of the mirror like that. All that remained of them was a mask, which was only supposed to look appealing to the guys on the motorcycles. It really pissed me off to see that. In a way, of course, it also reminded me of myself. I'd also hidden behind makeup and costumes in order to look good to the guys who had the drugs—first pot and then dope. And I'd also given up my own self, only to become a slave to heroin.

The whole class trip now revolved entirely around these cocky bikers, even though most of the girls already had steady boyfriends at home. Elke, my roommate, wrote a letter to her boyfriend on the first night. But on the second night, she went to the club and came back totally depressed. She said that she'd been making out with someone. I think she only did that so that she could prove to the other girls that she could get one of the bikers interested in her. She felt really guilty because of her boy-friend and even started to cry. She actually believed, though, that she'd fallen in love with the motorcycle guy. Her boyfriend, of course, didn't have a motorcycle. The next night she returned, totally devastated, and cried her eyes out. Her biker friend had, apparently, asked another girl in our class: "So, what's up: Is your friend ready for a ride yet or what?"

There was another girl, Rosi, who was even worse. A teacher caught her with one of those guys in a car, just as the two of them were getting busy. Rosi was so drunk she could barely walk. That guy knew what he was doing, and all night long he kept ordering her more rum and Cokes.

Rosi had been a virgin, but now she was a wreck. The other girls were calling a meeting to discuss what to do about her. They didn't get all upset about the guy who'd gotten Rosi drunk and then more or less raped her. No, they actually demanded that Rosi be sent home. I was the only one who objected. They were furious because our teachers had put a new rule in place that prohibited anyone from going back to the club. They were all upset over the fact that Rosi's little party had put an end to all the make-out sessions that they were looking forward to themselves.

It really sucked to see how no one cared at all about anyone else in this group: There was absolutely no sense of solidarity among the girls. Whenever a guy arrived on the scene, friendships were bound to break up. In a way, it really wasn't any different with heroin, which ruined the relationships among Stella, Babsi, and me over and over again.

Although I wasn't directly involved, the drama made me feel hopeless and emotionally drained. The last two days of the class trip, I had a relapse. I was absolutely gone the whole time.

In the meantime, however, I had resolved to cope with this world just the way it was. I didn't think about running away anymore. It was clear to me that "escaping" was really just another way of boxing myself into a life on drugs. And I kept pointing out to myself, as bluntly as I could, that it never amounted to anything good.

I thought that there had to be another way. There had to be a kind of compromise available, that would allow me to cope with the world, with society, without giving in and giving up completely.

Then I got a boyfriend, and he definitely had a calming effect on me. I could really talk to him. And despite everything, he always seemed to be able to keep his priorities in order; he knew what mattered. He could dream, yet he could also find a practical solution for everything. And at the same time, he wasn't blind to all the real problems that surrounded us. But he believed that if you could achieve some success yourself, then you could make your own, better world—no matter how small. That would make a difference. His plan was to become a businessman and make a bunch of money and then afterward buy a log cabin in the Canadian woods and live there. Canada was his big dream, just like for Detlef.

He was a student in the Gymnasium, the college preparatory track, and he got me excited about learning again. I realized that even the Hauptschule could offer me something as long as my goal was to actually learn—and not just get through the ridiculous, useless, moronic requirements for the Hauptschule diploma.

I read a lot. I picked up books almost at random. Goethe's *The Sorrows of Young Werther,* Hermann Hesse, and especially Erich Fromm.[52] His book *The Art of Loving* became like a bible

---

52 Erich Fromm was a renowned psychoanalyst and social philosopher who in 1956 wrote *The Art of Loving* which argues that true love involves four basic elements: care, responsibility, respect, and knowledge. One of the book's central concepts is the idea of self-love. According to Fromm, loving oneself is quite different from arrogance or egocentrism, and one must have achieved self-love before being able to love someone else.

to me. I learned whole pages by heart, simply because I felt that I had to read them over and over again. I also copied passages from the book and taped them above my bed. Fromm really had the right perspective on things. He understood what really mattered. If you listened to his advice and actually followed it, then your life would be meaningful because then you'd be able to make it into what you wanted it to be. At the same time though, it's so difficult to live by his rules because no one else has to follow them with you; most people don't even know about them! I wish I could have a conversation with Erich Fromm about how he lives in this world while also following his principles. But in any event, I realized that the real world sometimes escapes the grasp of his essential principles.

I thought that Fromm's book ought to have been the single most important book in our curriculum. But I never dared to bring it up in class because the others would've probably just turned it—and me—into a joke. Sometimes I took the book to school with me. Once, I was reading it during class because I thought I could find an answer in it to a question that had come up in class. The teacher saw that, looked at the title, and immediately took the book away from me. When I wanted to have it back at the end of class, he said, "So, the little miss likes to read pornography in class, does she? No, I'm sorry, this book will remain confiscated for the time being." He actually said that to me. The name Fromm didn't mean anything to him. And the title just sounded like porn to his ignorant ears, I guess. What else could love be for these frustrated men, anyway? So he came to the natural conclusion that Christiane just wanted to corrupt the kids in his class after spending time in Berlin as a drug-addicted hooker.

The next day, he gave me the book back and said it was okay. Still, he advised me not to bring it to school anymore because the title was misleading.

There were a lot of things like that, and this thing with the Fromm book was really only the tip of the iceberg. Other things made me way more upset. Like once, I got in trouble with the principal. He was another one of those totally frustrated, insecure guys. He was completely incapable of taking control of anything, even though he was the principal. He tried to compensate for that with yelling and a lot of senseless exercises. When we had class with him in the morning, we had to sing a song and do some exercises before we did anything else. He said it was meant to help us wake up. You only got good grades in his class if you did exactly what he said.

He was also our music teacher. And one time, he wanted to do us a favor (that at least was something new) and talk the about music that we cared about. He started by talking about "today's jazz music." I had no idea what he meant by that. I thought that maybe he was referring to pop, and so I said, "What do you actually mean when you say, 'today's jazz music'? If you're talking about pop and rock, that's not the word we use." Maybe I said it in the wrong tone of voice again or something. I'm sure I probably started spouting off without first thinking about what I really wanted to convey. In any case, the principal went ballistic. He screamed like a lunatic and sent me out of the class.

At the door, I turned around and tried to calm things down a bit. I said to him, "I think we must have misunderstood each other." So he called me back in. But in the end, I couldn't go back, so I spent the rest of the class out in the hall. At least I was under control enough to stick around the building and not just take off for home.

After class was over, I had to go to the principal's office. As soon as I walked in, I could see that he had my folder in his hand. He thumbed through the file and pretended to read it. Then he said that I wasn't in Berlin anymore. And incidentally,

I was only a guest at his school anyway. And under these circumstances, he could kick me out at any time. So I better start appreciating his hospitality.

I could feel myself losing it. I didn't want to go back to school at all. Even little things were still setting me off back then, and this was big. I didn't know what to do. I couldn't just shrug it off and tell myself that this idiot didn't really have any influence over my life. He did. But if he can only fight you with some paper files, then in a way he knows that he's already lost.

I managed to keep my big mouth shut in his office, and after that incident I tried my best to be inconspicuous. Before this, my boyfriend had encouraged me to try and do well on my finals at the Hauptschule and then to try to get into a comprehensive school after that.

But I knew how hard that would be, in real terms, as a student from the Hauptschule. And as things stood now, I didn't want to hear another word about school. I was sure that I wouldn't be able to hack it. The psychological fitness tests, the special permission from the superintendent, and all the other stuff you had to do if you wanted to get out of the Hauptschule were just too much. And I knew that my file from Berlin was always going to be one step ahead of me.

But at least I had my sensible boyfriend, and I was developing some friendships with the teenagers in the town who in their own way really appealed to me. They were pretty different from what I was used to, but they were way better than all the assholes from the club and the other town nearby. There was a real community spirit among them. There weren't any alpha males or hotshots among them. Everything had a sort of old-fashioned order, even if the boys did get drunk every now and then. And most of them accepted me, despite how unusual I must have seemed to them.

For a while, I thought I could be like them. I thought I could live a life like my boyfriend had. But I couldn't make it last. I broke up with my boyfriend as soon as he started pushing for sex. I just couldn't do it. I simply couldn't imagine sleeping with anyone besides Detlef.

So I guess I still loved Detlef. I thought a lot about him, even though I didn't want to. Sometimes I wrote him letters, which I intended to send to Rolf—the last person he'd lived with. But at least I still had enough sense left not to send the letters.

I heard that Detlef had wound up in jail again. Stella was there, too. I thought a lot about both of them. I missed them. But there were a lot of people around me now who I really liked, too. I felt much closer to them than I ever had to the kids in the village where I first grew up. They were easy to talk to, and we could talk about anything—including my problems. I felt accepted by them and didn't have to worry that they'd find out about my past. They saw the world like I saw it. I didn't have to pretend or adapt. We were on the same wavelength. Despite that, I was worried about getting any closer with them. Because at the time, they were all experimenting with drugs.

My mom, my aunt, and I, we all thought I'd landed in a corner of Germany that had been untouched by drugs—or at least by hard drugs. When the papers reported anything about heroin, it had happened in Berlin or Frankfurt. I looked at things the same way myself. I figured I had to be the only ex-junkie for miles around.

However, I grew to know better right after one of our first shopping expeditions. Early in 1978, we drove to Norderstedt —a kind of dormitory suburb of Hamburg, comprised of all-new high-rises—to go shopping. As I always did when we went on these road trips, I kept an eye on people who seemed like they were stoned. I'd been watching a couple of guys, and I was think-ing to myself, Are they shooting up? Smoking pot? Or maybe they're just students?

Before I got my answer, we went into a snack bar to get a hot dog. At one table, there were a few poor foreigners hanging around together. Two of them suddenly got up and moved to another table. I didn't know why, but I immediately had the feeling that heroin was involved. I made my aunt hurry up and leave without telling her about my suspicions.

Just a hundred yards further on, in front of a jeans shop, we walked right into the center of the Norderstedt heroin scene. There were junkies everywhere. Then I imagined that they were all looking at me. And that they had immediately recognized me as one of their own. I started freaking out. Heading for an all-out panic. I grabbed my aunt by the arm and told her that I had to leave immediately. She could kind of tell what was going on and said, "But why? You aren't involved with that sort of thing anymore." I said, "Just drop it. I'm not ready for this yet."

At that point, I already knew that I was done running. And when I knew that, I knew that I'd be able to stay away from heroin for the rest of my life if I wanted to. It shocked me that, despite my new resolve, they still had recognized me. So when I got home, I peeled off my clothes right away and scrubbed the makeup off my face. My high-heeled boots were fired—effective immediately. From that day, on I tried to look like the girls in my class.

But while at the club, I now hung out more frequently with the people who smoked pot and went tripping. Sometimes I smoked a pipe right along with them, and occasionally I "just said no." I really liked these kids. Most of them were apprentices somewhere and came from the surrounding villages. They all had brains and were interested in using them—so they were nothing like the helplessly defeated students at the Hauptschule. They thought about things, about politics and issues. When I had a conversation with any of them, I usually left excited, almost inspired. They were just good people. No one fought. The violence was elsewhere. This was a totally peaceful group.

One time—but only once—I asked some of them why we couldn't do what we were doing now without getting high. They blew me off. They said it was a stupid question. After all the shit that happens in the course of a day, how else were you supposed to relax?

They were all disappointed with their jobs. The one guy who wasn't was in a union and was working as an apprentices' ombudsman, he found meaning in his daily work. He looked after the interests of the other young people in that business, and that gave him satisfaction. He was also of the opinion that our society could be changed. He was on a pretty even keel. He didn't smoke at all, and when he drank it was usually just a glass of red wine.

The others didn't see any meaning in what they were doing. They were constantly talking about quitting. The only thing was, they didn't know what to do next. When they got off work, they were frustrated, bitter, and angry. When we got together, one of them always started talking about how he hated his boss or about how something had gone horribly wrong, until someone else would finally interrupt, "Enough about work!" Then a pipe would be passed around, and their postwork lives would begin.

I felt like in a way I was still better off than them. Sometimes I actually had some fun in school. On the other hand, I was just like them. There wasn't really any grand purpose behind all this studying and stress. By that time, it had become clear to me that I'd never be able to take my college exams or get into the Realschule. And I also knew that as a former addict, I wasn't eligible for a lot of the jobs I might be interested in later—no matter how well I did on my finals at the Hauptschule.

Still, when the time came, I did do well on my exams and got really good grades before I left. It didn't earn me an apprentice-ship, but I did get a temporary job (thanks to some law meant to keep unemployed young people off the streets). I haven't used heroin for almost a year. But I'm aware, of course, that it takes a couple of years before you're completely clean. And at the moment there are no big problems.

At night when we sit together, my friends and I, drinking wine and smoking, then all those small daily problems have a tendency to disappear. We talk about the books we're reading. We talk about the news and mysticism and whatever else comes up. We're all into Buddhism right now. We're looking for people who see the world in a different way than we do, so that we can learn from them. So far our own lives haven't proved to be quite what we'd hoped.

A girl in our clique is doing an apprenticeship as a nurse, and she brought some pills back one day. For a while, I was back on Valium. I won't touch acid, though, because I'm afraid to go on a horror trip. The others all seem to enjoy it.

There aren't any hard drugs in our small town. If anyone wants to get into that scene, they have to go to Hamburg. No one around has any H, so that makes it easy to avoid temptation. It's not like Berlin or Hamburg or even Norderstedt.

But if you're desperate to score, it's not really that hard. There are guys with connections. And sometimes a dealer passes through who has a real arsenal. If you ask somebody like that if he's got something to get high on, he'd most likely ask, What do you want? Valium, methadone, pot, acid, coke, or dope?

All the people that I hang out with these days believe they have the drug thing under control. There are definitely a few things that are different here than they were back at Gropiusstadt with all my old friends.

This new group is looking for something entirely different when they use drugs. It's not about getting away from ourselves now or numbing ourselves with pounding music and dancing. In fact, for these guys, the atmosphere at The Sound would be like torture. It would be the opposite of a high. We all hate the city. We're into nature now. On weekends, we drive all over Schleswig-Holstein, and then we just park the car and start walking until we find a good spot. Often we end up on the moors, in places where nobody else would ever think to go.

But the best place of all—the place we all really love—is the limestone quarry. It's an enormous crater right smack-dab in the middle of nowhere. More than half-a-mile long, two hundred yards wide, a hundred yards deep. The walls of the quarry are almost entirely vertical. It's warm at the bottom. No wind. There are plants growing down there—plants like we've never seen anywhere else. Incredibly clear streamlets flow through this crazy valley. Waterfalls come right out of the walls. The water turns the walls a rusty red. Everywhere you look you can see these bizarrely shaped white rocks, some of which look like the bones of ancient animals—maybe even mammoths. The gigantic excavator and the conveyor belts—which made so much noise during the week—on weekends looked like they'd been hibernating underground for centuries. The limestone covered them all in a blanket of white.

When we go there, we're all alone. All alone in this crazy magical hole. The rest of the world is kept at bay by the steep, vertical limestone walls. There's no noise that can reach us from the outside. All we can hear is the water cascading down the quarry walls.

We always imagine that someday we'll buy this quarry, once the mining operation is closed down. We want to build our log cabins down here, put in a huge garden, tend to our pets, and make sure we'd have whatever we need to live on. Then we'd blow up the only path out of the quarry.

We wouldn't ever want to come up again anyway.

Drug and Alcohol Abuse Resources

NIDA (National Institute on Drug Abuse)
www.drugabuse.gov
This organization conducts scientific research studies on the effects and prevalence of drug abuse in the United States.

SAMHSA (Substance Abuse and Mental Health Services Administration) Treatment Locaton
www.findtreatment.samhsa.gov
1-800-662-HELP (1-800-662-4357)
The SAMHSA website's treatment locator helps you find drug, alcohol, and mental health treatment resources in your city.

The Partnership at Drugfree.org
1-855-DRUGFREE (1-855-378-4373)
http://www.drugfree.org/
A guide for parents on how to prevent, intervene, treat, and recover from a teen drug problem.

TeenDrugAddiction.com
Teens and their families seeking help with an alcohol or drug addiction can find information on drug use, types of drugs, symptoms, intervention, and therapy.

The Alcohol & Drug Addiction Resource Center
www.addict-help.com
Drug and alcohol abuse information and online treatment locator.

Homelessness and Runaway Resources

National Runaway Switchboard
1-800-RUNAWAY (786-2929)
www.1800runaway.org
A resource for teen runaways or teens who are thinking of running away from home, and those who care about them.

Covenant House
1-800-999-9999
www.covenanthouse.org
A religious organization that provides shelter and resources for homeless kids and teens.

Suicide Resources

National Suicide Prevention Lifeline
1-800-SUICIDE (1-800-784-2433)
A hotline with resources for anyone feeling suicidal, or friends and family of someone who may be suicidal.

Sexual Health Resources

Sexually Transmitted Disease & AIDS/HIV Hotline
1-800-332-2437
This hotline provides information and resources for treating STD's, HIV, and AIDS.
CDC (Center for Disease Control) National Prevention Information Network
1-800-458-5231
http://www.cdcnpin.org/
Their website and hotline provide information about the prevention of HIV, AIDS, and other sexually transmitted diseases.

Rape and Abuse Resources

RAINN (Rape, Abuse, and Incest National Network)
1-800-656-HOPE (4673)
www.rainn.org
Their website and hotline offer resources for victims of sexual abuse.

National Domestic Violence Hotline
1-800-799-SAFE (7233)
A hotline providing resources for victims of domestic violence and those who care about them.

ChildHelp USA National Child Abuse Hotline
1-800-4-A-CHILD (1-800-422-4453)
Call for child abuse counseling and referrals.

General Resources

Boys Town
1-800-448-3000
www.boystown.org
Their website and hotline provide resources for suicide prevention, abuse, chemical dependency, depression, and more.

All About Counseling
1-800-521-7128
www.allaboutcounseling.com
Information about and resources for addiction, mental health issues, and abuse. Call for a free referral to a drug rehabilitation center.

Helpguide
www.helpguide.org
Information about addictions as well as abuse, suicide prevention, depression, grief, and other issues. Addiction resources include what to look out for, symptoms, and how to overcome a drug addiction.

Find Youth Info
www.findyouthinfo.gov
Information, tools, and resources for teens and their families regarding mental health, dating, violence, substance abuse, LGBT issues, and more.